ABU ZAKARIYA

JESUS

MAN MESSENGER MESSIAH

CONVEYING THE CALL

Dedicated to those who seek the truth

ISBN 978-1-910952-03-0

British Library Cataloguing in Publication Data.
A catalogue record for this book is available from the British Library.
© Copyright 2017 1st Edition by Abu Zakariya

Published & distributed by

CONVEYING THE CALL

iERA

Suite 321, Crown House, North Circular Road, London, NW10 7PN
T: 03000 111 365 : E: info@iera.org : W: www.iera.org

PREFACE

Some of my fondest memories, growing up as a child, were religious festivals. Religious celebrations with their feasts and presents are a magical time for children, and the annual calendar in my household had more than its fair share. Whilst I was raised as a Muslim, half of my family is Christian, so not only did we have the two festivals of Eid - the main celebrations on the Islamic calendar - but we also had two Christmases as well, 25th December as celebrated by the majority of Christians around the world, along with a celebration on 7th January because of my Eastern Orthodox Grandmother.

Whilst my body was well nourished, I still thirsted for an intellectual grasp of religion. Even with the little knowledge I possessed, I was struck by the similarities between both faiths. Both religions revere the one true God, and acknowledge the representatives of God, such as Abraham, Moses and Jesus, may God's peace be upon them all, as well as the Day of Judgement. Although they are very similar, in some ways they are also very different. It is a paradox that will be explored in this book, and continues to intrigue me to this very day.

My exposure to Christianity only developed beyond celebratory rituals when I started university. Many of my close friends were devout Christians, so for the first time in my life I had an intellectual exposure to the religion. I have fond memories of the many discussions we had about our respective faiths. At that particular point in my life, I possessed only a rudimentary knowledge about both faiths, so my interaction with my Christian friends was based on a zealous defence of Islam, rather than sincere discourse.

After leaving university my attitude matured from a knee-jerk "You are wrong!" to a more introspective "Am I right?". I began to properly research Islam, not because I doubted it, for I had believed it was the truth from a young age, but rather because I wanted to have a religious conviction based on sound knowledge, rather than blind following.

Some of my fondest memories, growing up as a child, were religious festivals. Religious celebrations with their feasts and presents are a magical time for children, and the annual calendar in my household had more than its fair share. Whilst I was raised as a Muslim, half of my family is Christian, so not only did we have the two festivals of Eid - the main celebrations on the Islamic calendar - but we also had two Christmases as well, 25th December as celebrated by the majority of Christians around the world, along with a celebration on 7th January because of my Eastern Orthodox Grandmother.

Whilst my body was well nourished, I still thirsted for an intellectual grasp of religion. Even with the little knowledge I possessed, I was struck by the similarities between both faiths. Both religions revere the one true God, and acknowledge the representatives of God, such as Abraham, Moses and Jesus, may God's peace be upon them all, as well as the Day of Judgement. Although they are very similar, in some ways they are also very different. It is

PRELIMINARY NOTES

In the Islamic tradition, when the Prophet Muhammad ﷺ is mentioned by name or title, the honorific phrase 'ﷺ' is used. It is a sign of love and respect. The phrase denotes 'May God's peace and blessings be upon him'. This phrase is used throughout this book.

The word God is used throughout this book. However, in the Islamic tradition, the name of God is Allah. Arabic linguists suggest that the name Allah comes from the word Al-Ilah, which means The-Deity. The name Allah has no plural, and is genderless.

CONTENTS

CONTENTS

CONTENTS

INTRODUCTION

I vividly remember explaining Islam to a Christian lady during an exhibition at a Cambridge library some years ago. Over the course of our conversation we discussed the death and resurrection of Jesus. After some discussion, the lady confessed to me that, even though she doubted the crucifixion, she would go to her grave holding onto the belief, no matter what. She explained that she was unable to abandon the belief that Jesus died for her sins because that's how she was raised and she didn't want to upset her family. She was willing to live a lie to maintain the status quo.

As I've met more and more Christians over the years, I've been struck by how much of an emotional attachment they have to their belief of the incarnation and crucifixion of God. Perhaps this should be no surprise, given the emotional language that permeates the New Testament, ***"for God so loved the world that He gave His only begotten Son, that whosoever should believe in him shall have everlasting life" [John 3:16].*** Throughout history, heroic tales of self-sacrifice have always appealed to mankind. I can understand why it is comforting to think that God Almighty is willing to become man and suffer and die as a redeeming sacrifice for us.

Although it's an emotional and perhaps beautiful notion, is it true? For many people, their commitment to their religion is not based on thorough research or an intellectual understanding of its teachings, but rather is based on powerful emotional and cultural influences. However, if religion is nothing more than blindly following our forefathers, then our present beliefs are arbitrary, for we didn't choose which religion we were born into. Had we been born in India, for example, then with this mindset we would be Hindu. Similarly, had we been born in Communist China, we would most likely be atheist. We need to examine our beliefs with a critical eye and that of others with an open mind. We should not allow our emotions to cloud our vision and thereby blind us from the truth.

No-one wants to dedicate their entire lives to a particular religion only to find out when we die that we were wrong. We only get one shot, we have only been given one life, so the stakes are very high. The only way that we may find the truth about God, or anything for that matter, is to approach it objectively. The fact that God endowed every one of us with the ability to reason is evidence that He doesn't want us to be blind followers. We must make use of our God-given intellect in order to weigh up the evidence and reason about religion systematically and logically. Our ability to reason is what distinguishes us from animals, which act purely on instinct. Only after determining what the objective truth is should we commit ourselves to it emotionally.

In both Christianity and Islam, there is the message that God wants to make Himself known to us; He wants a relationship, and that's why He has sent messengers and revelation to mankind throughout history. The question we need to ask ourselves is: "Are we willing to take the time and effort to seek out God's truth?" This is the key to fulfilling the purpose of our creation which will give us inner peace in this life and success in the eternal Hereafter.

The pursuit of truth is a noble endeavour; however, it's an objective. What will be our means of achieving this objective? The key to unlocking the truth lies in the person of Jesus Christ. Islam holds a unique position among the world's religions as it is the only religion, other than Christianity, that acknowledges Jesus as the Messiah. He is a pivotal figure in Christianity and Islam, so his life and teachings will be the focus of our study of both religions. Despite the fact that Jesus is one of the most significant personalities in the world today, with nearly two billion Christians and over 1.5 billion Muslims believing in him, he is also perhaps the most misunderstood and misrepresented person in history. As we are going to explore, while Christianity and Islam share much in common with regard to Jesus, they also make opposing claims. Since both religions can't be correct, how can we go about getting to the true message of Jesus?

If we were living in first-century Palestine, then it would be straightforward. We could simply walk up to Jesus and ask him about his message. Since we obviously don't have that opportunity today, we have to make use of the tools that are available to us, such as scripture, history and reason. Our quest for the truth will see us gathering key information, comparing competing claims and resolving differences. If this sounds a lot like the kind of investigative work that a detective would undertake, then you're not mistaken.

Along our journey we will see how the Qur'an challenges Church tradition about Jesus and ultimately brings to light his true message that has been buried under the myth and innovation that developed in the centuries following him. We will also see why the Qur'an is the solution that bridges the divide that exists between Judaism and Christianity, uniting all of the Abrahamic faiths.

Last, but by no means least, is our sincerity. In order to have any chance of arriving at the truth, we are going to have to challenge our own beliefs and suspend any preconceived notions we might have about that of others. It may not be a comfortable journey, but then anything in life that is valuable is worth struggling for. Isn't Paradise worth at least this much?

Please note that, unless stated otherwise, all verses referenced from the Bible have been taken from the New International Version.

May God's peace and blessing be upon you, and may He guide us all.

CHAPTER 1

THE CONCEPT OF GOD
IN CHRISTIANITY

The world around us, our very existence, everything, we owe it all to our Creator. God also sustains all life. Imagine what would happen if God withheld the rain, or blotted out the sun; life would cease to exist. Now, can you imagine if you gave someone a really expensive gift and they didn't thank you, or perhaps even worse, thanked someone else? What would you think about that person? God is our Master; we are but His servants. Our love, obedience and reverence are His rights upon us.

It's important to note that God is not in need of our worship; God is free of all needs. If the whole of humanity were to collectively worship God, it would not increase Him one iota. Similarly, if the whole of mankind were to cease worshipping God, it would not degrade Him one iota. God existed in all His majesty and splendour for an eternity before He created man. God does not need our worship, but He deserves it.

Thankfulness and gratitude is a key aspect of worship. This is why it's so important that we worship God properly, that we give Him His due reverence. Is it possible to have a meaningful relationship with a stranger? Would anyone want a relationship with the wrong concept of God? As you can see, in order for our worship to be effective, we need to know who God is. This is why the question of who Jesus is, what his true nature is, is so important. Thus, we begin by looking at the Christian concept of God.

THE DOCTRINE OF THE TRINITY

When it comes to the nature of God, beliefs differ significantly across the various denominations of Christianity. The most popular belief, promoted by the vast majority of churches in the world, is that God has a triune nature. This is the doctrine known as the Trinity, which defines God as one Being who exists eternally as three distinct persons — the Father, the Son and the Holy Spirit. Put simply, it is "one God in three persons". The persons of the Trinity are not to be confused, so the Father is not the Son, the Son is not the Holy Spirit and the Holy Spirit is not the Father. All three persons of the Trinity are said to be co-equal and co-eternal, and "each is God, whole and entire." However, each person is said to have a different role when it comes to how God relates to the world. For example, in God's plan of salvation for mankind, the Father is said to have sent the Son, Jesus, who died on the cross for the sins of mankind. The Holy Spirit is said to sanctify believers, inspiring Christians in their day-to-day lives.

Here is a diagram that is commonly used by Trinitarians to summarise the doctrine:

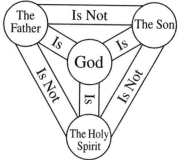

A key element of the doctrine of the Trinity is the incarnation of God. This teaches that the second person of the Trinity, the Son, took on human flesh in the bodily form of Jesus. Thus, when Mary gave birth to Jesus, God entered into the creation. Jesus is said to be the God-man, who has two natures — one divine, one human. Jesus is said to be both fully God and fully man. As a result of the incarnation, humanity has been permanently incorporated into the Godhead; the Son will forever have an inseparable divine and human nature. Jesus's humanity is not something that can be discarded or dissolved back into the Godhead. Even after his crucifixion, resurrection and ascension back to the Father, Jesus will forever exist in heaven as a glorified man, albeit God at the same time. Here is a diagram which summarises this concept:

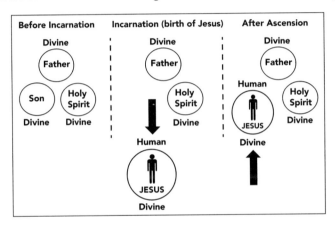

As a Muslim, I was raised to believe in the pure monotheism of Islam that teaches God is one, not only in essence, but also in personhood, and that God is distinct from human beings. So, it took me a long time to grasp the Trinitarian concept of God. It turns out that I'm not alone in struggling to grasp the Trinity. According to scholars of Christianity and defenders of the Trinity, many Christians who profess to believe in the Trinity in fact do not understand the doctrine. Dr James White, one of the foremost apologists for the Trinity today, wrote the following:

> **"For many Christians, the Trinity is an abstract principle, a confusing and difficult doctrine that they believe, although they are not really sure why in their honest moments." [1]**

This is evident when one discusses the doctrine with the average Christian. In my experiences of interacting with Christians, a common way of trying to explain the Trinity is the use of elaborate analogies.

The following examples are quite commonly put forward:

- *The Trinity is like the three parts of an egg: the shell, the white and the yolk.*

- *The Trinity is like three forms of water: ice, liquid and vapour.*

- *The Trinity is like a man who can exist as a father, a son and a husband, all at the same time.*

Such analogies, however, are highly problematic. The egg analogy doesn't work because the doctrine of the Trinity states that each person (Father, Son and Holy Spirit) is fully God. One wouldn't say that the shell is fully an egg, the white is fully an egg or that the yolk is fully an egg. It is only the totality of the three parts (shell, white and yolk) that make a complete egg. The water analogy doesn't work either, because it implies that God first manifested Himself as Father, then as the Son and then as the Holy Spirit. These 'forms' are temporary and never co-exist, thus violating the principle of the doctrine that the persons eternally co-exist. Finally, the man analogy also fails to encompass the doctrine of the Trinity. The Father, the Son and the Holy Spirit aren't simply three functions or roles of God, they are said to be three distinct persons.

The simple fact is that no analogy will ever be complete. Although this is not appreciated by the average Christian that I encounter on a day-to-day basis, it is something that is fully acknowledged by Christian theologians who freely admit that the Trinity cannot be explained. Many theologians have abandoned all hope of deriving a deep understanding of the doctrine and have resigned themselves to classifying it as a holy mystery. The Catholic Church states: **"The mystery of the Most Holy Trinity is the central mystery of Christian faith and life" [2].** The Catholic Church defines mystery in theology as something that remains veiled in darkness:

> **The Vatican Council has explained the meaning to be attributed to the term mystery in theology. It lays down that a mystery is a truth which we are not merely incapable of discovering apart from Divine Revelation, but which, even when revealed, remains "hidden by the veil of faith and enveloped, so to speak, by a kind of darkness. [3]**

Reconciling the plurality of the godhead, a threeness, within a monotheistic framework, continues to be one of the great challenges faced by Trinitarians. If Trinitarians embraced the polytheism that is inherent in the doctrine and explained it for what it really is – three Gods and not one – then there would be no confusion. The doctrine is inexplicable because Trinitarians try to reconcile a concept of threeness into a monotheistic context which does not, and cannot, fit. How can anyone, or anything, be three things and one thing, all at the same time? The fact is that the Trinity is something that believers must accept on blind faith; it cannot be rationalised.

The doctrine of the Trinity is also problematic when we consider the purpose of revelation, which boils down to guidance – the books of God were revealed in order to guide mankind. If guidance results in confusion (or misguidance), then it defeats the purpose of revelation. If the Trinity were some inconsequential aspect of Christian theology, then perhaps its mystery wouldn't be an issue. But it isn't; so entrenched has the belief in the Trinity become that it is the litmus test for whether or not a person is considered to be orthodox. Rejecting any aspect of the doctrine is enough for a Christian to be condemned as a heretic. Evangelical scholar Harold Lindsell and seminary professor Charles Woodbridge wrote the following:

> **The mind of man cannot fully understand the mystery of the Trinity. He who has tried to understand the mystery fully will lose his mind; but he who would deny the Trinity will lose his soul. [4]**

There you have it, "deny the Trinity and you lose your soul." This reveals a fundamental paradox with the doctrine: why would God reveal something that cannot be fully comprehended, and yet tie our salvation to it? What should we make of all this in the light of the purpose of revelation? Revelation is an opening up, an uncovering. How can the Trinity be a revelation when the most learned of biblical scholars write that it is a mystery? That is double-talk which directly conflicts with the very purpose of revelation: guidance.

Today, faith and the Trinity are synonymous in Christian thought. In fact, they are so intertwined that you would think the Trinity must have always been the dominant belief going all the way back to the early Church. As we are going to see, this could not be further from the truth.

THE DIFFERENT VIEWS OF JESUS IN THE EARLY CHURCH

Very early on in Christianity, almost from the beginning, different Christians in different churches in different regions had different views of Jesus. Here are some of the views about Jesus that existed in the first few centuries of Christianity:

1. Jesus was purely human.

This is the view that Jesus was born a human being with no divine aspect whatsoever. One such early Christian group that held this belief were the Ebionites. The word "Ebionite" is from Hebrew Ebyonim meaning "poor ones". The Ebionites were Jewish followers of Jesus and were concentrated in Palestine and its surrounding regions. The Ebionite Christians believed that Jesus was the Jewish Messiah sent from God to the Jewish people in fulfilment of the Jewish Scriptures. They also believed that to belong to the people of God, one needed to be Jewish. As a result, they insisted on observing the Sabbath, keeping kosher, and circumcising all males. Their insistence on staying Jewish should not seem peculiar from a historical perspective, since Jesus and his disciples were Jewish, as were the earliest Christians who were also Jewish followers of Jesus. At this early point, Christianity was a Jewish phenomenon. It was not yet a separate and distinct religion, but rather a sect of Judaism. It seems that the only thing that distinguished these early followers of Jesus from any other Jew was their belief that Jesus was the Messiah. The Book of Acts attests to their continued regular attendance at the Jewish Temple, as well as the goodwill they had from their fellow Jews, which would have been impossible had they preached that Jesus was God incarnate, a belief which is seen as blasphemous in Judaism:

> *And all that believed were together, and had all things common;*
> *And sold their possessions and goods, and parted them to all men,*
> *as every man had need. And they, continuing daily with one accord*
> *in the temple, and breaking bread from house to house, did eat*

their meat with gladness and singleness of heart, Praising God,
and having favour with all the people. And the Lord added to the
church daily such as should be saved. [Acts 2:44-47]

From what we know of the beliefs of the Ebionites, they saw Jesus as the adopted Son of God. They held that Jesus was born human and that he became God's son by adoption during his baptism, being chosen by God because of his sinless devotion to the will of God. It's important to note that, for the Ebionites, Jesus did not pre-exist and was never an object of worship because they believed he was inferior to God.

Many scholars believe that such views about Jesus were held by the earliest Christians. A New Testament scholar, Professor Bart Ehrman, states: **"... adoptionistic Christologies can be traced to sources that predate the books of the New Testament."** [5]

2. Jesus was purely divine and not human at all.

This view is an opposite extreme to that of the Ebionites. It is the belief that Jesus had no human aspect at all and was purely divine. One such group which held these beliefs were the Marcionites. Unlike the Ebionites, the Marcionites represented a highly attractive religion and had many pagan converts. Potential converts from among the pagans were not flocking to the Ebionite form of religion, which involved restricting activities on the Sabbath, giving up pork and other popular foods, and men getting circumcised. The Marcionites, on the other hand, had a comparatively easy religion to follow as it was avowedly Christian with nothing Jewish about it. In fact, everything Jewish was taken out of it as they had trouble reconciling what they saw as a wrathful, vengeful God of the Old Testament with the loving, merciful portrayal of God in the New Testament. They went so far as to even exclude the Jewish books of the Old Testament from their Bible.

The Marcionites believed that Jesus was not truly a part of this material world. He did not have a flesh-and-blood body, and was not actually born. Although he appeared to be human, his human form was merely an illusion. Jesus was purely divine with no human aspect whatsoever.

3. Jesus was both human and divine.

There were numerous sub-groups within this category. One group, known as Subordinationists, believed that Jesus was divine and that he was created by God the Father; thus, Jesus was not equal to the Father but subordinate to him. Origen of Alexandria, the most prolific Christian writer in history with over 1,000 books, was a Subordinationist.

Another group believed that Jesus was always divine and that when Jesus became human he became an additional person. So, Jesus existed as two beings: the man Jesus of Nazareth who was human and the Christ who was completely divine. People who held this belief are known as Separationists.

A third group believed that Jesus was always divine and when he became human he took on an additional nature. So Jesus is one person with two natures, one divine and one human. This is the Trinitarian view of Jesus that ultimately became orthodoxy. Today, it is the mainstream position in Catholicism, Protestantism and Eastern Orthodox Christianity. The official position of these churches is that all the other groups, with their different views about Jesus, are heretics, deviators from the truth of the orthodoxy of Trinitarianism.

Is it fair to casually dismiss these other views of Jesus as heretical? They can't be considered heretics from an early Church perspective because, as we've seen, there were many competing views about Jesus. During the first three centuries, Church doctrine had yet to be fixed. To take one example, Trinitarians like to quote early Church Fathers like Tertullian (155 – 240 CE) who spoke of a "trinitas" (Latin for 'threeness'). They cite them as proof that the Trinity was the standard belief of Christians in the early Church. However, such claims are misleading. When we properly examine the writings of individuals like Tertullian, we find that this is not the case:

> **For the Father is the entire substance, but the Son is a derivation and portion of the whole, as He Himself acknowledges: "My Father is greater than I." In the Psalm His inferiority is described as being "a little lower than the angels." Thus the Father is distinct from the Son, being greater than the Son. [6]**

In other words, one of the earliest sources in the early Church who spoke of a 'trinity' never actually taught a doctrine of three co-equal persons. Tertullian's understanding of Scripture was that the Father and Son cannot be co-equal, which goes against modern Trinitarianism. At this early stage in history, the doctrine of the Trinity was still in its infancy, so any talk of the Trinity being orthodoxy is not only anachronistic, but also a gross oversimplification. Many of the doctrine's finer details had yet to be formulated. This is why historians refer to the early Christians who believed in the deity of Jesus as "partially Trinitarian", or "proto-Trinitarian", as the doctrine hadn't yet been fully developed. Another issue with labelling these other views of Jesus as heretical is that proto-Trinitarianism wasn't even necessarily the majority belief in the early Church. Indeed, historians think that, at one point, there were more non-Trinitarian Christians than so-called orthodox Trinitarian believers. We can find evidence of this in the writings of Tertullian who commented:

> **The simple, indeed, (I will not call them unwise and unlearned,) who always constitute the majority of believers, are startled at the dispensation (of the Three in One)... are constantly throwing out against us that we are preachers of two gods and three gods... [7]**

Tertullian wrote the above in a chapter in his book "Sundry Popular Fears and Prejudices. The Doctrine of the Trinity in Unity Rescued from These Misapprehensions". This indicates that the proto-Trinitarian view was a minority belief in the early Church, which the masses rejected on the grounds that it was polytheistic. Another piece of historical evidence is a sermon delivered by the fourth century bishop Gregory of Nyssa:

> **If in this city you ask a shopkeeper for change, he will argue with you about whether the Son is begotten or unbegotten. If you enquire about the quality of the bread, the baker will answer, 'The Father is greater, the Son is less.' And if you ask the bath attendant to draw your bath, he will tell you that the Son was created ex nihilo [out of nothing]. [8]**

Gregory's wry comment is fascinating for what it says and what it implies. It suggests that ordinary tradespeople and workers felt perfectly competent to debate abstract theological issues. Gregory's shopkeeper questions whether

Jesus is "begotten or unbegotten" – that is, whether he is a creation of God or the Creator Himself. The bath attendant says that he was created "out of nothing", meaning that he was brought into existence like the rest of God's creatures. And the baker asserts that Jesus is separate from, and lesser than, God. All of these views go against the Trinity and seemed to be the popular belief among common people.

Proto-Trinitarianism was not even necessarily the default position of the bishops of the Roman Empire in the middle of the fourth century. For example, the high-ranking bishop of Constantinople, Macedonius, endorsed a non-Trinitarian position:

> **Towards the middle of the fourth century, Macedonius, Bishop of Constantinople, and, after him a number of Semi-Arians, while apparently admitting the Divinity of the Word, denied that of the Holy Ghost. [9]**

One of the most astounding historical facts about the Trinity is that the earliest Church Fathers who promoted a proto-Trinitarian belief (such as Tertullian and Origen) were all later condemned by the Roman Catholic Church as heretics. On the other hand, Church Fathers such as Ignatius, Polycarp and others, who taught a binitarian (not Trinitarian) view, are today considered to be saints by the Roman Catholic Church. This demonstrates the frivolity of assigning labels like orthodox and heretic in the early Church, as the orthodoxy of one age can (and did) become the heresy of the next.

We need to be more nuanced in our discussion of these subjects. We shouldn't evaluate these different views about Jesus as a popularity contest, but rather on the strength of the arguments that each view puts forward. We've seen that early Christianity was widely diverse, and that different groups of Christians in the ancient world held varying, even contradictory, points of view about the nature of Jesus. By the sixteenth century, the Trinity had a virtual monopoly in Christian thought. So dominant was the doctrine of the Trinity that toeing the line of orthodoxy was a matter of life and death. Michael Servetus was a sixteenth century Spanish theologian whose interpretations of the Bible brought him into conflict with the Church. In 1531 CE, Servetus published the book "Errors of the Trinity", in which he said those who believed in the Trinity were really Tritheists (believers in three gods). He was condemned as a heretic and burnt alive atop a pyre of his own books [10]. How did the Trinity go from being just another belief about Jesus to a position of absolute dominance to the point where dissent could cost you your life? We will now turn our attention to the tides of history to see just how the Trinity came to be the dominant, orthodox position of Christianity today.

HOW THE TRINITY BECOMES ORTHODOXY

Earlier, we saw how Christianity started out as a small movement within Judaism. When Christianity eventually spread to Gentiles (non-Jews), how was the religion perceived by the general Pagan populace in the Roman Empire? By 300 CE, Christians had accounted for approximately 10% of the Roman population, according to some estimates [11]. Up until that point, Christians had been a persecuted minority. This persecution culminated in the passing of legislation which compelled Christians to sacrifice to the Roman gods or face imprisonment and execution [12].

The coming to power of the Roman Emperor Constantine was a major turning point for Christianity. After his victory, Constantine supported the Church financially, granted privileges such as exemption from certain taxes to the clergy, promoted Christians to high-ranking offices and returned previously confiscated property to the churches [13]. Under the influence of Constantine, the Christian movement gradually underwent its major transformation from a previously underground, and even criminal, movement persecuted by the general Pagan populace into an officially-sanctioned religion of 'first rank' within the Roman Empire. Both Paganism and Christianity were now legal religions, with their respective adherents vying for power in the Roman Empire.

Perhaps the defining moment of Constantine's reign came with the Arian controversy. In the early fourth century, a debate raged within the Church with regard to the nature of Jesus and his precise relationship to God. Arius, a priest and theologian, and bishop Athanasius, a Church Father, were the chief proponents of both sides of the debate. Athanasius was a Trinitarian who promoted the idea that Jesus was equal to God, whereas Arius promoted the idea that Jesus was in fact a creation of God and therefore inferior to God. A major contention for Arius and his followers, the Arians, with regard to the Trinity was that if the Son were equal to the Father, then there would be more than one God. These disagreements about the nature of Jesus and his relationship to God deeply divided Christianity in the Roman Empire into two opposing theological factions. It's important to note that neither side was a niche group; in the fourth century, Arianism had the upper hand in the Eastern, Greek-speaking part of the Roman Empire, while the Trinitarians dominated the Western, Latin-speaking part.

Council of Nicea

Emperor Constantine, seeking to unify the Church, convened the Council of Nicea in 325 CE. The question to be settled was, "Is Jesus absolutely equal to the Father: always existing and of the very same substance, or not?" Bishops from all over the empire were summoned to the council where their differences would be debated with the aim of reaching agreement. This was the first time in Christian history that such a council had convened. Constantine told the delegates that they would enjoy the climate and also, with a hint of menace, that he intended to: *"be present as a spectator and participator in those things which will be done" [14].* It must be noted that Constantine was not interested in doctrinal purity; his motivation for calling the council was merely to assure the political stability of his empire. Constantine himself said: *"When I heard of your division, I was convinced that this matter should by no means be neglected... I shall feel my desire fulfilled only when I see the minds of all united in that peaceful harmony... Put away all causes of strife, and loosen all knots of discord by the laws of peace."* [15]

The Council of Nicea had three points of view represented at the meeting: the strict Arians, the semi-Arians and the strict Trinitarians. The strict Arians were a small minority who were led by Arius. They believed that Jesus is inferior to God and rejected the notion that Jesus is of the same substance as God. The strict Trinitarians were also a small minority and they were led by

Athanasius. They opposed Arianism because it questioned the deity of Jesus. The vast majority in attendance, however, took a middle position between Arianism and Trinitarianism. They were led by Eusebius of Caesarea and are referred to as "Semi-Arians". They rejected the Trinitarian doctrine that the Father, the Son, and the Holy Spirit are of the same substance. About this council, Church historian Philip Schaff wrote:

> *In reference to the theological question the council was divided in the beginning into three parties. The orthodox party... was at first in the minority... The Arians or Eusebians numbered perhaps twenty bishops... The majority, whose organ was the renowned historian Eusebius of Caesarea, took middle ground between the right and the left... [16]*

This is further evidence that the Trinity was not the orthodox position of the early Church, since the majority of bishops attending had not held a pro-Trinitarian, anti-Arian view before the council.

The council proceedings caused the mood of the undecided majority to move towards an anti-Arian view. Because of this sudden swing away from Arianism, the goal of the council quickly shifted from seeking compromise to condemning Arianism in no uncertain terms. Since it was difficult to do this on scriptural terms alone, the bishops decided to formulate a creed that specifically excluded Arianism from the scope of Christian belief. Key to it was a concept found nowhere in the Bible: homo-ousios (from the Greek 'homos', meaning "same", and 'ousia', meaning "essence"). The anti-Arians wanted to insert this concept of Jesus being of the same substance as God into the official creedal statement of the Church. This anti-Arian clause was proposed by Emperor Constantine himself [17]. Arius and his followers refused to accept it because they believed that Jesus was created by God and therefore they were materially separate from one another. Notice that the contention was not about passages of the Bible, but rather philosophy. This further reinforces the point that the Trinity is not a biblical concept but rather extraneous to the Bible. The Church had to come up with terms of "philosophical" (pagan/Greek) origin in order to explain it, as former Pope Benedict XVI states:

In order to articulate the dogma of the Trinity, the Church had to develop its own terminology with the help of certain notions of philosophical origin: "substance," "person," or "hypostasis," "relation" and so on. [18]

Faced with the awe-inspiring presence of the emperor, there could be little opposition: the majority of the bishops on the council ultimately agreed upon a creed, known thereafter as the "Nicene Creed": *"[The] majority eventually acquiesced in the ruling of the Alexandrians [trinitarians]; yet this result was due... partly to the pressure of the imperial will." [19]*

When the creed was finished, eighteen bishops still opposed it. Constantine at this point intervened to threaten with exile anyone who would not sign for it. Two Libyan bishops and Arius still refused to accept the creed. All three were exiled [20].

Although Constantine is usually remembered for the steps he took towards making Christianity an established religion in the Roman Empire, it would not be wrong to consider him as one of the chief driving forces behind the Nicene Creed. It was he who proposed and perhaps even imposed the expression homo-ousios ("same essence") on the Council of Nicea, and it was he who provided government aid to the so-called orthodox and exerted government pressure against non-conformists [21].

Councils of Rimini and Seleucia

The Council of Nicea, however, did not end the controversy, as many bishops of the Eastern provinces disputed the concept of homo-ousios, the central term of the Nicene Creed. The debates among these groups continued and resulted in numerous meetings, and no fewer than fourteen further creedal formulas between 340 CE and 360 CE, leading the pagan observer Ammianus Marcellinus to comment sarcastically: *"The highways were covered with galloping bishops." [22]*

Emperor Constantine's sons, among whom the empire was divided after his death, became even more embroiled in the theological disputes. The emperor in the West, Constans, sided with Nicea, while the emperor in the

East, Constantius, was anti-Nicea. Thus, a pattern was being set for political interference with theological issues on the part of civil rulers. Whether Arianism or the Nicene Creed had the upper hand at any particular time depended upon which one had the favour of the respective emperor.

With the death of Constans in 350 CE, his anti-Nicea brother Constantius became the sole ruler of the Empire. In 359 CE, he summoned two councils, one in the East at Seleucia and the other in the West at Rimini. These councils were attended by more bishops than at Nicea and were thus more representative of the entire Church. Like his father Constantine before him, Constantius also involved himself in the council proceedings, exerting pressure on the bishops attending. An anti-Nicean, pro-Arian creed was adopted, and thus Arianism gained the upper hand in the Roman Empire. Writing about these councils, Saint Jerome remarked that the world *"awoke with a groan to find itself Arian" [23].* The balance of power was now in favour of Arianism, and it looked like it had triumphed over Trinitarianism. So, if Trinitarians want to argue that today orthodoxy is on their side on the basis of popularity, then at one point Arianism was in the dominant position and was therefore orthodoxy!

Council of Constantinople

The seeming triumph of Arianism was short-lived. In 381 CE, the Council of Constantinople was summoned by Emperor Theodosius I. The main business of the council was to re-establish the doctrine that had been set forth in the Nicene Creed. They did this by writing a new creed to remove some of the language of the Nicene Creed that had proven controversial and problematic. This council *"sealed the final adoption of the faith of Nicea by the entire Church" [24].* So, the Nicene Creed, first set out on the Council of Nicea 55 years earlier, was ultimately victorious over Arianism.

It's important to note that on earlier councils, for example the Council of Nicea, they did not specify that the third person of the Trinity existed; they simply said they believed in the Holy Spirit. While the Council of Constantinople reaffirmed the tenets of the faith which were established in Nicea, one specific area where the doctrine of the Trinity had developed was related to the Holy Spirit. The divinity of the Holy Spirit was an important issue, as the Church debated and formalised its emerging view of the Trinity. The council attributed a number of things to the Holy Spirit, such as a divine title, 'Lord', and supreme worship equal to that rendered to the Father and the Son. Thus, the Holy Spirit was voted as the third Person of the Trinity. It should be pointed out that the disciples of Jesus had all been dead for hundreds of years before this position was agreed upon. The Catholic Church states: **"The apostolic faith concerning the Spirit was announced by the second ecumenical council at Constantinople (381 CE)." [25]**

Trinitarian and evangelical scholar Harold Brown gives some reasons for the slow adoption of the Holy Spirit as a person of the Trinity:

> **The language of the New Testament permits the Holy Spirit to be understood as an impersonal force or influence more readily than it does the Son...The attempt to develop an understanding of the Holy Spirit consistent with the trinitarian passages...came to fruition at Constantinople in 381. There were a number of reasons why the personhood of the Holy Spirit took longer to acknowledge than the Son: (1) the term pneuma, breath, is neuter in general and impersonal in ordinary meaning; (2) the distinctive work of the Holy Spirit, influencing the believer, does not necessarily seem as personal as that of the Father...in addition, those who saw the Holy Spirit as a Person, were often heretical, for example, the Montanists; (3) many of the early theologians attributed to the Logos or Word, the revelatory activity later theologians saw as the special, personal work of the Holy Spirit. [26]**

In other words, we can understand that:

1. A doctrine close to what modern Trinitarians teach about the Holy Spirit was not widely accepted until over 300 years after Jesus.

2. Normal understanding of the Greek of the New Testament suggests that the Holy Spirit is impersonal – not a person. This is in contrast to the portrayal of the Father and the Son.

3. The idea of treating the Holy Spirit as a person, as Trinitarians do today, was often associated with heretical groups in the early Church.

4. Early Christian theologians contradicted the current Trinitarian view of the Holy Spirit because they used to assign its functions, such as revelatory activity, to the Son.

At the close of the Council of Constantinople, Emperor Theodosius issued an imperial decree declaring that the churches should be restored to those bishops who confessed the equal divinity of the Father, the Son, and the Holy Spirit:

> *...let us believe in the one deity of the Father, Son and Holy Spirit, in equal majesty and in a holy Trinity. We authorize the followers of this law to assume the title Catholic Christians; but as for the others, since in our judgement they are foolish madmen, we decree that they shall be branded with the ignominious name of heretics, and shall not presume to give their conventicles the name of churches. They will suffer in the first place the chastisement of divine condemnation and the second the punishment of our authority, in accordance with the will of heaven shall decide to inflict... [27]*

Historical scholar Jonathan Roberts wrote:

> *Until Theodosius commanded his subjects to believe in the doctrine of the Trinity, and enforced his commands upon them by the most inhumane ways, that doctrine was rejected and resisted by the Greek and Roman followers of the Christos... That so senseless and unnatural doctrine should have been forced upon any people, by any means, however tyrannical is a mystery even more mysterious than the arithmetic that can make one three, and three one. [28]*

Thus, Arianism was officially outlawed. It was extinguished not by the force of scriptural truth, but by the force of imperial involvement. After over 55 years of battle, the Nicene Creed permanently gained the upper hand and Trinitarianism became the official doctrine of the Roman Catholic Church.

Council of Chalcedon

Even after Arianism was defeated, debate raged on about the nature of the incarnate Jesus as he walked upon the earth. While the Council of Nicea focused on the precise relationship of the Son to God the Father, the question that now had to be settled was: did Jesus have a single nature, meaning a mixture of human and divine, or a dual nature – human and divine, both distinct and not blurred together?

In 451 CE, the council of Chalcedon was summoned to address the nature of Jesus. The bishops arrived at the understanding of the two natures of Christ in one person. They adopted the Creed of Chalcedon, which stated:

We, then, following the holy Fathers, all with one consent, teach men to confess one and the same Son, our Lord Jesus Christ, the same perfect in Godhead and also perfect in manhood; truly God and truly man, of a reasonable [rational] soul and body; consubstantial [coessential] with us according to the manhood; in all things like unto us, without sin; begotten before all ages of the Father according to the Godhead, and in these latter days, for us and for our salvation, born of the Virgin Mary, the mother of God, according to the Manhood; one and the same Christ, Son, Lord, Only-begotten, to be acknowledged in two natures, inconfusedly, unchangeably, indivisibly, inseparably; the distinction of natures being by no means taken away by the union, but rather the property of each nature being preserved, and concurring in one person and one Subsistence, not parted or divided into two persons, but one and the same Son, and only begotten, God the Word, the Lord Jesus Christ, as the prophets from the beginning [have declared] concerning him, and the Lord Jesus Christ himself has taught us, and the Creed of the holy Fathers has handed down to us.

This concept of a dual human and divine nature in the person of Jesus is known as the Hypostatic Union, an essential component of modern Trinitarianism. Yet, it wasn't until the Council of Chalcedon that we saw the emergence of an official doctrine of the Trinity in a form that is recognisable with what Trinitarians believe in today. This took place in the fifth century, over 400 years after Jesus.

Evangelical theologian and professor Wayne A. Grudem sums this up as follows: **"[A] precise understanding of how full deity and full humanity" argues Grudem, "could be combined together in one person was formulated only gradually in the church and did not reach the final form until the Chalcedonian Definition in a.d. 451." [29]**

Some reflections on the Church councils

Regarding these various Church councils, I'd like to share with the reader some personal reflections:

1. The Trinity, as it is believed in today, did not emerge as the official doctrine of the Church until over 400 years after Jesus. Yet, today it is considered to be so pivotal to mainstream Christianity that anyone diverging from this is labelled a disbeliever or member of a cult. How central to the early Church could a doctrine, not fully formulated until a much later date, actually be? One would expect that anything that was truly fundamental to the Christian faith would have been clear and accepted by the Church from the first century.

2. The doctrine of the Trinity did not come into the Church easily, but rather through a great deal of dispute. Every fundamental aspect of the doctrine – the relationship of Jesus to God, the deity of the Holy Spirit, the dual nature of Jesus – was borne out of council proceedings spanning over a century. These were not dominated solely by scriptural discussion; politics and philosophy played significant roles.

3. Imperial involvement played a large part in determining which theological view was dominant at any given moment. Emperor Constantine was not a minister or even a theologian, but a political figure. However, he was a pivotal figure in establishing the Nicene Creed. To him, it was not a matter of true doctrine, but what was politically expedient. If Constantine or any subsequent emperors had favoured Arianism, then the tides of history could very well have turned in its favour and Arianism could be orthodoxy today!

So far, we have analysed the Trinitarian claim to orthodoxy from the historical angle. We will now look at the Bible to see whether it can stake a claim to orthodoxy from a scriptural standpoint.

IS THE TRINITY BIBLICAL?

Is the Trinity Biblical? To many people, this may sound like a strange question; in fact, many of the Christians that I interact with assume that everything they have been taught in church is based on the Bible. Is this really the case with the Trinity, is it Biblical? Through my research I was surprised to learn that the term 'Trinity' is not found anywhere in the Bible. Such terminology appears only in the writings of Church Fathers, much later in history. The position of the Catholic Church is that the term 'Trinity' was first mentioned late into the second century, about 150 years after Jesus:

> *In Scripture there is as yet no single term by which the Three Divine Persons are denoted together...The word trias (of which the Latin trinitas is a translation) is first found in Theophilus of Antioch about A.D. 180... Afterwards it appears in its Latin form of trinitas in Tertullian. [30]*

Its absence from the Bible is striking when one considers that this is the core doctrine of Trinitarianism. The Oxford Companion to the Bible, which has entries from over two hundred and sixty Bible scholars and academics from leading biblical institutes and universities in America and Europe, states: *"Because the Trinity is such an important part of later Christian doctrine, it is striking that the term does not appear in the New Testament..." [31]*

I often ask Christians about the absence of the term "Trinity" in the Bible. A common response that I receive is that, although the specific word "Trinity" is not present, its concept is found throughout the New Testament. When we examine the New Testament, is it really the case that there is a concept of God being three persons, Father, Son and Holy Spirit, who are co-equal and co-eternal? Since the Trinity is a fundamental doctrine, it's not unreasonable to expect to find a clear statement from the Bible that comprehensively defines the doctrine of the Trinity as it is believed in today. In my experience, the most common pieces of evidence put forward are the letters of Paul and the Gospels of John and Matthew. Here are some typical examples:

For in him [Jesus] dwelleth all the fullness of the Godhead bodily.
[Colossians 2:9]

In the beginning was the Word, and the Word was with God, and
the Word was God. [John 1:1]

Therefore go and make disciples of all nations, baptizing them
in the name of the Father and of the Son and of the Holy Spirit.
[Matthew 28:19]

Let's analyse each of these statements in turn to see if they are genuine proof texts for the concept of the Trinity as it is taught by the Church today. We will first deal with the statement by Paul: ***"For in him [Jesus] dwelleth all the fullness of the Godhead bodily" [Colossians 2:9].*** When one looks at other writings by Paul, we find mention of God "dwelling" in individuals other than Jesus: ***"and to know this love that surpasses knowledge—that you may be filled to the measure of all the fullness of God" [Ephesians 3:19].*** Here Paul prays that believers will be filled with "all the fullness of God". Clearly, Paul is not implying that believing Christians are literally divine persons. In other places, Paul talks of there being government in the Godhead, he gives a hierarchy of authority and responsibility: ***"But I want you to realize that the head of every man is Christ, and the head of the woman is man, and the head of Christ is God" [1 Corinthians 11:3].*** Here Paul evidently states that the Father is the head over all creation, including Jesus. Remember that the doctrine of the Trinity states that Jesus the Son and God the Father are co-equal, which of course conflicts with Paul's hierarchy of the Father as being the head of the Son. Even if we were to accept that Paul's mention of "Godhead" in **Colossians 2:9** indicates a plurality in the nature of God, can we conclude that God is three persons from this statement? We cannot; it is in fact ambiguous because it could mean two or more persons, there's no reason to conclude three. Nor is there any mention of the Holy Spirit, so **Colossians 2:9** is insufficient as it does not comprehensively support the concept of God being three persons who are all co-equal and co-eternal.

Now, if Paul had really believed in there being three persons in the Godhead, then he would have mentioned all three members in his letters to the church-es – he never did. Paul mentioned the Father and Jesus in every introduction of every letter he wrote **(Romans 1:7; 1 Corinthians 1:3; 2 Corinthians 1:2; Galatians 1:3; Ephesians 1:2; Philippians 1:2; Colossians 1:2; 1 Thessalonians 1:1; 2 Thessalonians 1:2; 1 Timothy 1:2; 2 Timothy 1:2; Hebrews 1:1-2),** but he never mentioned the Holy Spirit. If Paul were a Trinitarian, then such an omission is astounding. Clearly, Paul did not believe in a Triune God.

What about the Gospel of John, does it represent a proof text for the Trinity? The alleged proof text cited earlier was the following: **In the beginning was the Word, and the Word was with God, and the Word was God [John 1:1].** At face value, this may seem like conclusive evidence of Jesus being God, because Trinitarians interpret the Word to be Jesus and the verse apparently states **"and the Word was God."** The English translation that this particular version of the Bible has chosen is subjective. If one was to analyse the original Greek of the New Testament, one would find that it is far less clear. The English word translated as "God" **("and the Word was God")** lacks the definite article in Greek, so the verse can also be translated as **"and the Word was divine"** or **"and the Word was a god".** Origen of Alexandria, a teacher of Greek grammar of the third century and arguably the most important theologian and biblical scholar of the early Greek Church, wrote about the use of the definite article in **John 1:1:**

> **In some cases he [John] uses the article, and in some he omits it... He uses the article, when the name of God refers to the uncreated cause of all things, and omits it when the Logos [Word] is named God.... The true God, then, is 'The God'" [32]**

Origen concluded that John's intention in omitting the definite article was to show that Jesus is not truly God. Because of the ambiguity of **John 1:1**, we cannot use it as a basis to establish the divinity of Jesus. If we are serious about understanding Scripture, then we must interpret any ambiguous statements by an author in the light of their clear statements. The following verses of the Gospel of John provide the correct context for interpreting **John 1:1:**

> **After Jesus said this, he looked toward heaven and prayed: "Father, the hour has come. Glorify your Son, that your Son may glorify you. For you granted him authority over all people that he might give**

eternal life to all those you have given him. Now this is eternal life: that they know you, the only true God, and Jesus Christ, whom you have sent." [John 17:1-3]

Notice that Jesus is said to pray to the Father, evidently identifying the Father as the only true God to the exclusion of himself, the Son. If Jesus really were part of a Trinity, then he would have said *"the Father, Son and Holy Spirit are the only true God."* Remember that the doctrine of the Trinity states that the Father, the Son and the Holy Spirit are all fully God. Yet, Jesus isolates the Father as the only God to the exclusion of himself. Church Father Augustine, one of the greatest Trinitarian theologians in history, was so disturbed by these verses that he resorted to manipulating them in order to protect the doctrine of the Trinity. It was so difficult for Augustine to harmonise John 17:3 with his belief in the doctrine of the Trinity that he restructured the verse to make the Father and the Son equal in divinity. Augustine, in his "Homilies on John", changed the wording of **John 17:3** to say: **"This is eternal life, that they may know Thee and Jesus Christ, whom Thou hast sent, as the only true God."** [33] Notice how Augustine grouped the word "Jesus" with "Thee" (**"Thee and Jesus Christ"**) in order for both the Father and Jesus to be identified as "the only true God". Compare this to what John actually says: **"Now this is eternal life: that they know you, the only true God, and Jesus Christ, whom you have sent"**, which distinguishes Jesus from God. Augustine's change was subtle, but it seriously distorted the original meaning of the words in order to make Jesus equal to the Father in divinity.

With regard to this statement from the Gospel of Matthew: **"Therefore go and make disciples of all nations, baptizing them in the name of the Father and of the Son and of the Holy Spirit" [Matthew 28:19]**. Now this verse does have Jesus mentioning the three persons of the Trinity; however, it says nothing about their relationship with one another. It does not say that the Father, the Son and the Holy Spirit are all equal, nor does it say that they are all eternal, or that they are even God. Just mentioning the persons collectively does not equate to the doctrine of the Trinity, as even Muslims believe in the persons of God Almighty, Jesus and the Holy Spirit (whom we believe is the angel Gabriel). What's interesting about this verse in the Gospel of Matthew is that there are serious doubts about whether Jesus ever uttered the words attributed to him. The reason is, if Jesus really did say those words, then shouldn't we expect his loyal disciples to obey his command and baptise people using the formula that Jesus instructed? Although the Gospel of Matthew does not have any instances of disciples carrying out baptisms, other books of the New Testament, such as the Book of Acts, contain many such instances, and not once does any disciple baptise in the name of the Father, the Son and the Holy Spirit. Rather, they consistently baptise in the name of Jesus only:

> So he ordered that they be baptized in the name of Jesus Christ. Then they asked Peter to stay with them for a few days. [Acts 10:48]

> And now what are you waiting for? Get up, be baptized and wash your sins away, calling on his [Jesus] name.' [Acts 22:16]

Unless one is going to argue that the disciples of Jesus intentionally disobeyed him, then this indicates that the disciples were not aware of any such instruction, and therefore it is very likely that Jesus never uttered the words attributed to him in the Gospel of Matthew. We find support for this conclusion in the writings of the third century historian Eusebius. He wrote prolifically, quoting many verses of the New Testament in his writings. The verse in question, **Matthew 28:19**, is one that he happens to have quoted numerous times. However, he never quotes it as it appears today in modern Bibles, but always finishes the verse with the words **"in my name"**. For example, in his writings about the persecution of early Christians, we read:

> But the rest of the apostles, who had been incessantly plotted against with a view to their destruction, and had been driven out of the land of Judea, went unto all nations to preach the Gospel, relying upon the power of Christ, who had said to them, <u>"Go ye and make disciples of all the nations in my name."</u> [34]

We can be confident that if the New Testament Eusebius had in front of him read **"in the name of the Father, and of the Son and of the Holy Spirit"**, he would never have quoted it as **"in my name"**. Thus, the earliest manuscripts must have read **"in my name"**, which explains why the disciples used those exact words and not a Trinitarian formula when performing baptisms.

This is the case with all such proof texts put forward by Trinitarians. At best, they only allude to the divinity of Jesus, but this is only when they are taken in isolation. When we go beyond a superficial reading of Scripture, what we find is that all such proof texts fall short in comprehensively supporting the concept of the Trinity as it is believed in today. When Trinitarians try and argue for the divinity of Jesus as conclusive proof of the doctrine of the Trinity, they miss a big point. Even if, for the sake of argument, we grant the claim that there are some statements in the New Testament which can be interpreted to imply that Jesus is divine in some capacity, this in no way takes away from my point about the Trinity: nowhere do we find a clear definition of the doctrine of the Trinity, the idea that God is one Being consisting of three persons, Father, Son and Holy Spirit, who are all co-equal and co-eternal.

The fact is that nowhere in the New Testament is there any explicit mention of any such Trinitarian formula. Nor is God ever spoken of using terms like 'Being' and 'Persons' which is the language used by Trinitarians. These are not only my personal conclusions after years of study into the Bible, but also the findings of Christian scholarship. The Oxford Companion to the Bible, written by Bruce Metzger, one of the most influential New Testament scholars of the 20th century, and containing entries from over two hundred and sixty scholars and academics from leading biblical institutes and universities in America and Europe, states: **"...the developed concept of three co-equal partners in the Godhead found in later creedal formulations cannot be clearly detected within the confines of the canon" [35]**. Likewise, the New Catholic Encyclopedia explains that the doctrine of the Trinity is a product of history, developed over centuries:

> *There is the recognition on the part of exegetes and biblical theologians, including a constantly growing number of Roman Catholics, that one should not speak of Trinitarianism in the New Testament without serious qualification. There is also the closely parallel recognition on the part of historians of dogma and systematic theologians that when one does speak of an unqualified Trinitarianism, one has moved from the period of Christian origins to, say, the last quadrant of the 4th century. It was only then that*

> *what might be called the definitive Trinitarian dogma 'One God in three persons' became thoroughly assimilated into Christian life and thought...it was the product of three centuries of doctrinal development. [36]*

The New Bible Dictionary, an evangelical Trinitarian source, states that while the concept of God becoming man is present in Scripture from the perspective of how it relates to our salvation, the authors of the dictionary concede that the theological formulation of the doctrine is puzzlingly absent in the New Testament:

> *The only sense in which the New Testament writers ever attempt to explain the incarnation is by showing how it fits into God's overall plan for redeeming mankind...This evangelical interest throws light on the otherwise puzzling fact that the New Testament nowhere reflects on the virgin birth of Jesus as witnessing to the conjunction of deity and manhood in His person—a line of thought much canvassed by later theology. [37]*

If the Trinity is the true nature of God, why does the New Testament not clearly support it? If this doctrine is so important, then shouldn't it be evidently explained all over the New Testament, like other doctrines such as the death of Jesus for our sins and his resurrection from the dead? The doctrine must be read into Scripture – it is not derived from it. It is not developed from clear scriptural references, but rather by beginning with a premise and then proceeding to develop "proofs" from ambiguous statements in Scripture.

Any speculation about ambiguous verses of the Bible can be put to rest when we look to the clear, explicit statements that Jesus made regarding God's nature.

JESUS PREACHED PURE MONOTHEISM

There is an interesting incident in the New Testament where Jesus seems to affirm the theology of the Old Testament. One of the Jewish teachers of the law approaches Jesus and asks him which of the commandments is the most important:

"The most important one," answered Jesus, "is this: 'Hear, O Israel: The Lord our God, the Lord is one. Love the Lord your God with all your heart and with all your soul and with all your mind and with all your strength.' The second is this: 'Love your neighbour as yourself.' There is no commandment greater than these."

"Well said, teacher," the man replied. "You are right in saying that God is one and there is no other but him. To love him with all your heart, with all your understanding and with all your strength, and to love your neighbour as yourself is more important than all burnt offerings and sacrifices."

When Jesus saw that he had answered wisely, he said to him, "You are not far from the kingdom of God." And from then on no one dared ask him any more questions. [Mark 12:28-34]

This incident was the perfect opportunity for Jesus to correct misconceptions about God's nature and give the Jewish teacher of the law a Trinitarian understanding of God being three co-equal and co-eternal persons. As you can see, the exact opposite is the case; by quoting the Old Testament commandment about God being One, a direct quote of **Deuteronomy 6:4 ("Hear, O Israel: The Lord our God, the Lord is one")**, and by agreeing with the Jewish teacher's interpretation, Jesus is affirming an understanding of God that is purely monotheistic and rejects all notion of God being a Trinity. Not only is the Jewish teacher's wisdom about God acknowledged, but also Jesus goes so far as to compliment him, saying that he is close to the kingdom of God.

The reason why Jewish people do not believe in a Triune God is that He is never presented as such in the Old Testament. This is not surprising, given that God is described in purely monotheistic terms throughout the Old Testament. The Prophets of the Old Testament, such as Abraham, Noah and Moses, never preached that God is a Trinity. Their core message was simple: there is one God who is unlike His creation and He alone deserves our worship. Does it make sense that God sent countless Prophets, over a span of thousands of years, with a consistent message of pure monotheism, and then all of a sudden reveals that He is a Trinity, a radically different message which contradicts His previous Prophets' teachings?

How do Trinitarians explain this juxtaposition between their beliefs and the portrayal of God in the Old Testament? They claim that God reveals Himself gradually in stages; this is known as the concept of "Progressive Revelation":

> **The things that God revealed to humanity were not all given at once. His revelation was given in stages... Progressive revelation means that God did not unfold His entire plan to humanity in the Book of Genesis or, for that matter, in the entire Old Testament. The Old Testament revelation, though accurate, is incomplete. The fullness of certain teachings cannot be found in the Old Testament. [38]**

This is the idea that the sections of the Bible that were written later contain a fuller revelation of God, compared to the earlier sections. So, the New Testament is to be used to better understand and interpret the Old Testament. Such an explanation must be rejected because the progression from a purely monotheistic concept of God, who is unlike His creation, to a Trinity where God becomes His creation, is anything but gradual. Rather it is a radical overhaul of everything that came before it. Moreover, such an appeal creates more problems than it tries to solve. Because of Progressive Revelation, the Trinitarian concept of God's nature is, and continues to be, open to development. For example, when Trinitarians say that God is plural in personhood, how do they know to stop at three? Why not four or five? We've already seen that there is no verse in the Bible that says there are only three divine persons. At best, one can say that only three have revealed themselves to the Church so far. But how do you know there isn't a fourth lurking in the shadows, ready to reveal themselves? For example, couldn't it be revealed that Mary is also God, perhaps the Mother in the Godhead? Or could it later be revealed that the Holy Spirit is in fact seven persons and not just one **(see Revelation 1:4** which mentions **"the seven spirits before his [God's] throne")?** To reiterate, there is no explicit mention of 'three' either by name or concept, so with Progressive Revelation, there's nothing to stop God becoming four or more persons at some point in the future. Thus, Trinitarians can never lay claim to having a correct understanding of God, because they can never know for certain that God has revealed the full picture about Himself.

The New Testament touches upon an incident with Jesus and a fig tree in the Gospel of Mark:

> **The next day as they were leaving Bethany, Jesus was hungry. Seeing in the distance a fig tree in leaf, he went to find out if it had any fruit. When he reached it, he found nothing but leaves, because it was not the season for figs. Then he said to the tree, "May no one ever eat fruit from you again." And his disciples heard him say it. [Mark 11:12-14]**

Such an incident makes no sense in the light of the Trinitarian claim that Jesus is God. God is All Knowing, so if Jesus really is God, then that would make him the creator of fig trees, in which case how could he have not known that it was not the season for figs? Moreover, why would God curse the fig tree for doing something He himself willed it to do? If Jesus is God, then wouldn't it have been more befitting of him to command the tree to bear fruit? Why ruin a perfectly good tree? Come fig season, this tree would have had fruit and others could have eaten from it.

Some Trinitarians try to get around this problem by claiming that the verses about the fig tree and its lack of fruit are not to be taken literally but rather as a symbol of the nation of Israel and its lack of faith. Now, if the fig tree represents Israel in this particular incident, then this creates a problem. Notice that Mark makes it clear that the fig tree was not defective but just that it wasn't the right season, yet Jesus admonished a perfectly functioning fig tree to obey God's law by producing figs in certain seasons. This would mean that

Israel was being punished by God for obeying him! Such interpretations must be rejected because Mark very clearly gives us the reason as to why Jesus approached the fig tree: **"Jesus was hungry."** It doesn't say that "Jesus approached the fig tree because he saw an opportunity for a parable."

From the perspective of Trinitarian theology and the dual nature of Jesus, it would have been the limited human nature that made the mistake and the divine nature that had the power to curse the fig tree. However, this situation presents us with some difficult questions with regard to the interplay between the divine and human nature - why did the divine nature not inform him that there were no figs instead of acting upon the mistake of his human side? Is this a case of the human nature overriding the divine nature? Is such a thing possible?

Furthermore, such incidents bring to light the many paradoxes of the Trinity. For example, how can God be All Powerful and yet have weaknesses such as hunger? Such attributes are mutually exclusive. It would be like being asked to draw a square circle. Such a task is impossible, because each has incompatible properties: a shape cannot have four corners like a square and no corners like a circle at the same time. Yet, such paradoxes are what Trinitarians have to believe in in order for Jesus to not only be God, All Powerful and All Knowing, but also human with limitations such as hunger and possessing limited knowledge.

From this incident we can see that when it comes to the knowledge of Jesus, it seems that the divine nature is either lacking or completely absent. How then can the claim be made that Jesus is fully God? From what we've seen it seems that Jesus is human but not divine because he lacks essential attributes of God, such as possessing All Knowledge.

The fig tree incident is by no means an isolated case. Jesus plainly says elsewhere that the Son and the Holy Spirit do not know the hour, meaning the time of the Day of Judgement, but only the Father: **"But about that day or hour no one knows, not even the angels in heaven, nor the Son, but only the Father" [Mark 13:32].** From this we can see that the divine shortcomings of lacking All Knowledge aren't just restricted to Jesus; the Holy Spirit also lacks God's perfect knowledge. How then can the Father, the Son and the

Holy Spirit be said to be co-equal, as the doctrine of the Trinity teaches? If the Father possesses knowledge that the Son and the Holy Spirit lack, then the Father is a greater person of God than both Jesus and the Holy Spirit, in at least one area: knowledge.

In conclusion, we can see that the New Testament paints a picture of God and Jesus that is at odds with Trinitarian theology.

RECONCILING THE TRINITY WITH REASON

God is perfect in His knowledge, so it stands to reason that His true revelation will also be perfect. When we move beyond a basic understanding of the doctrine of the Trinity and dig beneath the surface even just a little, we will find that it is full of contradictions and inconsistencies. For example, the Bible says God is eternal and unchanging:

> *Your throne is established from of old; you are from everlasting.*
> *[Psalm 93:2]*

> *Every good and perfect gift is from above, coming down from the*
> *Father of the heavenly lights, who does not change like shifting*
> *shadows. [James 1:17]*

The Bible supports the notion that God does not change; indeed, God cannot change, because He transcends time altogether. Now the Trinitarian claim that God became flesh at the incarnation poses a problem. If the Son took on a dual nature, that is, a limited human nature alongside his divine nature, whilst at the same time still being God, then the implication is that in becoming man, the nature of God changed. The doctrine of the incarnation seems to contradict the Bible's statements that God is eternal and unchanging.

Trinitarians try to get around this issue by arguing that at the incarnation, nothing changed about God, and a human nature was merely added to God's divine nature. They reason that, since the two natures did not mix, the divine nature did not change at all in this "joining" and so God remained the same.

Can this be considered valid reasoning? Well, if God 'added' a new nature to Himself, then that is a change in state. Was God always a man? He was not. Did God later on become fully human? The answer, according to Trinitarian theology, is yes. Adding anything to oneself is clearly a change. To claim otherwise is nothing more than philosophical wordplay.

To illustrate why this is the case, let's take the example of a human being called John. Consider a hypothetical scenario in which God granted John a second nature - a divine nature. You can see that this scenario mirrors the incarnation; John took on an additional divine nature, much like Trinitarians believe God the Son took on an additional human nature. Even if John's first nature, humanity, remains unchanged and separate from his divinity, would you ever conclude that John has undergone no change at all? Would any reasonable person argue, "well, John hasn't really changed in nature, his original finite human nature is only being complemented by an additional infinite nature." Evidently, for anyone to claim that John, going from mere mortal to master of the universe, has undergone no change would be absurd.

Yet, the Trinitarian doctrine represents exactly the same scenario. In becoming divine, John has changed from one state (not being God) to another (being God). This mirrors the incarnation where God is said to have become flesh, which also entails a change from one state (not being human) to another (being human). The end result for both Jesus and John is the same; they've both become God-men. The only difference was their direction of change (God →God-man v.s. man →God-man). We must conclude that the incarnation involved an intrinsic change to the Son, and since Trinitarians claim that the Son is God, the implication is that God has changed. This directly conflicts with the Bible's statements that God is eternal and unchanging.

More issues with the doctrine of the incarnation emerge when we consider God's perfection. God is perfect in every way possible; both Muslims and Christians believe this to be true. Recall that Trinitarians believe that, at the incarnation, God entered into the creation as a human being in the form of Jesus. Humanity has been permanently incorporated into the Godhead; the Son will forever have an inseparable divine and human nature. This is in contrast to the nature of the Godhead before the incarnation, with all persons of the Trinity being purely divine into eternity past. This raises some uncomfortable questions. Since God is the pinnacle of perfection, then there is no need for Him to become anything. If God is perfect and something needs to be added to His nature, then doesn't that mean He lacked something before? Which state is considered more "godly", the pre-incarnation God, or post-incarnation God? You can see that the doctrine of the incarnation puts Trinitarians in a blasphemous predicament.

We've seen that such contradictions and inconsistencies are rampant through-out Trinitarian teaching. Can such a theology really be a true revelation from God when He is perfect in His knowledge?

THE INFLUENCE OF PAGANISM ON THE TRINITY

We've seen that the Trinity is not present in the Bible in either name or concept, and that its claim of a Triune God not only conflicts with the teachings of Jesus in the New Testament, but it is also inherently contradictory and inconsistent and therefore unlikely to be God's perfect revelation. So, where did the Trinity come from? In order to answer this question, we need to understand the world into which Christianity was born and developed. The disciples, the first believers in Jesus, were Jews. In fact, Christianity started out as a movement within Judaism. Like Jews since the time of Moses, these first believers kept the Sabbath, were circumcised and worshipped in the Temple: ***"One day Peter and John were going up to the temple at the time of prayer—at three in the afternoon." [Acts 3:1]*** The only thing that distinguished the early followers of Jesus from any other Jews was their belief in Jesus as the Messiah, that is, the one chosen by God who would redeem the Jewish people. Today, many Christian scholars agree that the authors of the New Testament, such as Matthew, were Jewish believers in Jesus. The influence of Judaism on the New Testament is important because it helps us to correctly understand its message. The New Testament is full of terminology like "son of God". Such language is interpreted literally by Trinitarians to mean that Jesus is God the Son, but is this correct? What was the intention of the Jewish writers of the New Testament when they used such language? What did these terms mean at the time of Jesus?

When we turn to the Old Testament, we find that such language permeates its pages. For example, Moses calls God "Father": **"Is this the way you repay the Lord, you foolish and unwise people? Is he not your Father, your Creator, who made you and formed you?" [Deuteronomy 32:6]**

Angels are referred to as "sons of God": **"Now there was a day when the sons of God came to present themselves before the Lord, and Satan came also among them." [Job 1:6]**

The Old Testament even goes so far as to call Moses a god: **"And the LORD said unto Moses, See, I have made thee a god to Pharaoh: and Aaron thy brother shall be thy prophet" [Exodus 7:1].**

The Israelites are also referred to as "gods": **"I said, 'You are "gods"; you are all sons of the Most High'" [Psalm 82:6].** What we can conclude is that such highly exalted language was commonplace and was intended to serve figurative purposes; it is not a literal indication of divinity. Even as late as the end of the first century, when the New Testament writers started penning their accounts of the life of Jesus, Jewish people were still using such language figuratively. In a conversation between Jesus and some Jewish teachers of the law, they say to Jesus: **"...The only Father we have is God himself" [John 8:41].** The Gospel of Luke calls Adam a son of God when it recounts the lineage of Jesus: **"the son of Enosh, the son of Seth, the son of Adam, the son of God" [Luke 3:38].**

Jesus even says that anyone who makes peace is a child of God: **"Blessed are the peacemakers, for they will be called children of God" [Matthew 5:9].** If the New Testament writers understood such language to be a claim to divinity, then they would have used it exclusively in relation to Jesus. Clearly, it denotes a person that is righteous before God, nothing more.

The turning point in history came when Christianity ceased being a small movement within Judaism and Gentiles (non-Jews) started to embrace the faith in large numbers. We need to look at the pagan world of the Gentiles in order to understand the mindset of the people that received the New Testament message. Since the time of Alexander the Great, Gentiles had been living in a Hellenistic (Greek) world. Their lands were dominated by Roman armies, with the Roman Empire being the superpower of the world at the time. The Roman Empire itself was heavily influenced by Hellenistic religion, philosophy and culture. Greek gods and goddesses, such as Zeus, Hermes and Aphrodite, as well as Roman gods and goddesses, like Jupiter, Venus and Diana, dominated the landscape. There were temples, priest-hoods, and feasts dedicated to the patron god or goddess of a city or a region; statues to the deities dotted the forums of the cities. Even rulers themselves were frequently worshipped as gods.

Gentiles from such a polytheistic background would have naturally understood Christian preaching about the "son of God" in the light of a Greek or Roman god having been begotten by another. We can see this mindset manifested in the New Testament. In the Book of Acts, there is an incident where the Gentile crowds think that Paul is a Greek god because he heals a crippled man:

> **When the crowd saw what Paul had done, they shouted in the Lycaonian language, "The gods have come down to us in human form!"**
>
> **Barnabas they called Zeus, and Paul they called Hermes because he was the chief speaker.**
>
> **The priest of Zeus, whose temple was just outside the city, brought bulls and wreaths to the city gates because he and the crowd wanted to offer sacrifices to them. [Acts 14:11-13]**

It is worthy of note that Paul and Barnabas did not take this opportunity to explain that it was not they but rather Jesus who was God come in human form. Such a clarification is what you would expect, if Trinitarian beliefs about Jesus are correct. Instead, they argued against such pagan beliefs and practices:

> **But when the apostles Barnabas and Paul heard of this, they tore their clothes and rushed out into the crowd, shouting:**

"Men, why are you doing this? We too are only men, human like you. We are bringing you good news, telling you to turn from these worthless things to the living God, who made heaven and earth and sea and everything in them. [Acts 14:14-15]

Here we see that the Greco-Roman peoples that Paul and Barnabas were preaching to were in the habit of taking humans for gods. Despite Paul protesting that he was not a god, the people persisted in their belief: *"Even with these words, they had difficulty keeping the crowd from sacrificing to them" [Acts 14:18].* From this example we can see that, according to Christian history, it was a common practice for people to attribute divinity to other humans. In spite of Paul openly denying being a god, the people continued to worship and sacrifice to him. We can conclude that, even if Jesus himself rejected being God at that time, the mindset of the people was such that they would still have found a way to deify him. This is not an isolated incident, as we read elsewhere that Gentiles believed Paul was a god because he survived a bite from a venomous snake:

Once safely on shore, we found out that the island was called Malta.

The islanders showed us unusual kindness. They built a fire and welcomed us all because it was raining and cold.

Paul gathered a pile of brushwood and, as he put it on the fire, a viper, driven out by the heat, fastened itself on his hand.

When the islanders saw the snake hanging from his hand, they said to each other, "This man must be a murderer; for though he escaped from the sea, the goddess Justice has not allowed him to live."

But Paul shook the snake off into the fire and suffered no ill effects.

The people expected him to swell up or suddenly fall dead; but after waiting a long time and seeing nothing unusual happen to him, they changed their minds and said he was a god. [Acts:28:1-6]

With this background in mind, it's easy to see how Judaic phrases like "son of God" took on a different meaning when transported out of their Jewish monotheistic context into pagan Greco-Roman thought. The Trinity doctrine arose neither in a vacuum, nor strictly from the text of Scripture. It was the result of the influence of certain beliefs and attitudes that prevailed in and around the Church after the first century. The Church emerged in a Jewish and Greek world, and so the primitive Church had to reconcile the notions it had inherited from Judaism with those it had derived from pagan mythology. In the words of historian and Anglican bishop John Wand, *"Jew and Greek had to meet in Christ."* [39]

It's interesting to note that the Greco-Roman religions were filled with tales of gods procreating with human beings and begetting god-men. The belief that God could be incarnate, or that there were sons of God, was common and popular. For example, the chief god in the Greek pantheon, Zeus, visited the human woman Danae in the form of golden rain and fathered Perseus, a "god-man." In another tale, Zeus is said to have come to the human woman Alcmena, disguised as her husband. Alcmena bore Hercules, another "god-man". Such tales bear a striking similarity to Trinitarian beliefs of God being begotten as a man. In fact, the early Christian apologist Justin Martyr, considered a saint in the Catholic Church, said the following in response to pagan criticisms that Christianity borrowed from their beliefs about the sons of God:

> **When we say that the Word, who is our teacher, Jesus Christ the first born of God, was produced without sexual union, and that he was crucified and died and rose again, and ascended to heaven, we propound nothing new or different from what you [pagans] believe regarding those whom you consider sons of Jupiter. [40]**

According to ancient Roman myth, Jupiter was the king of all the gods. Here Justin Martyr is telling Roman pagans that what the Christians believe about Jesus being the son of God is nothing different from what they believe about the sons of the god Jupiter. That the Church Fathers' conception of the Trinity was a combination of Jewish monotheism and pagan polytheism can be seen in the testimony of Gregory of Nyssa, a fourth century bishop who is venerated as a saint in the Roman Catholic and Eastern Orthodox Churches. He also happens to be one of the great figures in the history of the philosophical formulation of the Trinity doctrine. He wrote:

> *For the truth passes in the mean between these two conceptions, destroying each heresy, and yet, accepting what is useful to it from each. The Jewish dogma is destroyed by the acceptance of the Word and by belief in the Spirit, while the polytheistic error of the Greek school is made to vanish by the unity of the nature abrogating this imagination of plurality. [41]*

The Christian conception of God, argues Gregory of Nyssa, is neither purely the polytheism of the Greeks nor purely the monotheism of the Jews, but rather a combination of both.

Even the concept of God-men who were saviours of mankind was by no means exclusive to Jesus. Long before Jesus was born, it was not uncommon for military men and political rulers to be talked about as divine beings. More than that, they were even treated as divine beings: they were given temples with priests who would perform sacrifices in their honour. In Athens, for example, Demetrios Poliorcetes (Demetrios the Conqueror of Cities, 337–283 BCE) was acclaimed as a divine being by hymn-writers because he liberated them from their Macedonian enemies:

> *How the greatest and dearest of the gods are present in our city! For the circumstances have brought together Demeter and Demetrios; she comes to celebrate the solemn mysteries of the Kore, while he is here full of joy, as befits the god, fair and laughing. His appearance is solemn, his friends all around him and he in their midst, as though they were stars and he the sun. Hail boy of the most powerful god Poseidon and Aphrodite! For other gods are either far away, or they do not have ears, or they do not exist, or do not take any notice of us, but you we can see present here, not made of wood or stone, but real. So we pray to you: first make peace, dearest; for you have the power... [42]*

The Athenians gave Demetrios an arrival that was fit for a god, burning incense on altars and making offerings to their new deified king. It must be pointed out that, as time passed by, he did some other things that the Athenians did not approve of, and as a consequence they revoked their adoration of him. It seems that, in the days before Jesus, divinity could be stripped away from human beings just as easily as it was granted. Perhaps the best-known examples of God-men are the divine honours bestowed upon the rulers of the Roman Empire, starting with Julius Caesar. We have an inscription, dedicated to him in 49 BCE and discovered in the city of Ephesus, which says this about him [43]:

Descendant of Ares and Aphrodite

The God who has become manifest

And universal savior of human life

So, Julius Caesar was described as God manifested as man, the saviour of mankind. Sound familiar? Now, prior to Julius Caesar, rulers in the city of Rome itself were not granted divine honours. But Caesar himself was – before he died, the senate approved the building of a temple and statue for him. Soon after his death, his adopted son and heir, Octavian, promoted the idea that at his death, Caesar had been taken up to heaven and been made a god to live with the gods. There was a good reason that Octavian wanted his adopted father to be declared a God. If his father was a God, then what would that make him? This deification of Caesar set a precedent for what was to happen with the emperors, beginning with the first of them, Octavian himself, who became "Caesar Augustus" in 29 BCE. An inscription, which survived from his lifetime and was found in the city of Halicarnassus (modern Turkey), calls Augustus [44]:

...The native Zeus and

Savior of the human race

This is yet another example of a divine saviour of mankind. Now, Octavian happened to also be the "son of God" by virtue of his divine father Julius Caesar. In fact, Octavian became known as 'Divi filius' ("Son of the Divine One"). These, of course, are all titles widely used by Christians today to describe

Jesus. We must realise that the early Church did not come up with these titles out of the blue, for they are all things said of other men before they were said of Jesus. For early Christians, the idea was not that Jesus was the only person who was ever called such things; this is a misconception. The concept of a divine human being who was the saviour of mankind was a sort of a template that was applied to people of great power and authority. We've seen that the history of paganism is littered with such examples, and Jesus was just another divine saviour, in a long list of divine saviours who had preceded him.

THE STATE OF THE TRINITY TODAY

What is the situation with the Trinity today? Even after numerous councils and centuries of discussion and debate, there is still major disagreement among Trinitarians over the doctrine. The biggest issue relates to the Holy Spirit. As we've seen, the equality of the Holy Spirit with the Father and the Son was established on the Council of Constantinople in 381 CE. While the council concluded that the Holy Spirit proceeded from the Father, it said nothing concerning the procession of the Holy Spirit from the Son. Here is the last section of the Creed of the Council of Constantinople:

And in the Holy Spirit, the Lord, the giver of life,

who proceeds from the Father,

who with the Father and the Son is adored and glorified.

Note that the second line only specifies the Father. This section of the creed was later translated into Latin with the addition, "and the Son":

And in the Holy Spirit, the Lord, the giver of life,

who proceeds from the <u>Father and the Son,</u>

who with the Father and the Son is adored and glorified.

This addition to the creed is known as the Filioque (Latin for "and the Son"), a phrase that has been the subject of great controversy between Eastern and Western Churches. Whether one includes that phrase, and exactly how the phrase is translated and understood, can have important implications for how one understands the central Christian doctrine of the Trinity.

Eastern Churches believe that it proceeds from the Father only, whereas Western Churches believe that the Holy Spirit proceeds from both the Father and the Son. Here is a diagram which illustrates the difference:

The *Filioque* Controversy

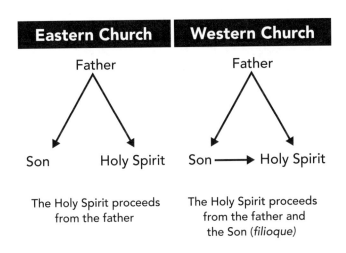

Eastern Church	Western Church
Father	Father
Son　Holy Spirit	Son ⟶ Holy Spirit
The Holy Spirit proceeds from the father	The Holy Spirit proceeds from the father and the Son (*filioque*)

Eastern Orthodox and Oriental Orthodox Churches reject the Filioque because it makes the Holy Spirit a subordinate, or a less important member of the Trinity. Thus, in their view it compromises the co-equality of the Persons of the Trinity. This issue is responsible for the largest schism in Church history. It divided Christianity into Western Catholicism and Eastern Orthodoxy. Differences over this doctrine still remain as a point of contention to this day [45].

Such lingering doctrinal disagreements are only one aspect of the issues with the Trinity today. Even after centuries of evolution and fine tuning, Trinitarians still walk a tightrope of heresy. To demonstrate this point, let us consider the question of who suffered and died on the cross, was it God or man?

If a Trinitarian claims that it is God who died, then this contradicts the Bible which teaches that God is immortal and cannot die: **"I lift my hand to heaven and solemnly swear: As surely as I live forever" [Deuteronomy 32:40].** This is why many Trinitarians believe that it was only the human side of Jesus that suffered and died, as the crucifixion is only meaningful with reference to his human nature; you cannot crucify the divine nature. However, in doing so, Trinitarians separate the divine nature from the human one at the crucifixion. The problem is that this violates the creed that was adopted on the Council of Chalcedon which states that Jesus is:

> **"... acknowledged in Two Natures unconfusedly, unchangeably, indivisibly..."**

Recall that the Chalcedonian Creed, today considered orthodoxy in the Catholic, Protestant and Eastern Orthodox churches, established that Jesus has a dual nature, with his divine nature and his human nature being eternally united (the doctrine of the Hypostatic Union). So, when Trinitarians state that it is only the human that died in Jesus, they are isolating the human nature from the divine one on the cross. Trinitarians are separating the natures of Jesus that are supposed to be eternally united, thus falling into heresy. We can see that every Trinitarian falls into some form of heresy in relation to the crucifixion, either by taking the view that it was the divine side of Jesus that died on the cross, which is in clear contradiction to what the Bible teaches about God's immortal nature, or by believing that only the human nature of Jesus was crucified, a violation of the "orthodoxy" of the Chalcedonian Creed. Trinitarians cannot avoid being involved in heresy; in practice, they almost have to decide which heresy they're going to commit. You have to walk on such a sharp edge that you're going to fall on one side or the other.

Today, such confusion is rampant throughout the Trinitarian doctrine. This is in spite of centuries of doctrinal fine-tuning by numerous Church councils and the collective efforts of the most brilliant minds that Christendom has had to offer. Is this really God's perfect revelation, or is it the fallible teaching of man? God's true guidance is surely perfect, free of conflict. This problem of holes appearing in one area of theology in the light of other areas is another sign that the doctrine of the Trinity is man-made. The whole doctrine is a patchwork; it joins things which cannot be joined, and the seams are always showing. Could this really be God's final revelation, would mankind be left to linger in the darkness of confusion until the Day of Judgement? As we will see in the next chapter, God has sent forth a light to guide us back to the truth.

CHAPTER 2

THE CONCEPT OF GOD IN ISLAM

"There is no god but God"

These words represent the first part of the Shahadah (the Muslim testimony of faith) which means that there is nothing worthy of worship except the One true God. This declaration is at the heart of Islam; the Oneness of God is the pivot around which everything else revolves. In Islam, this concept of God's Oneness is known as Tawheed. Linguistically, Tawheed is an Arabic word that means unification. It comes from the root word wa-ha-da which means making something one ("waahid"). Waahid is the opposite of plurality (two, three, etc.). So waahid is something that will continue to be singular and never become a partner of something else. Islamically, Tawheed means to single out God in all acts of worship and to abandon the worship of anything else. God is One with no partner or associate in His Lordship, divinity and attributes.

It's important to note that, unlike the issue with the word "Trinity" being absent in the Bible, the word "Tawheed" and its derivatives, such as "waahid", are found throughout the Islamic source texts. Tawheed is represented in the Qur'an, it's one of the names of God – al Waahid (meaning "the One"): ***"God is the Creator of all things, and He is the One..." [13:16]*** Prophet Muhammad ﷺ also explicitly spoke of Tawheed, for example:

> ***Some of the people of Tawheed will be punished in the Fire (on account of their sins) until they are coals. Then the Mercy (of God) will reach them, they will be taken out and tossed at the doors of Paradise." He said: "The people of Paradise will pour water over them, and they will sprout as the debris carried by the flood sprouts, then they will enter Paradise. [46]***

Whilst the word "Trinity" is absent in the Bible, the Qur'an does in fact mention it in the form of a stern warning: ***"Those people who say that God is the third of three are defying [the truth]: there is only One God. If they persist in what they are saying, a painful punishment will afflict those of them who persist." [5:73]***

The concept of Tawheed is summarised in the chapter of the Qur'an known as "Al Ikhlas" ("The Sincerity"):

> **Say, 'He is God the One,**
>
> **God the eternal.**
>
> **He begot no one nor was He begotten.**
>
> **No one is comparable to Him.' [Chapter 112]**

You can think of this chapter of the Qur'an as the manifesto of monotheism in Islam. It beautifully summarises Tawheed, the pure monotheism of the Islamic concept of God's nature. The first verse, **"Say, 'He is God the One'"**, tells us that God is One. This isn't one in the sense of one which can become two and two which can become three and so on. This is One and uniquely One, that cannot become two.

The next verse tells us that God is eternal: **"God the eternal..."** This means that He has no beginning and will never come to an end. The Qur'an rejects the idea that God can suffer or die, because anything which has weakness cannot be considered a supreme being.

The next verse tells us that God does not have any children or parents: **"He begot no one nor was He begotten..."** Why would a supreme God not have any children or parents? The final verse of the chapter answers this question, **"No one is comparable to Him"**. Everything within the creation has to reproduce in order for life to continue. In other words, we have offspring out of a need for survival. Some people have children for other reasons, such as wanting to be looked after when they become old and frail. This is also a need. But in Islam, God is unlike His creation, He does not have any needs, and He does not beget. God is also not begotten; He does not have parents, because that would mean there are other gods like Him, as children take after their parents. This uniqueness of God extends to all His attributes. There is nothing that is comparable to God.

We can see that the 112th chapter of the Qur'an needs only four short sentences, less than 20 words in the original Arabic, to describe God in crystal-clear terms that leave the reader in no confusion about the nature of our Creator and His distinction from the creation. This unique quality of the Qur'an, conciseness without compromising on clarity of meaning, means that Muslims have no need to resort to speculation in order to understand what God has revealed about Himself. God highlights the clarity of the Qur'an: *"These are the verses of the Scripture that makes things clear" [12:1].*

This distinction that the Qur'an presents between the Creator and the creation also extends to the messengers who were chosen by God. Throughout history, God has sent this message of His Oneness to mankind, through His chosen messengers such as Abraham, Moses, Jesus and the final messenger, Muhammad, peace be upon them all. Although these individuals represented the best of mankind in terms of their honesty, truthfulness and integrity, they are still human beings who did not share in any of the attributes of God.

Many Christians are not aware that Muslims revere individuals such as Abraham, Moses and Jesus. The Qur'an acknowledges their high status among mankind and contains many of their stories from the Bible. The Qur'an commands Muslims to hold all of them in equally high regard:

> *So [you believers], say, 'We believe in God and in what was sent down to us and what was sent down to Abraham, Ishmael, Isaac, Jacob, and the Tribes, and what was given to Moses, Jesus, and all the prophets by their Lord. We make no distinction between any of them, and we devote ourselves to Him.' [2:136]*

This commonality between the Qur'an and other Scriptures is a strong indication that the God who inspired the Prophet Muhammad ﷺ is the same God who inspired Abraham, Moses and Jesus. Muslims believe that the Qur'an is the literal word of God that was sent down to the Prophet Muhammad ﷺ via the angel Gabriel, the same angel who inspired other messengers such as

Abraham, Moses and Jesus. The entire Qur'an was revealed gradually to the Prophet Muhammad ﷺ over a period of 23 years.

Christians divide the Bible into the Old and New Testaments. Muslims believe that the Qur'an is the final testament sent to guide mankind. The Qur'an not only affirms the original revelation given to Moses and Jesus, the Torah and the Gospel, but also corrects Jews and Christians, respectfully referred to as "People of the Book", in the places where they have strayed from the original messages sent by God.

The Qur'an tells us that the Prophet Muhammad ﷺ is the last and final messenger: *"Muhammad is not the father of any one of you men; he is God's Messenger and the seal of the prophets..." [33:40]* Every messenger prior to Muhammad was sent to his own people and not the whole of humanity. Prophet Muhammad ﷺ is the only messenger who was sent to the whole of mankind: *"We have sent you [Prophet] only to bring good news and warning to all people..." [34:28]*

Whilst Tawheed is incompatible with the Trinity, it is in fact identical to the Jewish concept of God. Jews, like Muslims, believe in a purely monotheistic concept of God. Rabbi Moshe ben Maimon, widely considered to be one of the greatest Torah scholars in history, permitted Jewish and Muslim co-worship. Many Rabbis state that, if a Jew cannot find a synagogue to worship in, then it is permissible (and even encouraged) for them to pray in a mosque. This is only possible because they recognise that mosques are places of pure monotheism and that Muslims have absolutely no deviation in their views of the Oneness of the Divine. By comparison, Jews are discouraged from praying in churches because they are viewed as places of idolatry.

JESUS: MAN, MESSENGER AND MESSIAH

One of the most important individuals mentioned in the Qur'an is Jesus, peace be upon him. Muslims respect and love Jesus as a great messenger of God. You may be surprised to know that Jesus is mentioned more times by name in the Qur'an than Muhammad ﷺ, and that Mary, the mother of Jesus, even has a chapter of the Qur'an named after her, an honour not bestowed on her in the New Testament. The Qur'an even mentions details about the lives of Jesus and Mary that are not found in the New Testament. We are now going to spend some time analysing what the Qur'an has to say about Jesus and his mother Mary:

The birth of Jesus

God informs us in the Qur'an that one day Mary was given glad tidings by an angel of a special son she would give birth to:

> **The angels said, 'Mary, God gives you news of a Word from Him, whose name will be the Messiah, Jesus, son of Mary, who will be held in honour in this world and the next, who will be one of those brought near to God. [3:45]**

Mary reacts with surprise, for she had led a chaste life. This was to be a miraculous virgin birth:

> **She said, 'My Lord, how can I have a son when no man has touched me?' [The angel] said, 'This is how God creates what He will: when He has ordained something, He only says, "Be", and it is.' [3:47]**

This child would perform miracles from the cradle, be full of wisdom and righteous in the eyes of God:

> **He will speak to people in his infancy and in his adulthood. He will be one of the righteous... He will teach him the Scripture and wisdom, the Torah and the Gospel [3:46-48]**

When Mary became pregnant with Jesus, she withdrew herself from her people. She knew they would not believe her miraculous story and would slander her and accuse her of having committed fornication: "**And so it was ordained: she conceived him. She withdrew to a distant place."** [19:22]

When she went into labour, she was in great pain and utter despair. Then God, out of His mercy, provided her with sustenance:

> **And, when the pains of childbirth drove her to [cling to] the trunk of a palm tree, she exclaimed, 'I wish I had been dead and forgotten long before all this!' but a voice cried to her from below, 'Do not worry: your Lord has provided a stream at your feet and, if you shake the trunk of the palm tree towards you, it will deliver fresh ripe dates for you.' [19:23-25]**

God informed her that, when she returns to her people, she should not speak a word to them:

> **So eat, drink, be glad, and say to anyone you may see: 'I have vowed to the Lord of Mercy to abstain from conversation, and I will not talk to anyone today' [19:26]**

After giving birth to Jesus, Mary returned to her people. They confirmed her fears by implying she had committed fornication. This was a serious accusation, as under Jewish Law the punishment would be stoning to death:

> **She went back to her people carrying the child, and they said, 'Mary! You have done something terrible! Sister of Aaron! Your father was not an evil man; your mother was not unchaste!' [19:27-28]**

In this tense situation, Mary remained true to God's command. Honouring God's instructions to remain silent, Mary pointed to baby Jesus who proceeded to defend his mother's honour and proclaim his Prophethood:

> **She pointed at him. They said, 'How can we converse with an infant?' [But] he said: 'I am a servant of God. He has granted me the Scripture; made me a prophet; made me blessed wherever I may be. He commanded me to pray, to give alms as long as I live, to**

cherish my mother. He did not make me domineering or graceless. Peace was on me the day I was born, and will be on me the day I die and the day I am raised to life again.' [19:29-33]

The miracles of Jesus

The Qur'an affirms many of the miracles that Jesus performed in the New Testament: *"...I will heal the blind and the leper, and bring the dead back to life with God's permission; I will tell you what you may eat and what you may store up in your houses. There truly is a sign for you in this, if you are believers" [3:49].* It's important to understand that, even though Jesus performed numerous miracles throughout his life, this is not a reason to attribute divinity to him. The Qur'an states that God gifted His messengers with amazing signs in order to bring their people to faith: *"We sent Our messengers with clear signs..." [57:25]* One such example is Moses splitting the sea. The Qur'an informs us that Jesus is no exception in this regard: *"We gave Jesus, son of Mary, clear signs and strengthened him with the Holy Spirit." [2:87]*

Some people use the reasoning that because the birth of Jesus was miraculous and he had no earthly father, then he must have a heavenly one, and so they conclude that he is literally the Son of God. Is this really the case? The Qur'an puts forward a powerful argument: *"In God's eyes Jesus is just like Adam: He created him from dust, said to him, 'Be', and he was" [3:59].* The Qur'an's argument is thus: the creation of the first human being, Adam, was also a miracle, as he had no father or mother. Yet no-one attributes divinity to Adam by virtue of his miraculous creation. For that reason then, people should not attribute divinity to Jesus on account of his miraculous birth. Thinking along similar lines, the creation of Eve, the first woman, was also miraculous, for she was created from Adam's rib: a woman brought forth from a man. Note the consistency of the Qur'an, everything in the creation is a result of God's creative power: God merely says 'Be' and it is brought into creation. Jesus is no different in this regard.

The nature of Jesus

For the three Abrahamic faiths, the nature of Jesus is perhaps the most contentious issue. Was he just a Messianic imposter, as seen by Jews? Or perhaps a divine Son of God, as seen by Christians? The Islamic view of Jesus lies between these two extremes. The Qur'an clarifies for mankind that Jesus the Messiah was a messenger in a long line of messengers:

> **The Messiah, son of Mary, was only a messenger; other messengers had come and gone before him; his mother was a virtuous woman; both ate food [like other mortals]. See how clear We make these signs for them... [5:75]**

This verse illustrates one of the many beautiful qualities of the Qur'an: simplicity. The Qur'an contains a universal message for people of all ages and backgrounds, from the child to the adult, from lay people to scholars. Here, the example presented by the Qur'an, the need of sustenance by Jesus, is in fact profound if we reflect upon it. Anything that has a need, in this case food, cannot be God. What happens if the need is unfulfilled? In this case, Jesus would die from hunger. But we know that God is All Powerful, He cannot die. What happens to us, human beings, after we eat? We need to relieve ourselves. To entertain such a thought about God, however, would be blasphemous.

BELIEFS SHOULD STEM FROM REVELATION, NOT SPECULATION

Today, man worships a plethora of gods. From animals to the elements, even the worship of ourselves when we reject God's existence, the only limit seems to be our own wild imaginations. The best way to know the true reality of God is to pay careful attention to what He has revealed about Himself. This is why God has inspired messengers and sent down revelation throughout the ages, in order for us to know who He is so that we can have a proper relationship with Him. Without the light of revelation, mankind ends up in a state of confusion.

This brings us to an important principle in Islam. All of a Muslim's beliefs about the unseen are derived from revelation: *Say, [O believers], "We have believed in God and what has been revealed to us..." [2:136].* Muslims are forbidden from speculating about the nature of God:

> *Say [Prophet], 'My Lord only forbids disgraceful deeds... that you, without His sanction, associate things with Him, and that you say things about Him without knowledge.' [7:33]*

Without divine revelation to shine a light on the world of the unseen, mankind will inevitably fall into error when speculating about the nature of God. This is why a Muslim's beliefs about God are derived purely from revelation. Muslims believe that the Qur'an is the best source of revelation about God because the words of the Qur'an are His literal words. Although the Qur'an was first revealed to the Prophet Muhammad ﷺ, the voice of the Qur'an is not that of the Prophet Muhammad ﷺ or any other human being for that matter. The Qur'an was revealed by our Creator: *"And indeed, the Qur'an is the revelation of the Lord of the worlds." [26:192]*

One of the causes of speculation is when a reader has no guidance on how to interpret a book. Having revelation, or knowledge, is one thing. We also need a teacher to provide its correct interpretation in order for mankind to make use of the knowledge and implement it properly. It is God's messengers, those that have been inspired by Gowd with a special insight into the intended meaning behind the revelation, who are best placed to play the crucial role of teachers. The Qur'an tells us that the Prophet Muhammad ﷺ was tasked with explaining its verses to believers:

> *We sent them with clear signs and Scriptures. We have sent down the message to you too [Prophet], so that you can explain to people what was sent for them, so that they may reflect. [16:44]*

If Muslims happen to disagree about a theological issue, we are told to settle the disagreement by looking at what the Prophet Muhammad ﷺ taught:

> *By your Lord, they will not be true believers until they let you [Muhammad] decide between them in all matters of dispute, and*

find no resistance in their souls to your decisions, accepting them totally [4:65]

Here the Qur'an is referring to the Sunnah. The Arabic word "sunnah" broadly means a way, or manner of life. In Islamic literature, it has the very specific meaning of what the Prophet Muhammad ﷺ said, did, approved, and disapproved of. This information has been preserved along with the Qur'an to this very day. The Sunnah is another primary source of guidance for Muslims along with the Qur'an. The Qur'an is sufficient for a person to come to the realisation that it is the word of God; it covers all the key questions in life that a person who is seeking the truth may ask, such as explaining who God is, the purpose of life and what happens to us after we die. There are certain topics that the Qur'an mentions in general terms; it is the Sunnah that provides the detail. For example, the Qur'an commands believers to give charity. But it's the Sunnah that contains all the minute details, such as how much charity a Muslim should give, who is entitled to receive it, how often, etc.

There is always going to be the possibility of differences of interpretation; this is the case with any book. However, the Qur'an is unique because it is the only Scripture that comes with an explanation of how to interpret it correctly according to the understanding of its messenger. Because of the clarity of the Qur'an and its detailed explanation in the form of the Sunnah, the scope for any such dispute and differing is minimised. Muslims don't need to resort to speculation in order to understand the nature of God because the matter has been clarified in the Qur'an and Sunnah.

THERE IS NO CONFLICT BETWEEN ISLAM AND REASON

Contrary to what many secularists claim, there does not need to be conflict between religion and reason. The Qur'an highlights that God gave us the gift of our senses and reason: *"It is God who brought you out of your mothers' wombs knowing nothing, and gave you hearing and sight and minds, so that you might be thankful" [16:78].* Many of us use these gifts to excel in worldly affairs, such as work, recreation and sciences, but switch them off when it comes to the pursuit of spiritual truth. Is this logical, given that the Hereafter, Paradise and Hell, is eternal whilst our worldly life here on earth is temporary? The Qur'an describes people who do not make use of the gifts of God to heed His signs as being worse than cattle:

> *...They have hearts they do not use for comprehension, eyes they do not use for sight, ears they do not use for hearing. They are like cattle, no, even further astray: these are the ones who are entirely heedless. [7:179]*

Cattle were not created with the ability to reason; they act purely according to instinct. Our reasoning is one of the things that differentiate us from animals. If we don't use our God-given ability to reason, then we are in fact worse than cattle, because cattle are fulfilling their purpose of creation, whereas we are not. The Qur'an in fact admonishes those who follow blindly: *"Indeed, the worst of living creatures in the sight of God are the deaf and dumb who do not use reason." [8:22]* Revelation can only benefit us if we reflect upon it. The Qur'an is full of signs that it is the truth of God: *"We shall show them Our signs in every region of the earth and in themselves, until it becomes clear to them that this is the Truth..." [41:53].* But these signs are only of benefit for those who reflect. A state of heedlessness, like that of cattle, is not a state that God wants mankind to be in, and so the Qur'an is full of reminders to reflect deeply:

> *It is He [God] who spread out the earth, placed firm mountains and rivers on it, and made two of every kind of fruit; He draws the*

veil of night over the day. There truly are signs in this for people who reflect. There are, in the land, neighbouring plots, gardens of vineyards, cornfields, palm trees in clusters or otherwise, all watered with the same water, yet We make some of them taste better than others: there truly are signs in this for people who reason. [13:3-4]

The Qur'an encourages mankind to ponder, think and contemplate. God wants us to base our faith on intellect and not blind following. The Qur'an is full of rational arguments for Tawheed that address different mindsets and religious beliefs of its readers. Let's look at two examples:

Those who doubt the existence of God

The Qur'an puts forward a simple but powerful argument with regard to our origins: *"Or were they created by nothing? Or were they the creators (of themselves)? Or did they create heavens and earth? Rather, they are not certain" [52:35-36].* The Qur'an encourages those who doubt the existence of God to reflect upon their own existence. The Qur'an engages its audience by inviting us to ponder some rational, logical questions which we can use to arrive at a conclusion, not only about our origin, but also the origin of everything that exists in the material world: in other words, the entire universe. If we take these questions that the Qur'an poses and apply them to the universe, then there are three possibilities for its origin:

1. It was created from nothing

2. It was self-created

3. It has an external cause

The first possibility is that the universe was created from nothing. Can something really come from nothing? This is impossible. We know from our own personal experience of life, as well as the laws of the universe, that things don't just pop into existence out of nothing. Out of nothing, nothing comes!

This leads us to the next possibility: the universe was self-created. Can something create itself? This is a self-contradiction. Something creating itself requires its own pre-existence. Things cannot exist and not exist at the same time. That would be like saying that your mother gave birth to herself!

Since something cannot come from nothing, and self-creation is absurd, then what is the alternative? There is one final possibility: the universe has an external cause. When we observe the planets, solar systems, galaxies, stars and everything else in the universe, we can see that it is highly ordered, with intricate systems and laws in place. This implies that there is an intelligent mind behind the universe, a Creator.

<u>Those who worship idols</u>

The futility of idolatry is illustrated beautifully with the following story of Abraham:

> *Long ago We bestowed right judgement on Abraham and We knew him well.*
>
> *He said to his father and his people, 'What are these images to which you are so devoted?'*
>
> *They replied, 'We found our fathers worshipping them.'*
>
> *He said, 'You and your fathers have clearly gone astray.'*
>
> *They asked, 'Have you brought us the truth or are you just playing about?'*
>
> *He said, 'Listen! Your true Lord is the Lord of the heavens and the earth, He who created them, and I am a witness to this.*
>
> *By God I shall certainly plot against your idols as soon as you have turned your backs!'*
>
> *He broke them all into pieces, but left the biggest one for them to return to.*
>
> *They said, 'Who has done this to our gods? How wicked he must be!'*

Some said, 'We heard a youth called Abraham talking about them.'

They said, 'Bring him before the eyes of the people, so that they may witness [his trial].'

They asked, 'Was it you, Abraham, who did this to our gods?'

He said, 'No, it was done by the biggest of them– this one. Ask them, if they can talk.'

They turned to one another, saying, 'It is you who are in the wrong,'

but then they lapsed again and said, 'You know very well these gods cannot speak.'

Abraham said, 'How can you worship what can neither benefit nor harm you, instead of God? [21:51-66]

This is a story about Abraham that is found only in the Qur'an. The Qur'an shows us that worshipping anything created, such as idols, is illogical. As the story of Abraham demonstrates, he was able to smash the idols to pieces. Since idols are not able to defend themselves, then they obviously cannot benefit or harm us, so why should mankind take them as gods? Rather, we should worship God - the one who gave us life, sustains us and will take our souls when we die.

The Qur'an is unique because it is the only religious Scripture that gives its reader the tools needed to reason to the truth: ***"Will they not think about this Qur'an? If it had been from anyone other than God, they would have found much inconsistency in it" [4:82].*** Here the Qur'an has provided us with an important principle that allows us to determine whether something is from God or not. If one reasons about theology and finds that there are glaring inconsistencies, then it cannot be from God. God is perfect in knowledge and, therefore, it stands to reason that His revelation will be perfect and free of inconsistencies. So, we can use this principle as a falsification test to determine whether a doctrine is divine or man-made. If we apply this to the Qur'an, we find that the concept of God it presents is consistent, despite the fact that it uses numerous different approaches in conveying monotheism when addressing its reader. We've already seen one example by engaging intellectually with those who doubt God's existence, but there is also the use of analogies, storytelling the lives of the Prophets and recalling the history of past nations, among others. Even though the Qur'an is diverse in the way it addresses its reader, we find that it consistently serves to reinforce the central theme of Tawheed. Every page of the Qur'an reminds the reader of the idea that God is One and Unique, with no partner or peer in His Essence and Attributes.

HOW ISLAM ELIMINATED IDOLATRY

Pre-Islamic Arabia was a dreadful place to live in. Slavery was an economic institution, with male and female slaves being bought and sold like animals. Illiteracy was common among the Arabs, as were alcoholism and adultery. Those with power and money took advantage of the poor by charging extremely high interest on loans. Arabia was a male-dominated society; men could marry any number of women. When a man died, his son would inherit all his wives, except his own mother. Women had virtually no legal status; for example, they had no right to possess property and had little to no inheritance rights. Female infanticide was widely practised, with daughters often being buried alive.

It was not only the rights of human beings that were violated, but also the rights of God. The Arabs were a highly idolatrous people. The idolatry of pre-Islamic Arabia seeped into every facet of day-to-day life. Idols adorned their places of worship. Today, the Ka'aba, situated in Saudi Arabia and the holiest place of worship for Muslims, contains neither idols nor images. But before Islam, the pagan Arabs housed 360 different idols in the Ka'aba. Idols were their travel partners whenever they set out on a journey, for the Arabs were very superstitious and believed that they would provide protection in a land plagued by highway robbery and kidnapping. They were also the source of their livelihoods; so central was the Ka'aba to idolatry that pagans from all over Arabia would make pilgrimage there.

In just 23 years, Islam managed to completely reform not only the social ills of Arabian society, but also its idolatry, taking people away from the worship of carved images and stones to the worship of the One true God of Abraham. This is the testimony of Ja'far bin Abi Talib, who was a contemporary of the Prophet Muhammad ﷺ. Here he informed the king of Abyssinia about the condition of his people and the positive change that Islam brought for them:

> *O King, we were an uncivilised people, worshipping idols, eating corpses, committing abominations, breaking natural ties, treating guests badly, and our strong devoured our weak. Thus we were until God sent us an apostle whose lineage, truth, trustworthiness, and clemency we know. He summoned us to acknowledge God's unity and to worship Him and to renounce the stones and images which we and our fathers formerly worshipped. He commanded us to speak the truth, be faithful to our engagements, mindful of the ties of kinship and kindly hospitality, and to refrain from crimes and bloodshed. He forbade us to commit abominations and to speak lies, and to devour the property of orphans, to vilify chaste women. He commanded us to worship God alone and not associate anything with Him, and he gave us orders about prayer, almsgiving, and fasting. We confessed his truth and believed in him, and we followed him in what he had brought from God, and we worshipped God without associating aught with Him. [47]*

Just how did the Qur'an go about winning the hearts and minds of people, completely transforming every level of Arabian society in such a short space of time? In the previous section, we saw some of the intellectual arguments the Qur'an uses to address its reader. The Qur'an also takes into account the psychology of its audience, which is demonstrated in its use of language. In defining the relationship between God and mankind, the Qur'an avoids terms like "Father" when referring to God and "sons of God" when referring to human beings. Such language can be easily misunderstood, especially in the minds of those who come from a background of idolatry and are used to interpreting such language literally. There are even those who might take advantage of such ambiguous language in Scripture, by interpreting it in such a way as to try and justify idolatry. The Qur'an warns us, mankind, against using ambiguity as the foundation for our beliefs:

It is He who has sent this Scripture down to you [Prophet]. Some of its verses are definite in meaning – these are the cornerstone of the Scripture – and others are ambiguous. The perverse at heart eagerly pursue the ambiguities in their attempt to make trouble and to pin down a specific meaning of their own. [3:7]

The Qur'an confirms that those who believe that Jesus is the literal Son of God are imitating an ancient pagan concept: *"The Christians said, 'The Messiah is the son of God': they said this with their own mouths, repeating what earlier disbelievers had said" [9:30].* When the Qur'an defines the relationship between God and mankind, it instead uses terms like Creator when referring to God, and we as the creation. Such terms leave no room for confusion and clearly distinguish between what is God and what is not – everything else. Such careful use of language shows the Qur'an's author's wisdom and insight into the human condition. Our Creator knows the inner thoughts of man: *"We created man - We know what his soul whispers to him: We are closer to him than his jugular vein." [50:16]*

THE PURITY OF TAWHEED THROUGH THE AGES

The foundations of Muslim belief were set during the lifetime of the Prophet Muhammad ﷺ. The message given to Muhammad ﷺ, the Qur'an, represents perfection in the way of life for human beings to live: *"Today I have perfected your religion for you, completed My blessing upon you, and chosen as your religion Islam..." [5:3].* If something has been perfected, then it cannot be further improved, and so there is no need to send any additional messengers or messages to mankind.

As well as setting a solid theological foundation early on, the Qur'an and Sunnah (teachings and actions of the Prophet Muhammad ﷺ) expressly forbid believers from adding to the religion of Islam. The Qur'an warns mankind against inventing doctrine and claiming it is from God:

So woe to those who write the "scripture" with their own hands,

then say, "This is from God," in order to exchange it for a small price. Woe to them for what their hands have written and woe to them for what they earn. [2:70]

Likewise, the Sunnah also warns mankind against tampering with the religion. The Prophet Muhammad ﷺ said: **"Whoever tells lies about me deliberately, let him take his place in Hell." [48]**

When we study history, we will find that Islamic monotheism, Tawheed, has undergone no historical evolution in the nearly 1,500 years that have passed since the Qur'an was first revealed to the Prophet Muhammad ﷺ. Muslims hold to the same creed to this very day. All who have tried to introduce something new into the creed of Islam have been rejected, purely on the basis that it was not taught by the Prophet Muhammad ﷺ. This is the standard that Muslim scholars have held to since the beginning of Islam. These strict standards have been built into the religion since its inception, preserving the purity of its teachings, such as Tawheed.

It's important to note that, like with any religion, various sects and innovations have sprung up throughout Islamic history. The Prophet Muhammad ﷺ himself foretold that this would be the case: **"My nation will split into seventy-three sects, all of whom will be in Hell except one group - (those who follow) that which I and my companions follow" [49]**. However, the key point is that thanks to the Sunnah, a Muslim alive today in the 21st century is able to avoid all innovations and stay upon the correct, pure understanding of Tawheed as it was understood by the Prophet Muhammad ﷺ and his companions in the 7th century.

WHY THE QUR'AN IS A MERCY TO MANKIND

God, out of His mercy for mankind, resolved all of the confusion surrounding His nature in the 7th century by revealing the Qur'an to the Prophet Muhammad ﷺ. We've seen that the main theme in the Qur'an is the purely monotheistic nature of God. It teaches that God is unique and separate from His creation; there is no confusion about who God is, and what His creation is. Jesus, like all the messengers sent before him, such as Abraham and Moses, and like the final messenger Muhammad ﷺ after him, is simply the creation of God. The Qur'an puts forward a clear picture of both God and Jesus that is easy to understand:

> *People of the Book [Jews and Christians], do not go to excess in your religion, and do not say anything about God except the truth: the Messiah, Jesus, son of Mary, was nothing more than a messenger of God, His word, directed to Mary, a spirit from Him. So believe in God and His messengers and do not speak of a 'Trinity'– stop [this], that is better for you– God is only one God, He is far above having a son, everything in the heavens and earth belongs to Him and He is the best one to trust. [4:171]*

Thus, in one short verse, the Qur'an unravels centuries of myth-making and demystifies for us who the real Jesus was. Jesus is not God, or even the literal Son of God; rather, he is a man, messenger and Messiah.

In the previous chapter, we saw that the Trinity is a product of history, borne not out of Scripture but centuries of evolving Church tradition. A Trinitarian can't open their Bible and point to one chapter that explains the Triune nature of God, the idea that God is three persons who all are co-equal and co-eternal. Instead, Trinitarians need to quote creeds from outside the Bible, such as the Nicean Creed and Chalcedonian Creed, which were developed long after the disciples of Jesus lived and died. Moreover, a Triune concept of God has more in common with paganism than the message of pure monotheism that Jesus himself preached in the New Testament. If we are sincere in our pursuit of the truth, then we must put the teachings of Jesus at the forefront of our beliefs. This leaves us with a message that is not fundamentally different from that of Islam. The conclusion might be shocking, but it is undeniable: Jesus preached Tawheed.

One of the benefits of such doctrinal clarity is that it facilitates contemplation. God wants us to reflect on His revelation and ponder its meanings:

> **[This is] a blessed Book which We have revealed to you, [O Muhammad], that they might reflect upon its verses and that those of understanding would be reminded. [Qur'an 38:29]**

The believer benefits from such contemplation, which reminds us of who our Creator is and strengthens our relationship with our Creator by bringing us closer to Him. If God wanted us to know about Him, the Qur'an provides the simplest, easiest and most accessible description about the nature of God. Now, that's not to say there aren't any concepts in Islam that are complex – there are, for example the laws governing the distribution of inheritance – but such specialist knowledge is only needed by a few and is not tied to the believer's salvation. This is the opposite of the situation with Trinitarians. Not only is the Trinity inconsistent and paradoxical in nature, but also Christian theologians relegate the doctrine to a holy mystery that cannot be fully grasped. So, they are in the awkward position of being compelled to believe in something that cannot be comprehended, which creates tension between the heart and mind. Can such a person ever truly be at peace? By comparison, Tawheed, the first pillar of Islam, is something that can be grasped by anyone. This is one of many reasons why Islam brings about inner peace in those who embrace it. A healthy relationship with the creator is only possible when we understand who He is. One cannot properly worship a stranger, or something that goes against all rationality. It's interesting that one of the root meanings of the Arabic word Islam is in fact "peace" – in essence, Islam means "the attainment of peace by submitting to our Creator". The Qur'an describes this peace that Muslims have when they remember God: **"truly it is in the remembrance of God that hearts find peace." [13:28]**

CHAPTER 3

THE PORTRAYAL OF JESUS AND OTHER PROPHETS IN SCRIPTURE

The previous chapter focused on the nature of God in the light of revelation. However, there is much more to revelation than giving insight into the unseen; it also serves as a practical guide on how to live our lives in a way that pleases God and brings the most benefit to mankind. When it comes to the means by which God has delivered revelation to mankind, throughout history, God's guidance has always been imparted to us through His Prophets, may God's peace and blessings be upon them all. This shows us that Prophethood plays an important role in revelation. Not only did the Prophets act as teachers, but, by embodying the message and values conveyed by the Divine text, they also served as a practical and spiritual example for us to follow. From this perspective, the Divine revelation is what to do and the Prophets' lives explain to us how to do it.

CONCEPT OF PROPHETHOOD

Prophethood is a concept that is common to all three Abrahamic faiths. Significant portions of both the Qur'an and the Bible are dedicated to the lives of the Prophets. Throughout the Qur'an, Prophethood is described in highly noble terms:

> **There has certainly been for you in the Messenger of God an excellent example for anyone whose hope is in God and the Last Day and [who] remembers God often. [33:21]**

Likewise, the Bible also describes Prophethood in highly noble terms:

...Have faith in the Lord your God and you will be upheld; have faith in his prophets and you will be successful. [2 Chronicles 20:20]

Although the Lord sent prophets to the people to bring them back to him, and though they testified against them, they would not listen. [2 Chronicles 24:19]

Bringing people back to God doesn't just mean believing in God. It also involves righteous actions, and avoiding sins. From that point of view, God chose the best of mankind to be His representatives. Prophets were role models of holiness and closeness to God; they set the standards for the entire community. This is why it was essential that the Prophets God chose had good characters and behaviour so that they could be successful in their missions of calling people back to God. Such sentiment is also echoed by Jesus, who even goes so far as to say that bad actions are a sign of false prophets:

Watch out for false prophets. They come to you in sheep's clothing, but inwardly they are ferocious wolves. By their fruit you will recognize them. Do people pick grapes from thornbushes, or figs from thistles? Likewise, every good tree bears good fruit, but a bad tree bears bad fruit. A good tree cannot bear bad fruit, and a bad tree cannot bear good fruit. Every tree that does not bear good fruit is cut down and thrown into the fire. Thus, by their fruit you will recognize them. [Matthew 7:15-20]

We can conclude that both the Qur'an and the Bible define Prophets as those who were sent in order to bring mankind closer to God. Both the Qur'an and the Bible paint a very noble, honourable picture of the concept of Prophethood. So, we should expect God's Prophets to embody these ideals by being the best people in character, with their behaviour and lives representing a practical example for us to follow in order to come closer to God.

There is a lot of overlap between the Qur'an and the Bible when it comes to the stories of the Prophets, with both Scriptures sharing many similar events and themes. However, when it comes to the character and conduct of the Prophets, the Scriptures are radically different:

LIVES OF THE PROPHETS IN THE QUR'AN AND THE BIBLE

Jesus and his alleged harsh speech

The Bible has numerous instances where Jesus addresses strangers, his disciples and even God in a very harsh manner. Here, Jesus is alleged to have called a non-Jewish woman a 'dog', a term of great insult during his time:

> *A Canaanite woman from that vicinity came to him, crying out, "Lord, Son of David, have mercy on me! My daughter is demon-possessed and suffering terribly." Jesus did not answer a word. So his disciples came to him and urged him, "Send her away, for she keeps crying out after us." He answered, "I was sent only to the lost sheep of Israel." The woman came and knelt before him. "Lord, help me!" she said. He replied, "It is not right to take the children's bread and toss it to the dogs." [Matthew 15:22-26]*

What makes this incident even worse is that the woman was coming to Jesus out of desperation for help, and even though she addressed him with titles of great respect ("Lord", "Son of David"), she was greeted with abuse in return. We find that such harshness isn't just limited to strangers, as Jesus is alleged to have treated his disciples in a similar fashion. Here, Jesus allegedly calls Peter 'Satan':

> *Jesus turned and said to Peter, "Get behind me, Satan! You are a stumbling block to me; you do not have in mind the concerns of God, but merely human concerns." [Matthew 16:23]*

Even his blessed mother Mary is spoken about in a disrespectful manner:

> *Someone told him, "Your mother and brothers are standing outside, wanting to speak to you." He replied to him, "Who is my mother, and who are my brothers?" Pointing to his disciples, he said, "Here are my mother and my brothers. [Matthew 12:47-49]*

Perhaps worst of all, Jesus allegedly goes so far as to blaspheme when speaking to God:

> *About three in the afternoon Jesus cried out in a loud voice, "Eli, Eli, lema sabachthani?" (which means "My God, my God, why have you forsaken me?") [Matthew 27:46]*

The portrayal of Jesus in the Qur'an is very different. Throughout the Qur'an, his manner of speaking, whether to his own mother, strangers or God, is always respectful:

> *[Jesus] said, "Indeed, I am the servant of God. He has given me the Scripture and made me a prophet. And He has made me blessed wherever I am and has enjoined upon me prayer and charity as long as I remain alive. And dutiful to my mother, and He has not made me insolent, unblessed. [19:30-32]*

> *And when Jesus brought clear proofs, he said, "I have come to you with wisdom and to make clear to you some of that over which you differ, so fear God and obey me. [43:63]*

> *And [beware the Day] when God will say, "O Jesus, Son of Mary, did you say to the people, 'Take me and my mother as deities besides God?'" He will say, "Exalted are You! It was not for me to say that to which I have no right. If I had said it, You would have known it. You know what is within myself, and I do not know what is within Yourself. Indeed, it is You who is Knower of the unseen. I said not to them except what You commanded me - to worship God, my Lord and your Lord. And I was a witness over them as long as I was among them; but when You took me up, You were the Observer over them, and You are, over all things, Witness. [5:116-117]*

Aaron and the golden calf

The Bible smears Aaron with involvement in the worst of sins, idolatry:

> *So all the people took off their earrings and brought them to Aaron. He took what they handed him and made it into an idol cast in the shape of a calf, fashioning it with a tool. Then they said,*

"These are your gods, O Israel, who brought you up out of Egypt."
[Exodus 32:3-4]

This is a violation of the most important of the Ten Commandments, "You shall have no other gods before me." Monotheism was the very essence of the message that God tasked Moses and Aaron to impart on the Israelites, so from this point of view a Prophet of God failed in their most basic of duties. The Bible then goes on to tell us that God punished the Israelites who worshipped the calf idol with a plague:

"And the LORD struck the people with a plague because of what they did with the calf Aaron had made" [Exodus 32:35].

Prophet Aaron, however, was spared any such punishment, even though he was the individual who made the idol. Shouldn't Prophets be more accountable before God than common people, owing to the greater knowledge that they possess and their higher positions of responsibility? From this point of view, if anyone was to be punished, then Aaron should have been the first person to be punished by God. This is because he was the chief instigator and actually encouraged and supported the people worshipping the idol he made. What makes matters even worse is that when Moses confronted Aaron about the golden calf incident, he was unrepentant and even put forward excuses:

"Do not be angry, my lord," Aaron answered. "You know how prone these people are to evil." [Exodus 32:22]

This story is told quite differently in the Qur'an. In the story that the Qur'an narrates to us, we can see that Aaron is free of the major sin of idolatry; he in fact orders the Israelites not to worship the golden calf:

Aaron did say to them, 'My people, this calf is a test for you. Your true Lord is the Lord of Mercy, so follow me and obey my orders,' but they replied, 'We shall not give up our devotion to it until Moses returns to us.' [20:90-91]

However, Aaron is only one man, and without Moses he was not in a position to physically restrain such a large number of people from worshipping the calf idol (the Qur'an does not give a number, but the Bible narrates that there were around three thousand people who were involved in the incident). Moreover, the Qur'an points out that it was not Prophet Aaron, but rather an individual called Samiri, who made the golden calf: **"Moses said, 'And what was the matter with you, Samiri?' He replied, 'I saw something they did not; I took in some of the teachings of the Messenger but tossed them aside: my soul prompted me to do what I did'" [20:95-96]**. The Qur'anic account not only presents Aaron in a manner that is befitting of a great Prophet of God, but also it does not contain any of the inconsistencies present in the biblical narrative.

<u>David and the accusation of adultery</u>

The Bible relates a story about David in which he passes judgement on a case involving a dispute between two parties. After passing judgement, David is accused of committing some very serious sins:

> *The Lord sent Nathan to David. When he came to him, he said, "There were two men in a certain town, one rich and the other poor. The rich man had a very large number of sheep and cattle, but the poor man had nothing except one little ewe lamb he had bought. He raised it, and it grew up with him and his children. It shared his food, drank from his cup and even slept in his arms. It was like a daughter to him.*

> *"Now a traveller came to the rich man, but the rich man refrained from taking one of his own sheep or cattle to prepare a meal for the traveller who had come to him. Instead, he took the ewe lamb that belonged to the poor man and prepared it for the one who had come to him."*

> *David burned with anger against the man and said to Nathan, "As surely as the Lord lives, the man who did this must die! He must pay for that lamb four times over, because he did such a thing and had no pity."*

> *Then Nathan said to David, "You are the man! This is what the Lord, the God of Israel, says: 'I anointed you king over Israel, and I delivered you from the hand of Saul. I gave your master's house to*

you, and your master's wives into your arms. I gave you all Israel and Judah. And if all this had been too little, I would have given you even more. Why did you despise the word of the Lord by doing what is evil in his eyes? You struck down Uriah the Hittite with the sword and took his wife to be your own...'" [2 Samuel 12:1-9]

These sins relate to an earlier story in which David is said to have committed the acts of adultery and murder:

One evening David got up from his bed and walked around on the roof of the palace. From the roof he saw a woman bathing. The woman was very beautiful, and David sent someone to find out about her. The man said, "Isn't this Bathsheba, the daughter of Eliam and the wife of Uriah the Hittite?" Then David sent messengers to get her. She came to him, and he slept with her. (She had purified herself from her uncleanness.) Then she went back home. The woman conceived and sent word to David, saying, "I am pregnant."... In the morning David wrote a letter to Joab and sent it with Uriah. In it he wrote, "Put Uriah in the front line where the fighting is fiercest. Then withdraw from him so he will be struck down and die."... When Uriah's wife heard that her husband was dead, she mourned for him. [2 Samuel 11:2-26]

It turns out that Bathsheba was married, and so when David found out she was pregnant with his child, he had her husband killed. Perhaps even more strangely, God allegedly struck the child that was born from the adulterous relationship with a lethal illness: **"But because by doing this you have shown utter contempt for the Lord, the son born to you will die." [2 Samuel 12:14]** This contradicts a basic principle of justice laid out in the Bible: **"Parents are not to be put to death for their children, nor children put to death for their parents; each will die for their own sin." [Deuteronomy 24:16]** So according to Old Testament law, it was David and Bathsheba that both deserved death for their sins, not their innocent child. Such stories don't just reflect badly on David, they also portray God as being unjust.

Contrast the biblical account with the Qur'an. Like the biblical account, the Qur'an also relates a story about David in which he passes judgement on a case involving a dispute between two parties:

> *Have you heard the story of the two litigants who climbed into his private quarters? When they reached David, he took fright, but they said, 'Do not be afraid. We are two litigants, one of whom has wronged the other: judge between us fairly– do not be unjust– and guide us to the right path. This is my brother. He had ninety-nine ewes and I just the one, and he said, "Let me take charge of her," and overpowered me with his words.'*
>
> *David said, 'He has done you wrong by demanding to add your ewe to his flock. Many partners treat each other unfairly. Those who sincerely believe and do good deeds do not do this, but these are very few...' [38:21-24]*

However, the Qur'an has David immediately repenting to God for having made a mistake in judging the dispute that was brought before him. The Qur'anic account tells us that the two disputants were in fact angels sent by God to test how fairly he would judge between them:

> *...[Then] David realized that We had been testing him, so he asked his Lord for forgiveness, fell down on his knees, and repented: We forgave him [his misdeed]. His reward will be nearness to Us, a good place to return to. [38:24-25]*

David was too hasty in judging the case; he passed judgement without hearing both parties in the dispute. As soon as David realised this, he immediately repented. There is no mention of adultery and murder, so the Qur'an exonerates David of such an accusation. Thus, the Qur'anic account is consistent: David is portrayed as a Prophet who was thankful for all that he was given. The Qur'an makes no mention of David committing major sins; in fact, the opposite is the case; he shows righteous conduct throughout the Qur'an. This is the conduct that we would expect of someone whom God had personally handpicked to lead Israel, not a selfish man who is enslaved to his lowly desires as the Bible claims.

Noah and the accusation of drunkenness

The Bible tells us that after the great flood, one of the first things Noah did was to plant a vineyard and fall into a state of naked drunkenness:

> **Noah, a man of the soil, proceeded to plant a vineyard. When he drank some of its wine, he became drunk and lay uncovered inside his tent. [Genesis 9:20-21]**

We are led to believe that this is the same great Prophet who had the self-discipline to build an ark by hand. Moreover, after claiming that Noah was lying on the floor in a naked, drunken state, the Bible goes on to tell us that his youngest son, Ham, walks in on him: **"Ham, the father of Canaan, saw his father naked and told his two brothers outside" [Genesis 9:22].** Ham immediately notifies his two older brothers and they come to Noah and cover up his nakedness. When Noah wakes up, he proceeds to curse Canaan, the son of Ham: **"When Noah awoke from his wine and found out what his youngest son [Ham] had done to him, he said, 'Cursed be Canaan! The lowest of slaves will he be to his brothers'" [Genesis 9:24].** Ham's only crime seems to be that he told his older brothers about the state of their father. Even if we assume that Ham had committed a sin, and it certainly seems that Noah was angry with him, one cannot help questioning Noah's conduct. Even if cursing was justified, then wouldn't it make more sense, and be more just, for Noah to curse Ham, rather than Ham's son Canaan, Noah's grandson, who was an innocent party?

The Qur'an paints a very different picture of Noah. He is portrayed throughout the Qur'an as a man of righteous conduct:

> **He said, 'My Lord, I have called my people night and day, but the more I call them, the further they run away: every time I call them, so that You may forgive them, they thrust their fingers into their ears, cover their heads with their garments, persist in their rejection, and grow more insolent and arrogant. [71:5-7]**

Noah warned his people day and night; he announced his message in public and he spoke quietly to people privately; yet all, but a few, denied his words. Noah called his people back to God for 950 years: **"We sent**

Noah out to his people. He lived among them for fifty years short of a thousand but when the Flood overwhelmed them they were still doing evil" [29:14]. It is unthinkable that a man of such discipline, who had the patience to preach to his rebellious people for 950 years, would lose all self-control by getting into a state of naked drunkenness soon after he set foot off the ark, which is what the Bible states. So, what does the Qur'anic portrayal have Noah doing when the waters subsided and the ark came to rest? He enquires about his son who refused to board the ark:

> *It sailed with them on waves like mountains, and Noah called out to his son, who stayed behind, 'Come aboard with us, my son, do not stay with the disbelievers.'*
>
> *But he replied, 'I will seek refuge on a mountain to save me from the water.' Noah said, 'Today there is no refuge from God's command, except for those on whom He has mercy.' The waves cut them off from each other and he was among the drowned.*
>
> *Then it was said, 'Earth, swallow up your water, and sky, hold back,' and the water subsided, the command was fulfilled. The Ark settled on Mount Judi, and it was said, 'Gone are those evildoing people!' Noah called out to his Lord, saying, 'My Lord, my son was one of my family, though Your promise is true, and You are the most just of all judges.' [11:42-45]*

Again, notice the stark contrast with the biblical portrayal. Rather than getting drunk and cursing his family, the Qur'an shows Noah's concern for his family. The Qur'an tells us that Noah, a great Prophet and leader of men, but also a father, turned to God with sadness for his dead son.

Job and his many alleged blasphemies

The Story of Job in the Bible is one of a Prophet being severely tested. The story begins with God highly praising Job for his righteousness. God says to Satan: **"Have you considered my servant Job? There is no one on earth like him; he is blameless and upright, a man who fears God and shuns evil." [Job 1:8]** Satan proceeds to challenge God, stating that the only reason Job is upright is because Job has a good life, with a large family and plenty of wealth. Satan predicts that, if God were to test Job 'properly', then Job would "curse God": **"But now stretch out your hand and strike his flesh and bones, and he will surely curse you to your face." [Job 2:4]** God allows Satan to test Job by afflicting his health: **"The Lord said to Satan, 'Very well, then, he is in your hands; but you must spare his life'" [Job 2:6].** Once the trials commence, Job fails to remain patient and proceeds to complain about his sorry state, even going so far as to blaspheme against God numerous times:

> **I will say to God: Do not condemn me, but tell me what charges you have against me. Does it please you to oppress me, to spurn the work of your hands, while you smile on the schemes of the wicked? [Job 10:2-3]**

> **Then know that God has wronged me and drawn his net around me. "Though I cry, 'I've been wronged!' I get no response; though I call for help, there is no justice." [Job 19:6-7]**

> **Job says, 'I am innocent, but God denies me justice.' [Job 34:5]**

> **For he [Job] says, 'It profits a man nothing when he tries to please God.' [Job 34:9]**

We are told that a man called Elihu, who had witnessed Job's tirade against God, is angered by Job's blasphemy:

> **So these three men stopped answering Job, because he was righteous in his own eyes. But Elihu son of Barakel the Buzite, of the family of Ram, became very angry with Job for justifying himself rather than God. [Job 32:1-2]**

Elihu asks Job to listen to him so that he might impart some wisdom: **"But if not, then listen to me; be silent, and I will teach you wisdom." [Job 33:33]**

Elihu is very direct with Job; he accuses him of speaking without knowledge, lacking wisdom, and showing conduct that has been like that of a wicked man:

> **Men of understanding declare, wise men who hear me say to me,**

'Job speaks without knowledge; his words lack insight.' Oh, that Job might be tested to the utmost for answering like a wicked man! To his sin he adds rebellion; scornfully he claps his hands among us and multiplies his words against God. [Job 34:34-37]

After chastising Job, Elihu proceeds to give him the correct insight into his condition:

Then Elihu said: "Do you think this is just? You say, 'I am in the right, not God.' Yet you ask him, 'What profit is it to me, and what do I gain by not sinning?' I would like to reply to you and to your friends with you." [35:1-4]

The Bible goes on to tell us that God eventually intervenes and Job repents from his sins. He is forgiven by God and has his full heath restored. Now, the way that the story unfolds is highly problematic for a number of reasons. First, the Bible describes Job as a righteous man, that he is **"blameless and upright".** Now, it's very easy to be happy with God when times are good. True piety, however, is being happy with God when one has nothing. Showing gratitude to God and remaining steadfast in the face of trials is a sign of strong faith. So, from this point of view, hasn't Satan effectively "one-upped" God – Satan challenged God when he predicted that Job would curse God, and so haven't Job's blasphemies proven Satan to be correct? Secondly, how is it that the young man Elihu, who, unlike Job, is not a Prophet, demonstrates more wisdom in religious matters than a Prophet of God? Recall that the Bible stated that there was **"no one on earth"** like Job, yet this young man seems to possess more insight into Job's situation than Job himself.

The Qur'an resolves all of these inconsistencies and issues in just a few short verses. Rather than complaining about his situation to other people, Job calls on God for help. Notice that Job doesn't blaspheme against God; rather, he blames Satan for his hardship: **"Bring to mind Our servant Job who cried to his Lord, 'Satan has afflicted me with weariness and suffering'"** **[38:41].** God rewards Job's unwavering faith by healing him and replacing everything that Satan took away from him:

'Stamp your foot! Here is cool water for you to wash in and drink,'

and We restored his family to him, with many more like them: a sign of Our mercy and a lesson to all who understand. [38:42-43]

God compliments Job for his patience in the face of such trials: *"We found him patient in adversity; an excellent servant! He, too, always turned to God" [38:44].* Job's righteous conduct in the Qur'an is exactly what we would expect of a Prophet of God. Moreover, we learn a great lesson, that no matter what trials we face, no matter how severe an affliction we are tested with, we should always remain patient, for in the end the righteous are rewarded.

ANALYSIS OF THE STORIES OF THE PROPHETS

We've seen that both the Qur'an and the Bible paint a very noble and honourable picture of the concept of Prophethood. However, after analysing the stories of the Prophets, it is only the Qur'an that presents the Prophets in such a way that satisfies this ideal. By contrast, the Bible shows the Prophets in an extremely negative light; it seems that no sin is too great for them to commit. Here are some reasons why the negative picture of the Prophets painted by the Bible is problematic:

1. It goes against the very nature and purpose of Prophethood as stated in the Bible itself. The word used for Prophet in Hebrew in the Bible, 'navi', means "spokesperson" which emphasises the prophet's role as a speaker. So, for Prophets to commit the worst of sins (idolatry, murder, adultery etc.) contradicts the very concept of Prophethood. How can a Prophet ever be an effective spokesperson if his community can turn his calling to God around on him by pointing out that he himself can't even keep the most important of God's commands?

2. As human beings, we learn by example and naturally aspire to follow role models; so, in order to encourage piety, the examples set before us should be positive. Anyone with children will recognise this. So, this makes a mockery

of God's wisdom, since His intention is to bring us closer to Him but the bad examples of His Prophets achieve the opposite of what God intended.

3. The Bible states that all Scripture is good for training in righteousness: **"All Scripture is God-breathed and is useful for teaching, rebuking, correcting and training in righteousness" [2 Timothy 3:16].**

But what morals can be derived from stories that are filled with Prophets committing idolatry, murder, adultery and blasphemy against God?

Please note that this does not mean that Prophets are infallible, as only God is perfect and free of error. However, a distinction has to be made between making honest mistakes, which all human beings fall into, Prophets included, and the committing of the worst of sins as portrayed in the Bible. This is one of the reasons why God revealed the Qur'an, in order to defend His righteous Prophets against slander and falsehood. In the previous chapter, we saw how the Qur'an restores the original theological message of Jesus about the nature of God. In this chapter, we've seen how the Qur'an goes even further by shining light on the life of not only Jesus, but also other great Prophets of the Old Testament, such as Aaron, David, Noah and Job. Thus, the Qur'an provides excellent guidance for those who want the best examples to follow in order to be successful in the Hereafter: **"There is a lesson in the stories of such people for those who understand..." [12:111]**

CHAPTER 4

THE ATONEMENT RELATIONSHIP BETWEEN MAN AND GOD

We owe so much to our Creator. Our eyesight, for example, is something that we could never repay God for. Since God bestowed countless gifts on humanity without us even asking for them, what does this tell us about God's attributes? The very act of creation bears witness to God's abundant love and mercy. This is why when we worship God, we should do so with a feeling of love and gratitude. Unlike God, however, our expressions of love and gratitude are flawed. We inevitably fall short in our worship because of our sins.

Does our Creator's love and mercy extend itself to the forgiveness of our sins? This is the key question of this chapter, and as we will see, Islam and Christianity provide very different answers. Before getting into the specifics of what Islam and Christianity teach on this subject, let's reflect on the following point. If we think about it, during the act of creation we were the recipients of God's love and mercy without even asking for it, so how could we be denied it when we ask God for it directly? Belief in God doesn't just entail an acknowledgement of His existence, but it also includes the affirmation of His attributes. Denying any of God's attributes is in fact an act of disbelief. This is why we have to be very careful when it comes to atonement as our understanding of it has serious implications on the attributes of God such as His love and mercy.

IN ISLAM, GOD IS THE LOVING, THE MOST MERCIFUL

Islam teaches that God created man in the best of states; each baby that is born is pure and sinless: *"We create man in the finest state" [95:4]* Nevertheless, mankind is prone to making mistakes because we are fallible beings, an inevitable consequence of the free will that God gifted us. When God created man He did not expect us to be angels, for He already had countless angels, perfect in their compliance, to do His bidding. In the creation of Adam, God brought into existence something different: a creature of free will, submitting to Him out of choice. A consequence is that we commit sins, and God knew we would fall into sin even before He created us. In Islam, it is up to every human being to take responsibility for their own sins, as long as they have reached the age of discernment and are of sound mind: *"Whoever accepts guidance does so for his own good; whoever strays does so at his own peril. No soul will bear another's burden..." [17:15]*

Not having the safety blanket of another person carrying our sins means that Muslims have to strive in bettering themselves from the cradle to the grave, in turn making the true believer a force for good in society. In Islam, two of the names of God are Al-Wadud and Al-Raheem, "The Loving" and "The Most Merciful". These attributes manifest themselves in God's attitude towards our sins. The Qur'an tells us: *"O my servants who have transgressed against their souls! Despair not the Mercy of God. Verily, God forgives all sins: for He is Oft-Forgiving, Most Merciful" [39:53]* God sees the sins we commit, but He waits for us to repent, and when we do, He forgives us. That is the part that God loves: the repentance, the voluntary return. The Prophet Muhammad ﷺ taught that *"God turns with mercy to him who turns to Him in repentance." [50]*

In Islam, God's love and mercy transcends all other types of love and mercy. His love and mercy is greater than all worldly and human forms of love and mercy – even motherly love and mercy. God is an independent being who is self-sufficient and perfect. He doesn't need or require anything. A mother's love and mercy, although selfless, is based on her internal need to love her child. It completes her and through her sacrifices she feels whole and fulfilled However, God's love and mercy is not based on a need or want; it is therefore the purest form of love and mercy, because He gains absolutely nothing from loving and being merciful. The Prophet Muhammad ﷺ said: **"God is more affectionate to His servants than a mother to her young ones."** **[51]**

THE THEOLOGY OF THE CROSS: NO BLOOD, NO FORGIVENESS

By comparison, Christian theology teaches that sin is like a debt that must be repaid; it cannot simply be forgiven by God: **"For the wages of sin is death"** **[Romans 6:23].** God is portrayed as a Being whose mercy is contingent on the shedding of blood: **"In fact, the law requires that nearly everything be cleansed with blood, and without the shedding of blood there is no forgiveness" [Hebrews 9:22].** The Church teaches that this is why Jesus was sent to die on the cross; his sinless life represents the ultimate sacrifice to appease God's wrath and wash away the sins of the whole of humanity, reconciling us with God. The theology that underpins the crucifixion is that humanity is inherently sinful, a consequence of Adam eating from the forbidden tree. So, when Adam violated God's command not to eat from the tree, sin entered into humanity and has remained ever since: **"Therefore, just as sin entered the world through one man, and death through sin, and in this way death came to all people, because all sinned" [Romans 5:12].** The solution, according to the New Testament, is thus: Jesus died on the cross in order to undo Adam's "original sin":

> **For if, by the trespass of the one man, death reigned through that one man, how much more will those who receive God's abundant provision of grace and of the gift of righteousness reign in life through the one man, Jesus Christ! [Romans 5:17]**

So, we can see that the Christian concepts of atonement and divine mercy are diametrically opposed to Islam. In Islam, we are responsible for our own sins and God grants forgiveness to all those who call upon Him and sincerely repent. In Christianity, we have the paradoxical situation of the whole of mankind being held accountable for something we didn't do – Adam's original sin – and forgiven for something someone else did – Jesus' sacrifice at the crucifixion. When you factor the Trinity into the atonement equation, things get stranger still. If Jesus is God, then the crucifixion effectively amounts to God incarnating Himself into the creation and committing suicide in order to forgive sinners from Himself. According to Christianity, God can only forgive sin if He punishes Himself first, even though He is the one whom the crime was committed against. Imagine someone wronged you. If we follow this doctrine, the only way you can forgive that person is if you punish yourself first. How much sense does that make? If Jesus died on the cross for our sins, then we already have our golden ticket to heaven. There's no need for us to strive, or to repent, because Jesus has already done the hard work for us.

BLOOD ATONEMENT COMPROMISES GOD'S JUSTICE, LOVE, AND MERCY

God's love for mankind lies at the heart of the Gospel message: ***"For God so loved the world that he gave his one and only Son, that whoever believes in him shall not perish but have eternal life" [John 3:16].*** However, the crucifixion of Jesus would be a gross act of injustice on the part of God. In Christian theology, God effectively demonstrates His love by torturing and killing His son. Such a system of justice is one that we human beings ourselves wouldn't use in an everyday practical setting. Suppose one day a judge throws you into prison for no apparent reason. Upon questioning your arrest and imprisonment, the judge says that, although he knows you are innocent, he decided to punish you as a substitutionary atonement for the crimes of another who had now been set free. Would you accept the judge's ruling? No-one would accept such a situation; we would all protest and ask why we are being punished when we are innocent. Such a system is anything but just; if anyone is to be punished, then it should be the guilty party. A human court that punished the innocent in place of the guilty would be considered corrupt; it would be a miscarriage of justice. How much more unjust then would it be if God were behind such a system? Yet, such a system is exactly what we have with the Christian theology of blood atonement.

Furthermore, if God always requires a blood sacrifice in order to forgive, then the question that has to be asked is whether God ever really forgives. Imagine if someone punched you and gave you a bloody nose. You have two options: in the spirit of an eye for an eye and a tooth for a tooth, you could punch them back and that would be justice, or you could just forgive them. Both these options are valid in Islam. What is not logical is that you punch the person back and say "now I forgive you." That's not forgiveness, because you got your revenge. In a similar way, the Christian portrayal of God is one of getting His blood payment, His ransom, and only then does He let you go. So, we can see that, with the crucifixion, forgiveness is not being fulfilled by God.

By comparison, the Qur'an's concept of divine justice and forgiveness is natural. God can forgive our transgressions without blood atonement if we ask him to, simply by calling upon Him and sincerely repenting. No-one has to die; no blood has to be spilt. God doesn't require blood to forgive; He can simply forgive, just as we forgive each other when we wrong one another in everyday life. Shouldn't God, the creator of the love and mercy that exists among His creation, be even more capable of love and mercy? The reality is that the concept that "Jesus paid the price for our sins" is an alien creed which is incompatible with God's love and mercy. To claim that mankind was only able to properly access God's forgiveness the moment Jesus shed his blood on the cross is an intolerable challenge to the principles of God's love and mercy. We now know that the human story is so old, going back tens of thousands and perhaps hundreds of thousands of years, that to say it's only been 2,000 years since a proper relationship between man and God has been made possible, makes a mockery of the idea of divine love, because that is not loving. A God who coherently shows mercy, compassion and forgiveness for His creation doesn't stuff all of salvation into a single moment in human history at the crucifixion. The Qur'anic vision is very different: **"For every people there has been a guide" [13:7].** In Islam, the salvation offered through all of the Prophets has been the same throughout history: submission to our

Creator and forgiveness granted through sincere repentance. That's the true understanding of God as having love and mercy inscribed on His very nature.

DOES BLOOD ATONEMENT HAVE A FOUNDATION IN THE BIBLE?

The foundation of the crucifixion stands on the doctrine that blood sacrifice alone expiates sin and reconciles man with God. At face value, the notion of Jesus sacrificing himself to redeem mankind may appear to be a noble act and undoubtedly is an aspect of Christianity that resonates deeply with its followers. But we have to ask the question, is it Biblical? When we look at the Old Testament, we find that the notion that only unblemished sacrificial blood can appease God's wrath and atone for sin is explicitly denounced by the prophets of Israel. One such example is King Solomon. While dedicating the Temple of Jerusalem to God Almighty, Solomon makes a special plea on behalf of the Israelites:

> *When they sin against You—for there is no one who does not sin... and if they turn back to you with all their heart and soul in the land of their enemies who took them captive, and pray to you toward the land you gave their ancestors, toward the city you have chosen and the temple I have built for your Name; then from heaven, your dwelling place, hear their prayer and their plea, and uphold their cause. And forgive your people, who have sinned against you; forgive all the offenses they have committed against you, and cause their captors to show them mercy. [1 Kings 8:46-50]*

This entire passage seems to have foreshadowed the exile of the Israelites into Babylonian captivity which took place in the 6th century BCE. The words of Solomon represent a total refutation of the Christian theology of God's forgiveness being contingent on blood atonement – the exiled Israelites would be able to attain forgiveness through repentance and prayer.

If we fast forward to the time of Prophet Ezekiel, we will find the Israelites living in exile in Babylon after the destruction of Jerusalem, just as foreshadowed by

Solomon. The entire chapter of **Ezekiel 18** is devoted to sin and atonement. The Jewish people, perhaps under the influence of Babylonian pagan practices and beliefs, had the misapprehension that God punishes the innocent for the sins of the guilty. They ask Ezekiel: *"Why does the son not share the guilt of his father?" [Ezekiel 18:19].* This idea that an innocent can die as atonement for the sins of the wicked was widely known throughout the world as a practice among pagan communities. Prophet Ezekiel's response to his people is a clear rejection of such beliefs:

> **But if a wicked person turns away from all the sins they have committed and keeps all my decrees and does what is just and right, that person will surely live; they will not die. None of the offences they have committed will be remembered against them. Because of the righteous things they have done, they will live. Do I take any pleasure in the death of the wicked? declares the Sovereign LORD. Rather, am I not pleased when they turn from their ways and live? [Ezekiel 18:21-23]**

So, we can see that God is pleased when the guilty stop sinning and make sincere repentance. Much like God's nature being purely One and not a Trinity, the Old Testament concept of a loving and merciful God agrees with Islam; it's Christian theology that is the odd one out. Furthermore, in the Old Testament God's love and mercy is not just restricted to the Jewish people; even Gentiles (non-Jews) were freely forgiven by God through sincere repentance. For example, the Old Testament describes the people of Nineveh as a wicked nation. God sent Prophet Jonah to warn them: *"The word of the Lord came to Jonah son of Amittai: 'Go to the great city of Nineveh and preach against it, because its wickedness has come up before me'" [Jonah 1:1-2].* This was a nation of considerable size, numbering over 120,000 inhabitants:

> **And should I not have concern for the great city of Nineveh, in which there are more than a hundred and twenty thousand people who cannot tell their right hand from their left—and also many animals? [Jonah 4:11]**

This entire nation was spared God's punishment in the end because they repented from their wicked ways:

> *When Jonah's warning reached the king of Nineveh, he rose from his throne, took off his royal robes, covered himself with sackcloth and sat down in the dust. This is the proclamation he issued in Nineveh:*
>
> *"By the decree of the king and his nobles:*
>
> *Do not let people or animals, herds or flocks, taste anything; do not let them eat or drink. But let people and animals be covered with sackcloth. Let everyone call urgently on God. Let them give up their evil ways and their violence. Who knows? God may yet relent and with compassion turn from his fierce anger so that we will not perish."*
>
> *When God saw what they did and how they turned from their evil ways, he relented and did not bring on them the destruction he had threatened. [Jonah 3:6-10]*

An entire nation of over 120,000 condemned to destruction were forgiven by God when they simply repented and fasted, without ever offering any sacrifice. In fact, even though they had many animals at their disposal, which God could have easily commanded them to sacrifice, they weren't sacrificed, but rather the animals were made to fast along with the people. From these examples we can see that the Christian theology that only unblemished sacrificial blood can appease God's wrath and atone for sin has no foundation in the Bible.

JESUS TAUGHT OTHERS TO SEEK FORGIVENESS

During the Sermon on the Mount, Jesus makes some interesting statements with regard to the forgiveness of sin:

> **This, then, is how you should pray:**
>
> **"Our Father in heaven,**
>
> **hallowed be your name,**
>
> **your kingdom come,**
>
> **your will be done,**
>
> **on earth as it is in heaven.**
>
> **Give us today our daily bread.**
>
> **And forgive us our debts,**
>
> **as we also have forgiven our debtors.**
>
> **And lead us not into temptation,**
>
> **but deliver us from the evil one."**
>
> **For if you forgive other people when they sin against you, your heavenly Father will also forgive you. But if you do not forgive others their sins, your Father will not forgive your sins. [Matthew 6:9-15]**

So, according to this prayer that Jesus taught, we are to ask God to "forgive us" our debts as "we also forgive our debtors." We are to forgive others their sins if we are to see God forgive our sins.

If we take Jesus' analogy of debt and apply it to the theology of the cross, it is highly problematic. If someone owes you money and you wanted to "forgive this debt", that would mean that you would forgo the money owed to you by writing the debt off. If, however, someone owes you money and then you tell them you don't have to pay it anymore on the condition that someone else pays it on their behalf, can it be said that you have forgiven the debt? It cannot, because the burden of settling the debt has just been transferred onto someone else. True forgiveness is the virtuous act of letting go of a wrong without exacting any form of payment or punishment in return. But the theology of the cross teaches that Jesus bore the punishment of sinners on the cross in order to fully pay off the debt of our sins.

In another incident, we see an example where Jesus informs a person that their sins have been forgiven on account of their repentance:

> *Jesus entered Jericho and was passing through. A man was there by the name of Zacchaeus; he was a chief tax collector and was wealthy. He wanted to see who Jesus was, but because he was short he could not see over the crowd. So he ran ahead and climbed a sycamore-fig tree to see him, since Jesus was coming that way.*
>
> *When Jesus reached the spot, he looked up and said to him, "Zacchaeus, come down immediately. I must stay at your house today." So he came down at once and welcomed him gladly.*
>
> *All the people saw this and began to mutter, "He has gone to be the guest of a sinner."*
>
> *But Zacchaeus stood up and said to the Lord, "Look, Lord! Here and now I give half of my possessions to the poor, and if I have cheated anybody out of anything, I will pay back four times the amount."*
>
> *Jesus said to him, "Today salvation has come to this house, because this man, too, is a son of Abraham. For the Son of Man came to seek and to save the lost." [Luke 19:1-10]*

Notice that the man's virtuous act of repentance resulted in him being forgiven and receiving salvation that very day – not at a later date as a result of Jesus's death on the cross.

We can see from these examples that, much like when it comes to the nature of God, Jesus had an Old Testament understanding of atonement; he taught others to seek God's forgiveness.

CONCLUSION

Islamic theology paints a picture of God that is loving and merciful. No sin is too great to be forgiven; the doors of mercy are never shut. All we have to do is turn to God in repentance with a sincere heart and our sins will be washed away. A Muslim never despairs of the love and mercy of God. Such a positive outlook on the nature of God in turn instils in us a deeper and further love for God.

By comparison, Christian theology claims that without the cross, without the innocent blood of Jesus being spilt, mankind is cut off from God's forgiveness. These claims bear a striking resemblance to the pagan blood sacrifices of old. In fact, there have been all kinds of pagan deities throughout history who needed the blood of an innocent human to appease them. If one believes that God's wrath at sin necessitated the blood sacrifice of Jesus in order to calm His wrath, we are not describing a god who is fundamentally different – we are simply describing another version of an angry god who needs an innocent thrown into the volcano. We've seen that when we look at the teachings of the Old Testament, the claim that God's forgiveness is contingent on the shedding of blood is an alien concept with no basis in Scripture. Likewise, Jesus taught others to seek God's forgiveness, not by blood sacrifice, but by asking for it. Christianity changed this message of Jesus: the one who sought God's forgiveness and taught others to do the same became the object of forgiveness on the cross. This has big implications on the crucifixion itself, as blood atonement is the foundation upon which it stands.

CHAPTER 5

THE CRUCIFIXION: INDISPUTABLE FACT, OR THE MOST MISUNDERSTOOD EVENT IN HISTORY?

After the deity of Jesus, the crucifixion is perhaps the most contested issue about his life between Christians and Muslims. The crucifixion sees a rare convergence of opinion between Christians and secular historians. His death on the cross is taken as an almost indisputable fact of history, to the point where it's not even questioned. Yet, the Qur'an makes the bold claim that he was not crucified. Is it possible that the Qur'an, written some 600 years after Jesus, could be right? In this chapter, we are going to see that, contrary to what many tend to think, far from going against the tides of history, the Qur'an is in fact in perfect harmony with the historical account. The key to understanding this lies in appreciating the nature of the New Testament and the Qur'an.

WERE THE NEW TESTAMENT AUTHORS WRITING UNDER DIVINE INSPIRATION?

The earliest accounts we have for the crucifixion are the books of the New Testament. Within the New Testament, it is the four Gospels of Matthew, Mark, Luke and John that provide the details of the crucifixion. Other books may allude to the crucifixion, but it's the Gospels that contain the details of the events that led up to the crucifixion, the crucifixion itself and the events after the crucifixion. Are the Gospel accounts divinely inspired? This question is critical in determining the reliability of their claims about the death of Jesus because only divine inspiration provides certainty. Human endeavours are limited in what can be discovered about the past because human beings can only deal with what is apparent.

A good example to illustrate this concept is the late Mother Teresa. She was a Roman Catholic nun who dedicated her life to the poor, sick and dying in India. Such was her dedication to charitable work that she has been dubbed the Saint of the Poor. She was the recipient of numerous honours, including the 1979 Nobel Peace Prize. In 2003, she was beatified by the Catholic Church as "Blessed Teresa of Calcutta". At the time of writing, the Catholic Church has announced that she will soon be officially recognised as a saint. For a long time, historians held her as an example of piety. No credible historian questioned her faith because of what was apparent; everyone judged her by her public persona. All of this changed ten years after her death with the release of some of her private letters [52]. They revealed for the first time that throughout her life she was deeply tormented about her faith and suffered periods of doubt about God. This stands in marked contrast to her public image as a selfless and tireless minister for the poor who was driven by faith. Literally overnight she went from being the Saint of the Poor to a doubting Thomas. Because these letters were kept secret by her colleagues and seniors, historians held to a distorted picture of her even long after her death. What this example serves to demonstrate is that the reality of a situation can, and often is, at odds with what we, as human beings, are able to perceive using our limited senses.

Coming back to the Gospels, is it the case that they are divinely inspired and therefore their accounts of the death of Jesus represent certain knowledge? Let's look at some reasons why they were not divinely inspired. First, from what is apparent the authors were merely writing accounts about the life of Jesus, albeit ones that were theologically based. None of the authors of these books claimed to be writing under divine inspiration. The divine inspiration of the Gospels is a conclusion that Christians arrived upon later. Without any explicit statements by the Gospel authors, it is impossible to say with certainty what each author thought of their own writings. There is a verse, **2 Timothy 3:16**, which is frequently cited as evidence that the Gospels are inspired by God: ***"All Scripture is God-breathed and is useful for teaching, rebuking, correcting and training in righteousness" [2 Timothy 3:16]***. The reasoning is that since this verse mentions "All Scripture" as being "God-breathed", then that would include the four Gospels. Now, this understanding of the verse assumes that these writers viewed the term "God-breathed" the same way as it is viewed by Christians today. What is meant by "God-breathed", from the Greek 'theopneustos'? We can't say for certain, as this word was not used by other biblical authors, and appears only once in the entire New Testament, so we cannot assume it was a common term early Christians ascribed to the Scriptures. Putting this to one side, did the writer of **2 Timothy** have the Gospels in mind when they wrote this statement? We can look to the history of the compilation of the New Testament for an answer to this question. The New Testament canon, that is, the compilation of books that make up the New Testament today, was not determined until after the first century, so the author of **2 Timothy** could not have been referring to the New Testament when they mentioned "All Scripture" because the New Testament had not yet existed. Rather, they must have been referring to the Old Testament Scriptures which did exist at the time the author penned **2 Timothy**.

We can look to how the authors of the New Testament viewed each other's writings for a conclusive answer as to whether they personally believed the Gospel accounts are divinely inspired. When we analyse the Gospels, we will find that there is a lot of overlap in the content of Matthew, Mark and Luke. All three of them narrate the same events, often with identical wording and in the same chronological sequence. Hence, scholars classify these Gospels as Synoptic, meaning "giving an account of the events from the same point of view or under the same general aspect". This strong parallelism among the Synoptic Gospels has been widely attributed by scholars to literary interdependence [53]. Let's look at some compelling evidence of copying between the Gospels of Matthew and Mark. Compare the speech of Jesus in **Matthew 24:15-16** and **Mark 13:14** and notice the identical editorial comments by both authors:

So when you see the abomination of desolation spoken of by the prophet Daniel, standing in the holy place (let the reader understand), then let those who are in Judea flee to the mountains. [Matthew 24:15-16]

But when you see the abomination of desolation standing where he ought not to be _(let the reader understand)_, then let those who are in Judea flee to the mountains. [Mark 13:14]

These comments in parenthesis, **"(let the reader understand)"**, are almost certainly the authors' editorial comments directed to their readers, rather than a quote of the words of Jesus. Yet, both authors, Matthew and Mark, add the exact same comment in the exact same location in the discourse. It is highly unlikely that two writers would by coincidence insert into their accounts exactly the same editorial comment at exactly the same place. The most likely explanation is that one of the writers was using the other as a source and copied not only the bulk of the discourse, but also the same editorial comment. By comparing the details found within the stories of the Synoptic Gospels, we can see that not only were the authors copying from one another, but they were also making significant changes to each other's accounts:

i. The incident of the woman in the crowd.

MARK 5:25-34	MATTHEW 9:20-22
And a woman was there who had been subject to bleeding for twelve years. She had suffered a great deal under the care of many doctors and had spent all she had, yet instead of getting better she grew worse. When she heard about Jesus, she came up behind him in the crowd and touched his cloak, because she thought, "If I just touch his clothes, I will be healed." Immediately her bleeding stopped and she felt in her body that she was freed from her suffering. At once Jesus realized that power had gone out from him. He turned around in the crowd and asked, "Who touched my clothes?" "You see the people crowding against you," his disciples answered, "and yet you can ask, 'Who touched me?'" But Jesus kept looking around to see who had done it. Then the woman, knowing what had happened to her, came and fell at his feet and, trembling with fear, told him the whole truth. He said to her, "Daughter, your faith has healed you. Go in peace and be freed from your suffering."	Just then a woman who had been subject to bleeding for twelve years came up behind him and touched the edge of his cloak. She said to herself, "If I only touch his cloak, I will be healed." Jesus turned and saw her. "Take heart, daughter," he said, "your faith has healed you." And the woman was healed at that moment.

The Gospels of Mark and Matthew narrate a story about a woman who seeks to be cured by touching Jesus's cloak. In Mark, Jesus does not seem to know who touched him; he even asks the crowd. Only after the woman comes forward and confesses does Jesus know who touched him. Contrast this with Matthew's account which omits a large portion of the story and instead has Jesus immediately spotting who touched him. Matthew seems to want to portray Jesus in a more powerful light.

ii. The incident of Jesus and the question of eternal life.

The Gospels of Mark and Matthew mention an incident about a man who approaches Jesus and questions him. In Mark, Jesus rejects the questioner's praise of him being good. Contrast this with Matthew's account which subtly re-phrases Jesus's response:

MARK 10:17-18	MATTHEW 19:16-17
As Jesus started on his way, a man ran up to him and fell on his knees before him. "Good teacher," he asked, "what must I do to inherit eternal life?" "Why do you call me good?" Jesus answered. "No one is good—except God alone."	Just then a man came up to Jesus and asked, "Teacher, what good thing must I do to get eternal life?" "Why do you ask me about what is good?" Jesus replied. "There is only One who is good. If you want to enter life, keep the commandments."

Matthew seems to have been troubled by the implication of the statement "Why do you call me good?" and therefore re-phrased it (very slightly) to "Why do you ask me about what is good" so as to avoid the difficult implication that Jesus might be admitting to not being wholly 'good'.

iii. The disciples and Jesus sailing on a boat.

The Gospels of Mark and Luke provide an account of the disciples on a boat with Jesus during a storm. The attitudes of Jesus and the disciples are portrayed very differently:

MARK 4:38-40	LUKE 8:23-25
Jesus was in the stern, sleeping on a cushion. <u>The disciples woke him and said to him, "Teacher, don't you care if we drown?"</u> He got up, rebuked the wind and said to the waves, "Quiet! Be still!" Then the wind died down and it was completely calm. <u>He said to his disciples, "Why are you so afraid? Do you still have no faith?"</u>	As they sailed, he fell asleep. A squall came down on the lake, so that the boat was being swamped, and they were in great danger. <u>The disciples went and woke him, saying, "Master, Master, we're going to drown!"</u> He got up and rebuked the wind and the raging waters; the storm subsided, and all was calm. <u>"Where is your faith?" he asked his disciples.</u>

Mark portrays the disciples as rather disrespectful towards Jesus, as they accuse him of being uncaring. Even the response of Jesus is harsh, **"Do you still have no faith?"** Luke neutralises these negative portrayals by having the disciples address Jesus more respectfully, and softens Jesus's response to **"Where is your faith?"**

iv. The last words of Jesus on the cross.

MARK 15:34	LUKE 23:46
And at three in the afternoon Jesus cried out in a loud voice, "My God, my God, why have you forsaken me?"	Jesus called out with a loud voice, "Father, into your hands I commit my spirit."

The Gospels of Mark and Luke record the last words of Jesus. In Mark, Jesus utters the blasphemous words of despair **"My God, my God, why have you forsaken me?"** Luke's account deletes these troubling words and replaces them with the far more submissive statement **"Father, into your hands I commit my spirit."**

In my experiences of engaging with Christians over the years, the vast majority of people that I've spoken to are unaware of such changes. This is not surprising, because the Gospels are typically read in a vertical fashion. It's only when you read them horizontally, comparing the accounts with each other side by side, that the changes become apparent. Evidently, the authors of the Gospels were sometimes troubled by one another's depictions of Jesus and his disciples and made changes accordingly. These examples are important because they have serious implications for the doctrine of divine inspiration. The copying and modification between the Gospel authors implies they didn't consider one another's writings to be inspired; otherwise, they wouldn't have omitted material, added their own and revised the wording. Even if one rejects the evidence for literary interdependence, we still have the problem of the significant differences between the Gospel accounts. If the authors were writing under divine inspiration, then wouldn't God have inspired them to record the same details? We must conclude that the Gospel accounts themselves were not divinely inspired, but rather very human endeavours.

THE CLAIM THAT THE CRUCIFIXION IS FORETOLD IN THE OLD TESTAMENT

An argument commonly put forward to provide divine backing for the crucifixion is that it is foretold in the Old Testament. The reasoning is that even if the Gospel authors themselves are not writing under divine inspiration, they are in fact recording the fulfilment of an Old Testament prophecy that Jesus was to suffer and die on the cross for our sins. The 53rd chapter of the Book of Isaiah is the most popular proof text put forward. Here is the chapter in full:

Who has believed our message and to whom has the arm of the Lord been revealed?

He grew up before him like a tender shoot, and like a root out of dry ground.

He had no beauty or majesty to attract us to him, nothing in his appearance that we should desire him.

He was despised and rejected by mankind, a man of suffering, and familiar with pain.

Like one from whom people hide their faces he was despised, and we held him in low esteem.

Surely he took up our pain and bore our suffering, yet we considered him punished by God, stricken by him, and afflicted.

But he was pierced for our transgressions, he was crushed for our iniquities; the punishment that brought us peace was on him, and by his wounds we are healed.

We all, like sheep, have gone astray, each of us has turned to our own way; and the Lord has laid on him the iniquity of us all.

He was oppressed and afflicted, yet he did not open his mouth; he was led like a lamb to the slaughter, and as a sheep before its shearers is silent, so he did not open his mouth.

By oppression and judgement he was taken away.

Yet who of his generation protested?

For he was cut off from the land of the living; for the transgression of my people he was punished.

He was assigned a grave with the wicked, and with the rich in his death, though he had done no violence, nor was any deceit in his mouth.

Yet it was the Lord's will to crush him and cause him to suffer, and though the Lord makes his life an offering for sin, he will see his offspring and prolong his days, and the will of the Lord will prosper in his hand.

After he has suffered, he will see the light of life and be satisfied; by his knowledge my righteous servant will justify many, and he will bear their iniquities.

Therefore I will give him a portion among the great, and he will divide the spoils with the strong, because he poured out his life unto death, and was numbered with the transgressors.

For he bore the sin of many, and made intercession for the transgressors. [Isaiah 53:1-12]

In Isaiah, statements such as *"for the transgression of my people he was punished"* and *"he bore the sin of many"* do, at face value, seem to bear a striking resemblance to the theology of the crucifixion. However, when we analyse this chapter in its entirety, we will see that it cannot be a prophecy about Jesus. When it comes to prophecies in Scripture, you can think of each detail that the prophecy provides as a criterion that must be satisfied. So, if we consider **Isaiah 53** to be a prophecy about the future, then in order for it to be fulfilled by Jesus, every detail provided in the prophecy has to be satisfied by the life of Jesus as he is portrayed in the New Testament. If not, then Jesus fails as a candidate and the prophecy remains unfulfilled. We also find mention of the following in verse 10:

"...he will see his offspring and prolong his days"

The Hebrew word used for "offspring", 'zera', carries the meaning of progeny and semen. So, in the context of this verse, it means he will see his children. This can't be a reference to Jesus as nowhere does the New Testament state that Jesus had children. Trinitarians might want to think twice before trying to argue that silence on this matter leaves the possibility that it could be true, as from their perspective, any children of Jesus would also be God-men and we'd have the troubling prospect of grandchildren of the Father. The verse above also mentions that his days will be prolonged. This statement makes no sense in the light of the Trinitarian belief that Jesus is God. A mortal man's days can be prolonged, but God is eternal. A being that is eternal cannot have their lives prolonged.

Now, those who consider **Isaiah 53** to be a prophecy about Jesus tend to interpret these verses metaphorically, as a literal interpretation is problematic.

The issue with this approach is one of inconsistency. Why interpret the mention of those things that support the crucifixion, such as suffering, literally, whereas those things that go against Jesus, such as having children and a prolonged life, are interpreted metaphorically? The suffering, offspring and prolonged days are all mentioned together within verse 10, and yet there is nothing within the context of the verse which indicates a mixture of literal and metaphorical interpretation:

> **Yet it was the Lord's will to crush him and cause him to suffer, and though the Lord makes his life an offering for sin, he will see his offspring and prolong his days, and the will of the Lord will prosper in his hand.**

So, to be consistent, we should interpret all the statements literally or metaphorically, rather than picking and choosing according to our desires.

So, if **Isaiah 53** is not talking about Jesus, then whom or what is it referring to? The Jewish people have historically associated the chapter with the suffering of the Israelites. There are even prominent Christian sources which agree with the common Jewish perspective. For example, the *Harper Collins Study Bible* says: **"The early church identified the servant in this passage [Isaiah 52:13-53:12] with Jesus, and Jesus' own sense of identity and mission may have been shaped by this figure. In the original historical context, however, the servant appears to have been exiled Israel"** [54]. The commentary found in the *Oxford Study Edition of The New English Bible* associates Isaiah's mention of death with the destruction and exile of Israel: **"The crowds, pagan nations, among whom the servant (Israel) lived, speak here (through v. 9), saying that the significance of Israel's humilia-tion and exaltation is hard to believe... The death probably refers to the destruction and Exile of Israel."** [55]

In fact, **Isaiah 53** can be applied to any people of God that suffer. We find support for this interpretation in the Old Testament book of Jeremiah. Prophet Jeremiah faithfully communicated God's words to the people of Israel, warning them about the impending Babylonian captivity that was sure to come unless they repented. But no-one listened to him; he was rejected, even by his own family: **"Your relatives, members of your own family— even** *they have betrayed you" [Jeremiah 12:6].* Jeremiah suffered greatly as he was beaten and imprisoned: *"They were angry with Jeremiah and had him beaten and imprisoned in the house of Jonathan the secretary, which they had made into a prison." [Jeremiah 37:15]* Here Jeremiah seems to quote **Isaiah 53** and applies it to himself:

JEREMIAH 11:18-19	ISAIAH 53:7-8
Because the Lord revealed their plot to me, I knew it, for at that time he showed me what they were doing. I had been like a gentle lamb led to the slaughter; I did not realize that they had plotted against me, saying, "Let us destroy the tree and its fruit; let us cut him off from the land of the living, that his name be remembered no more"	He was oppressed and afflicted, yet he did not open his mouth; he was led like a lamb to the slaughter, and as a sheep before its shearers is silent, so he did not open his mouth. ...For he was cut off from the land of the living; for the transgression of my people he was punished.

We can in fact look elsewhere in the Old Testament to settle the question of whether **Isaiah 53** is about Jesus. There are prophecies in the Old Testament which specifically relate to the Messiah, and these explicitly rule out any possibility of the Messiah being crucified. In the New Testament, Jesus affirms an Old Testament prophecy about himself:

Then the devil took him to the holy city and had him stand on the highest point of the temple. "If you are the Son of God," he said, "throw yourself down. For it is written:

"'He will command his angels concerning you,

and they will lift you up in their hands,

so that you will not strike your foot against a stone.'"

Jesus answered him, "It is also written: 'Do not put the Lord your God to the test.'" [Matthew 4:5-7]

We can see that Satan challenged Jesus by applying an Old Testament prophecy to him. Jesus responds by affirming the prophecy (*"It is also written..."*). The prophecy being quoted can be found in **Pslam 91:**

PSALM 91:10-15	MATTHEW 4:5-7
no harm will overtake you, no disaster will come near your tent. *For he will command his angels concerning you to guard you in all your ways;* *they will lift you up in their hands, so that you will not strike your foot against a stone.* *You will tread on the lion and the cobra; you will trample the great lion and the serpent.* *"Because he loves me," says the Lord, "I will rescue him; I will protect him, for he acknowledges my name.* *He will call on me, and I will answer him; I will be with him in trouble, I will deliver him and honor him.*	*Then the devil took him to the holy city and had him stand on the highest point of the temple. "If you are the Son of God," he said, "throw yourself down. For it is written:* *"'He will command his angels concerning you,* *and they will lift you up in their hands,* *so that you will not strike your foot against a stone.'"* *Jesus answered him, "It is also written: 'Do not put the Lord your God to the test.'"*

We can see that the verses of **Psalm 91** mention that no harm will come to Jesus ("no harm will overtake you"), that the angels will guard him ("they will lift you up in their hands, so that you will not strike your foot against a stone"), that God will rescue and protect him ("I will rescue him; I will protect him"), and that God will deliver him from all trouble ("will be with him in trouble, I will deliver him"). Clearly, this prophecy eliminates any possibility of a crucified Messiah. If we are going to be objective in our interpretation of Scripture, then surely the explicit words of Jesus that confirm **Psalm 91** as a prophecy about himself override the comparatively speculative interpretation of **Isaiah 53**.

In summary, far from there being Old Testament prophecies about the crucifixion of Jesus, there are in fact prophecies which explicitly state that the Messiah would not be harmed in any way. The only way you can arrive at a crucified Messiah in the Old Testament is to ignore explicit verses like those found in **Psalm 91**, and instead interpret comparatively ambiguous verses, like **Isaiah 53,** through the Gospel claims about the life, death and resurrection of Jesus.

NOT DIVINELY INSPIRED OR FORETOLD, BUT EYEWITNESS TESTIMONY?

So far in this chapter we've seen that there is no divine backing for the crucifixion, neither in the uninspired writings of the Gospels, nor in the prophecies of the Old Testament. Remember that only divine revelation provides absolute certainty, whereas humans are limited to what is apparent. You may be thinking, even if the Gospel claims about the crucifixion don't have divine backing, weren't their authors eyewitnesses to the life of Jesus, and therefore we can be confident that their claims about the death of Jesus are historically reliable?

To be able to make the claim that the Gospel authors were eyewitnesses to the event of the crucifixion, we need to look at three key pieces of information about the authors:

- *Their identities*

- *The content of their writings*

- *The date of their writings*

To appreciate this point, imagine you are a member of a jury at a trial. The prosecution claims to have a witness who saw the accused commit the crime which they are standing trial for. If the accused is found guilty, then they face the prospect of life in prison. The stakes are high, and the fate of the accused lies in your hands. Since the witness represents the key piece of evidence against the accused, you quite naturally want to be sure, beyond any reasonable doubt, that their testimony is reliable. You make the request that the prosecution bring forward the witness so that you can question them, and to your surprise they state that they can't reveal their identity as they wish to remain anonymous. However, they can provide a written statement on their behalf. You examine the written statement of the witness and find that it contains details that conflict with the other evidence that has been presented about the case. Would you feel confident condemning the accused to life in prison in such circumstances? This hypothetical scenario mirrors the crucifixion. You can think of the crucifixion as being on trial, and the Gospel authors as the potential witnesses. Each and every one of us is the jury, and we need to examine the claims of the Gospel authors and decide whether they are true eyewitnesses. If we get it wrong, then we don't stand to condemn another individual, but rather ourselves as it is our own eternal Hereafter that is at stake.

When we scrutinise the Gospel authors in the light of their identities and the content and date of their writings, we will find that they are not credible eyewitnesses to the crucifixion. To begin with, it's important to recognise that the Gospels themselves are, strictly speaking, anonymous [56]. While today in the New Testament you see the headings "The Gospel according to..." at the start of each of the Gospels, it's important to note that none of the authors identify themselves by name within the texts. They were quoted anonymously by Church Fathers in the first half of the second century (i.e. 100 - 150 CE) and the names by which they are currently known appeared suddenly around the year 180 CE, nearly 150 years after Jesus [57]. We find this in the writings of early Church apologists such as Justin Martyr who was writing in the middle of the second century. Justin quotes from the Gospels on numerous occasions, but the striking thing is that he does not call the Gospels by their names. Instead, he regularly calls them "Memoirs of the Apostles". He does not say that he thinks that the disciples themselves wrote the books, only that these books preserve their "memoirs" (meaning, their recollections of the life and teachings of Jesus). These are some of the reasons that have led scholars to believe that the names Matthew, Mark, Luke and John were assigned to the Gospels long after they were first authored.

The authors of the Gospels of Mathew, Mark and Luke do not make the claim of being first-hand eyewitnesses to the life of Jesus. In fact, the author of the Gospel of Luke openly states that they are not an eyewitness, in the prologue of the Gospel:

> **Many have undertaken to draw up an account of the things that have been fulfilled among us, just as they were handed down to us by those who from the first were eyewitnesses and servants of the word. [Luke 1:1-2]**

There are some important points to note here. The author speaks in the first person ("us"), but they do not say who they are. They claim that many others – who are also not named – preceded them in writing an account of "the things that have been fulfilled among us". These "things", of course, are the events of Jesus's life. The predecessors based their accounts on traditions that had been handed down by "eyewitnesses and servants of the word". The author of Luke does not say that they themselves have had access to eyewitnesses, only that the materials that both they and their predecessors provided in their books were based on reports that ultimately go back to eyewitnesses and "servants of the word". The Gospel of John is the only Gospel that makes the claim to have been written by a disciple of Jesus: **"This is the disciple who testifies to these things and who wrote them down. We know that his testimony is true" [John 21:24].** This disciple seems to be a reference to the "disciple Jesus loved" who is mentioned five times throughout the Gospel of John (**John 13:23, 19:26, 20:2, 21:7, 21:2**). Although this beloved disciple is traditionally associated with John the Evangelist, this is a view rejected by modern scholarship [58]. They are another anonymous figure and we can only speculate as to their true identity.

We can turn to the content of the Gospel of John to reach a conclusion on whether it is a reliable first-hand account of the life of Jesus. Before that, let's imagine ourselves in the shoes (or perhaps that should be sandals) of the disciple John who walked, talked and lived with Jesus. If you were to write an account of your personal experiences with Jesus, would you write using the first or third person narrative? For example, if you witnessed Jesus making a particular speech, would you record this in the first person as "I heard Jesus say...", or in the third person as "Jesus said to John..."? Human beings typically write in the third person when they are reporting something they heard from someone else, so if you really did witness the speech first-hand you would most likely write your account from a first person perspective. When we analyse the narration style of the Gospel of John, we will find that the disciple that Jesus loved, who is said to be the author of the Gospel, is referred to in the third person so the author clearly can't be the disciple: *"One of them, the disciple whom Jesus loved, was reclining next to him" [John 13:23]*. This disconnected, third person style narrative is employed throughout the Gospel of John, and in fact the other Gospels of Matthew, Mark and Luke as well. Clearly, the Gospels were not written by first-hand witnesses of Jesus, but rather later authors who had no connection with the events they narrate, hence the detached third person narrative – much like that of a history book – being employed throughout their writings.

Another interesting point about the author of the Gospel of John is the way they present Jesus. In the Gospels of Matthew, Mark and Luke, Jesus preaches in parables and short, compact sayings. However, in John, the method is with long discourses – Jesus sounds like a Greek philosopher. If the Gospel of John were read in isolation, then one would never guess that the parable was a common teaching method of his (**John 15:1-8** being a rare example of a parable in the Gospel of John).

We can also look to the social conditions of the Holy Land for further insight into the content of the Gospels. Illiteracy rates in first-century Palestine were staggeringly high. It has been estimated that the total literacy rate for Jews during the time of Jesus was likely less than 3 percent [59]. This is not surprising, given that it was a predominantly oral society. Furthermore, the uneducated and the poor, who represented the majority of the population, would have had little reason to learn to read and write as their primary lines of work were agriculture and fishing. We see these social conditions reflected in the New Testament which describes the disciples, including John, as being "unschooled" and "ordinary": *"When they saw the courage of Peter and John and realized that they were unschooled, ordinary men, they were*

astonished and they took note that these men had been with Jesus"
[Acts 4:13]. Strong's Bible Dictionary has this to say about the original Greek used for the words translated as "unschooled" and "ordinary":

> **Agrammatos – illiterate, without learning.**
>
> **Idiōtēs – an unlearned, illiterate, man as opposed to the learned and educated: one who is unskilled in any art.**

With this in mind, it is highly unlikely that disciples such as John, who the New Testament describes as illiterate and uneducated, are the authors of the Gospels, works that are written in highly eloquent Greek. Rather, it is much more plausible that later unknown authors, highly skilled in Greek philosophy, rhetoric and literature, were behind the Gospel accounts.

Finally, let's consider the dates of the writing of the Gospels. New Testament scholars have widely agreed that the earliest Gospel was Mark, written around 70 CE; that Matthew and Luke were some years later, around 80 - 85 CE; and that John was the last Gospel, around 90 - 100 CE. It's out of the scope of this book to go into detail about how scholars could arrive at those dates, but let's cover a few points to give some sense of why these particular dates are so widely preferred. To begin with, Jesus ascended to God around the year 30 CE, so we can use that date as an initial lower bound as the Gospels must have been written after that. The first really convincing quotations of the Gospels come in the writings of Justin Martyr, around the year 150 CE. Justin does not name the Gospels as Matthew, Mark, Luke, and John, but he quotes them explicitly. If we use this as an upper bound, then this means that the Gospels probably date to somewhere between 30 - 150 CE.

To narrow down the dates further, we can look to the writings of Paul. Paul wrote his letters around 50 - 60 CE. Paul never mentions or quotes any of the Gospels, so it seems that they were not written in his lifetime. Paul was an extraordinarily well-travelled and well-connected person. So, if anyone would have known about the existence of written accounts of Jesus's life, it would have been him. From this, it appears that the Gospels were not in circulation yet in the 50s. So, that narrows the dates to some time after 60 CE. Based on the literary relationship between the Gospels, as well as the links between the issues that the authors are writing about and real historical events, scholars narrow the dates down further to around 70 – 100 CE. It is always very hard to come up with precise dates for ancient narratives. Unless they refer to people or events that can be reliably dated from other sources, or unless their authors actually tell you when they were writing, then dates have to be estimated. But these parameters (between 70 - 100 CE for all four Gospels) are agreed on by most scholars. New Testament scholar Christopher Tuckett states that all four Gospels were written by later Christians: **"Thus in reading all the Gospels, we have to be aware of the fact that we are reading accounts of Jesus' life as mediated by later Christians and hence we may learn much, if not more, about the latter as about Jesus himself in studying the Gospel texts." [60]**

In summary, when it comes to their dates, not one of the Gospels was written during the lifetime of Jesus, nor during the lifetimes of any witnesses, as the disciples would have most likely long passed away by that stage. When we also factor in their unknown identities together with the contents of the Gospels, we must conclude that they were not written by eyewitnesses.

WERE THE STORIES ABOUT JESUS PASSED ON RELIABLY?

So far in this chapter we've seen that not only is there no divine backing for the crucifixion in the Gospel accounts, but also that their authors were not eyewitnesses to the event of the crucifixion. This means that, in terms of their sources, they would have been limited to recording the stories about Jesus that were passed down to them by other people. Just what was the situation in the decades following Jesus, were there just the stories that can be found in the New Testament today, or were there other competing traditions in circulation? There were in fact many competing traditions, as is demonstrated in the writings of Paul:

> **For if someone comes to you and preaches a Jesus other than the Jesus we preached, or if you receive a different spirit from the Spirit**

you received, or a different gospel from the one you accepted, you put up with it easily enough. [2 Corinthians 11:4]

So, we can see that even as early as the 50s CE, when Paul was writing, there were many competing traditions about the life of Jesus. Unfortunately, the only traditions that survive from the first century are the accounts that we find in the New Testament today. We don't have access to any of these other traditions, but we shouldn't be so quick to write them off by virtue of the attacks by their opponents or their exclusion from the New Testament. We must remember that history is written by the winners, but that doesn't mean that the traditions that made it into the New Testament are necessarily the most correct. Just as we saw with the doctrine of the Trinity in the first chapter of this book, political and social factors play a big role in determining which points of view became dominant.

Although Paul's writings represent the earliest surviving works by Christians, we can't turn to his writings to examine the reliability of the New Testament crucifixion narrative because he does not go into any detail about the crucifixion. He believes that Jesus was crucified, but he is silent on the details. By his own admission, he wasn't an eyewitness to the crucifixion: **"For what I received I passed on to you as of first importance: that Christ died for our sins according to the Scriptures" [1 Corinthians 15:3].** Here Paul is saying that he is conveying information that he has received from others. In order for the crucifixion of Jesus to be reliable, the stories on which it was based had to have been reliable. The Gospels represent the earliest surviving works that provide detail about the events leading up to, during and after the crucifixion, so the Gospels are where we must focus our attention. When we examine Gospel accounts about the crucifixion and the key events surrounding it, such as the resurrection, we will find that there is evidence of changes, contradictions and even fabrications:

The Gospel of John changes the date of the crucifixion

According to the Gospels of Mark, Matthew and Luke, the Last Supper is the Passover meal which Jesus ate with his disciples:

MARK 14:16-18	MATTHEW 26:19-21	LUKE 22:13-15
The disciples left, went into the city and found things just as Jesus had told them. So they prepared the Passover.	So the disciples did as Jesus had directed them and prepared the Passover.	They left and found things just as Jesus had told them. So they prepared the Passover.
When evening came, Jesus arrived with the Twelve.	When evening came, Jesus was reclining at the table with the Twelve.	When the hour came, Jesus and his apostles reclined at the table.
While they were reclining at the table eating, he said, "Truly I tell you, one of you will betray me—one who is eating with me."	And while they were eating, he said, "Truly I tell you, one of you will betray me."	And he said to them, "I have eagerly desired to eat this Passover with you before I suffer."

The Gospel of John also indicates that Jesus had a last meal with his disciples. However, unlike the accounts in Mark, Matthew and Luke, we're told he never got to eat the Passover meal as his final meal took place before the festival of Passover:

> **It was just before the Passover Festival. Jesus knew that the hour had come for him to leave this world and go to the Father. Having loved his own who were in the world, he loved them to the end. The evening meal was in progress... [John 13:1-2]**

John goes on to state that Jesus was crucified on the day of preparation for the Passover:

Now it was the day of Preparation of the Passover. It was about the sixth hour. He said to the Jews, "Behold your King!" They cried out, "_Away with him, away with him, crucify him!_" Pilate said to them, "Shall I crucify your King?" The chief priests answered, "We have no king but Caesar." [John 19:14-15]

Remember that in the other Gospels, Jesus actually eats the Passover meal with his disciples before his arrest. John's timing of the story is different - he has Jesus die before the Passover meal is eaten. Why did John's author alter the story? We find a clue in the Gospel of John when he refers to Jesus as the "Lamb of God": **_The next day John saw Jesus coming toward him and said, 'Look, the Lamb of God, who takes away the sin of the world!'_" [John 1:29]**

It's crucial to note that John is the only Gospel that identifies Jesus as the "Lamb of God". Thus, the Gospel of John portrays Jesus as the Passover lamb, slaughtered on the day of preparation of Passover. For John, Jesus was the Lamb of God – he died at the same time, in the same place (Jerusalem), and at the hands of the same people (the Jewish priests) as the Passover lamb. In other words, the author has told a story that is not historically accurate, even though in their judgement it may be theologically true. Therefore, we can see that the author of the Gospel of John was willing to change the biography of Jesus in order to make him conform to their beliefs. This is one of the many reasons why New Testament scholars conclude that the Gospel of John is not historically accurate. Liberal and conservative Christian scholars alike no longer believe that Jesus actually said the words attributed to him by the author of John. New Testament scholar and Anglican priest Christopher Tuckett has this to say:

In terms simply of historical reliability or 'authenticity', it seems impossible to maintain that both John and the synoptics [Mark, Matthew and Luke] can be presenting us with equally 'authentic' accounts of Jesus' own life. By 'authentic' accounts I mean here historically accurate representations of what Jesus himself actually said and did. The theological 'authenticity' of John's account is quite another matter. The differences between the two are too deep seated and wide ranging for such a position to be sustainable.

If there is a choice, it is almost certainly to be made in favour of the synoptic picture, at least in broadly general terms. The picture John then presents us with is a view of the Jesus tradition which has been heavily coloured and influenced by John and his own situation. [61]

Evangelical Professor Richard Bauckham concludes that John is a highly interpreted account of the life and ministry of Jesus:

All scholars, whatever their views of the redactional work of the Synoptic Evangelists and of the historical reliability of the Gospel of John, agree that the latter presents a much more thoroughly and extensively interpreted version of the story of Jesus. [62]

The Mary Magdalene Problem

The various Gospel accounts of the resurrection are so different that it's hard to know what to focus on, but the visit of Mary Magdalene to the tomb of Jesus is central. In particular, the accounts of Matthew and John cannot be harmonised:

MATTHEW 28:1-9	JOHN 20:1-2
After the Sabbath, at dawn on the first day of the week, Mary Magdalene and the other Mary went to look at the tomb.	Early on the first day of the week, while it was still dark, Mary Magdalene went to the tomb
There was a violent earthquake, for an angel of the Lord came down from heaven and, going to the tomb, rolled back the stone and sat on it.	and saw that the stone had been removed from the entrance
His appearance was like lightning, and his clothes were white as snow	
The guards were so afraid of him that they shook and became like dead men.	
The angel said to the women, "Do not be afraid, for I know that you are looking for Jesus, who was crucified	
He is not here; he has risen, just as he said. Come and see the place where he lay	
Then go quickly and tell his disciples: 'He has risen from the dead and is going ahead of you into Galilee. There you will see him.' Now I have told you."	
So the women hurried away from the tomb, afraid yet filled with joy, and ran to tell his disciples	
Suddenly Jesus met them. "Greetings," he said. They came to him, clasped his feet and worshipped him	So she came running to Simon Peter and the other disciple, the one Jesus loved, and said, "They have taken the Lord out of the tomb, and we don't know where they have put him!"

We can see that in the Gospel of Matthew, Mary Magdalene is presented as having found the tomb empty, but after that she actually encountered Jesus as she was running away from the tomb. In the Gospel of John, Mary Magdalene is also presented as having found the tomb empty. However, after she flees the tomb she doesn't encounter Jesus but instead runs to the disciples and tells them that the body of Jesus had been stolen. Now, these two accounts of the resurrection are a contradiction; if Mary Magdalene met Jesus at the tomb, as Matthew says, then why did she report that the body had been stolen, according to John?

Since it's important to have a firm grasp of the chronological sequence of events as described in Matthew and John, I have summarised the key information in a diagram:

MATTHEW

[1] After the Sabbath, at dawn on the first day of the week, Mary Magdalene and the other Mary went to look at the tomb

[2] There was a violent earthquake, for an angel of the Lord came down from heaven and, going to the tomb, rolled back the stone

[3] So the women hurried away from the tomb, afraid yet filled with joy, and ran to tell his disciples. Suddenly Jesus met them. "Greetings," he said.

JOHN

[1] Early on the first day of the week, while it was still dark, Mary Magdalene went to the tomb

[2] and saw that the stone had been removed from the entrance.

[3] So she came running to Simon Peter and the other disciple and said, "They have taken the Lord out of the tomb, and we don't know where they have put him "

We can see that Matthew and John must be talking about the same visit to the tomb. This is because in **John 20:1**, the stone was removed before Mary Magdalene's first visit. This mirrors **Matthew 28:2** which says that the stone was removed as Mary Magdalene was arriving. Moreover, Matthew mentions the day of the visit to the tomb (**"after the Sabbath"**), as does John (**"first day of the week"**). In the Jewish calendar, the day after Sabbath is the first day of the week. So, we know Matthew and John are referencing the same day. Matthew also mentions the time of the visit to the tomb (**"towards the dawn of the first day"**), as does John (**"while it was still dark"**), so we know they are referencing the same time frame. We must conclude that these contradictory accounts cannot be explained away: Matthew, who has Mary Magdalene meet Jesus and touch him after leaving the tomb, conflicts with John who reports that she left the tomb and told the disciples that the body of Jesus had been stolen and she didn't know where it was.

The Gospel of Matthew invents many resurrections

In the Gospel of Matthew, we are told that something extraordinary, perhaps miraculous, happened after Jesus was crucified:

> **At that moment the curtain of the temple was torn in two from top to bottom. The earth shook, the rocks split and the tombs broke open. The bodies of many holy people who had died were raised to life. They came out of the tombs after Jesus' resurrection and went into the holy city and appeared to many people. [Matthew 27:51-53]**

Now, none of the other Gospels mention this astonishing incident of the walking dead, only Matthew reports it. Compare the accounts of Matthew and Mark regarding the events surrounding the crucifixion:

MATTHEW 27:48-56	MARK 15:36-41
Immediately one of them ran and got a sponge. He filled it with wine vinegar, put it on a staff, and offered it to Jesus to drink. The rest said, "Now leave him alone. Let's see if Elijah comes to save him."	Someone ran, filled a sponge with wine vinegar, put it on a staff, and offered it to Jesus to drink. "Now leave him alone. Let's see if Elijah comes to take him down," he said.
And when Jesus had cried out again in a loud voice, he gave up his spirit.	With a loud cry, Jesus breathed his last.
At that moment the curtain of the temple was torn in two from top to bottom. The earth shook, the rocks split	The curtain of the temple was torn in two from top to bottom.
and the tombs broke open. The bodies of many holy people who had died were raised to life. They came out of the tombs after Jesus' resurrection and went into the holy city and appeared to many people.	
When the centurion and those with him who were guarding Jesus saw the earthquake and all that had happened, they were terrified, and exclaimed, "Surely he was the Son of God!"	And when the centurion, who stood there in front of Jesus, saw how he died, he said, "Surely this man was the Son of God!"
Many women were there, watching from a distance. They had followed Jesus from Galilee to care for his needs. Among them were Mary Magdalene, Mary the mother of James and Joseph, and the mother of Zebedee's sons.	Some women were watching from a distance. Among them were Mary Magdalene, Mary the mother of James the younger and of Joseph, and Salome. In Galilee these women had followed him and cared for his needs. Many other women who had come up with him to Jerusalem were also there.

Notice that even though Mark's account of the crucifixion is virtually identical to that of Matthew, Mark does not mention the rising of the dead saints. If such a miraculous event really happened, then there would be no rational reason for it to be omitted from the Gospel of Mark. Bizarrely, when it comes to relatively mundane events like Jesus riding into Jerusalem, all four Gospels corroborate one another (*"on a donkey and a colt" [Matthew 21:5], "on a colt" [Mark 11:7]; [Luke 19:35], "on a young donkey" [John 12:14]*), but all the Gospels, apart from Matthew, are silent on the story of the rising of the dead saints.

Christian apologists may try to argue that the other Gospel authors chose not to mention the walking dead because the story didn't interest them or that it wasn't deemed to be theologically significant. This argument is refuted by the writings of Paul. Consider that Paul had the perfect opportunity to cite this story when he was preaching to an audience that were sceptical about life after death: *"But if it is preached that Christ has been raised from the dead, how can some of you say that there is no resurrection of the dead?" [1 Corinthians 15:12].* Why didn't Paul just cite Matthew's report about the many resurrections that took place at Jesus's death? Paul fails to mention Matthew's mass resurrection, even when it could have been used to his advantage. It appears Paul never knew anything about Matthew's rising dead saints either.

Matthew's claim is also dubious from the perspective of the historians that lived around the first century. Historian Josephus (37 CE – 100 CE), a contemporary of Jesus from Jerusalem who wrote much about his city, fails to mention this most public of miracles. To put it into modern terms that are easy to appreciate, this would be like a graveyard full of dead people in a major city like London suddenly coming back to life, with these zombies mingling with Londoners and only a single newspaper reporting the event. It is simply inconceivable that such an event wouldn't be reported by masses of people.

Even conservative Christian scholarship rejects the historicity of this event. New Testament scholar and evangelical apologist Mike Licona stated that the resurrection of the saints narrative in Matthew 27:51-54 is *"a weird residual fragment" [63]* and a *"strange report" [64]*. He called it *"poetical"*, a *"legend"*, an *"embellishment"*, and literary *"special effects"* *[65]*. He claims that Matthew is using a Greco-Roman literary genre which is a *"flexible genre"* in which *"it is often difficult to determine where history ends and legend begins"* *[66]*. Dr. William Lane Craig, an American Christian apologist, concludes that there are *"probably only a few [contemporary] conservative scholars who would treat the story as historical"* *[67]*. Note that these are not liberal or atheist scholars but rather conservative, Bible-believing Christians.

We must conclude that the author of the Gospel of Matthew embellished the crucifixion narrative by inventing the story about the rising of the dead saints. Therefore, the early Christian writers were indeed involved in the act of myth-making. If the rising of many dead people can be invented, then why can't the rising from the dead of one man, Jesus, similarly be invented? If early Christians could invent stories about many dead persons rising from the grave and believe in it, then it is equally as plausible that they could invent a less fantastical scenario about one man rising from the dead.

In summary, when it comes to the crucifixion and its related events such as the resurrection, we've seen examples of changes, contradictions and fabrications in the Gospels of Matthew and John. Recall that the Gospel authors were not divinely inspired nor were they eyewitnesses and so they would have been reliant on the stories about Jesus that had been passed down to them. If we're seeing changes, contradictions and fabrications at the written level, then this would also likely be the case with the stories that were being circulated by word of mouth in the decades preceding the Gospels. The conclusion is that the Gospel crucifixion narratives are unreliable and not a historical certainty. Now, it's important to note that this does not mean that the Gospels contain no truth about Jesus whatsoever. To adopt such a position would be extreme, and we must be fair and balanced when approaching these texts. What we can conclude is that when it comes to the crucifixion narrative in the Gospels in general, their claims cannot be taken at face value.

WHY THE QUR'AN HAS THE TRUE INSIGHT INTO THE CRUCIFIXION

This is what the Qur'an says about the crucifixion of Jesus:

> *They did not kill him, nor did they crucify him, though it was made to appear like that to them; those that disagreed about him are full of doubt, with no knowledge to follow, only supposition: they certainly did not kill him. God raised him up to Himself. God is almighty and wise. [4:157-158]*

We can see that the Qur'an states that Jesus was not crucified; rather, it was made to appear so. What **"though it was made to appear like that to them"** means is a topic of discussion among scholars. A major view is that God gave someone else Jesus's appearance and it was this other person who was substituted for Jesus on the cross, causing his enemies to believe that Jesus was crucified. We find support for this view in the narrations of one of the companions of the Prophet Muhammad ﷺ, Ibn Abbas. He stated:

"Just before God raised Jesus to the Heavens, Jesus went to his disciples, who were twelve inside the house. When he arrived, his hair was dripping with water (as if he had just had a bath) and he said, 'There are those among you who will disbelieve in me twelve times after you had believed in me.' He then asked, 'Who among you will volunteer for his appearance to be transformed into mine, and be killed in my place. Whoever volunteers for that, he will be with me (in Heaven).' One of the youngest ones among them volunteered, but Jesus asked him to sit down. Jesus asked again for a volunteer, and the same young man volunteered and Jesus asked him to sit down again. Then the young man volunteered a third time and Jesus said, 'You will be that man,' and the resemblance of Jesus was cast over that man while Jesus ascended to Heaven from a hole in the roof of the house. When the Jews came looking for Jesus, they found that young man and crucified him..." [68]

We can see that the Qur'an and other Islamic sources are crystal clear: God saved His beloved messenger from crucifixion. Jesus was raised up to God, alive and unharmed, where he remains until this day.

From an observational perspective, would anyone be able to tell the difference between Jesus being crucified, and it being made to appear like he was? Whether it was the real Jesus, or someone who looked, sounded and acted in an identical manner to Jesus, or even an illusion of it being Jesus that tricks the eyes, most casual observers would not be able to distinguish between them. If you think about it, these various scenarios would appear identical for all intents and purposes and would end up being recorded the same way.

Can the Qur'an's claim that Jesus was not crucified, but that it was made to appear so, be accurate? How can a book, revealed over 600 years after Jesus, have such an insight into the crucifixion? Unlike the Gospels, the Qur'an states in no uncertain terms that it is divinely revealed:

> **Nor could this Qur'an have been devised by anyone other than God. It is a confirmation of what was revealed before it and an explanation of the Scripture– let there be no doubt about it– it is from the Lord of the Worlds. [10:37]**

If the Qur'an is from God, then this means that it is not limited by the apparent; in fact, it reveals the reality of history. The Qur'an proclaims that it reveals knowledge of the unseen: **"That is from the news of the unseen which We reveal to you, [O Muḥammad]. You knew it not, neither you nor your people before this..." [11:49].** Having knowledge of the unseen is a quality of God, not human beings. The verses of the Qur'an that discuss the crucifixion show remarkable insight when we analyse them in detail. The Qur'an states that those who differ with its claims about the crucifixion are "full of doubt": **"They did not kill him, nor did they crucify him, though it was made to appear like that to them; those that disagreed about him are full of doubt..."** As we've seen, this is exactly the situation that we found with the Gospel crucifixion narratives with all their changes, contradictions and fabrications. Another important point is that the Old Testament actually supports the Qur'anic narrative on the crucifixion. Recall that Jesus endorsed **Psalm 91** as a prophecy about himself, and that it rules out any possibility of a crucified Messiah:

> *No harm will overtake you, no disaster will come near your tent.*
>
> *For he will command his angels concerning you to guard you in all your ways;*
>
> *they will lift you up in their hands, so that you will not strike your foot against a stone.*
>
> *You will tread on the lion and the cobra; you will trample the great lion and the serpent.*
>
> *"Because he loves me," says the Lord, "I will rescue him; I will protect him, for he acknowledges my name.*
>
> *He will call on me, and I will answer him; I will be with him in trouble, I will deliver him and honor him. [Psalm 91:10-15]*

We can see from the above verses that the Old Testament even supports the Qur'anic narrative on *how* Jesus was saved from the crucifixion, as **Psalm 91** foretold that the angels would "lift him up" and the Qur'an states that "God raised him up":

PSALM 91:11-12	QUR'AN 4:157-158
For he will command his angels concerning you to guard you in all your ways; they will lift you up in their hands...	*... they certainly did not kill him. God raised him up to Himself*

So, we can see that just like with the issue of the nature of God and the Trinity, the Old Testament goes against the Christian understanding and backs up the theology of the Qur'an on the Messiah not being crucified. What the Qur'an reports about Jesus is in fact the fulfilment of an Old Testament prophecy that the Messiah would not be harmed. This is a very important point as it has far-reaching implications. One of the reasons that the Jewish people reject Jesus as the Messiah is because the crucifixion is an obstacle for them. They know that the Messiah cannot be crucified, as stated in the Old Testament prophecy. The Messiah, by definition, is supposed to be victorious, the establisher of the kingdom of God's law, so the idea or notion that the Messiah was crucified is an oxymoron. If he was crucified, he cannot be the Messiah, so the claim that Jesus was put to death in fact justifies their rejection of him. The Qur'an removes this stumbling block of a crucified Messiah and paves the way for the Jewish people to accept Jesus.

An important point that must be highlighted is that we find the claims of the Qur'an also reflected in the New Testament traditions about Jesus. In the following incident, Jesus prays to God just before his arrest, asking to be saved from the crucifixion:

> *Then he [Jesus] said to them, "My soul is overwhelmed with sorrow to the point of death. Stay here and keep watch with me." Going a little farther, he fell with his face to the ground and prayed, "My Father, if it is possible, may this cup be taken from me. Yet not as I will, but as you will." [Matthew 26:38-39]*

These words that have been attributed to Jesus are a clear indication that he did not want to be crucified, supporting the Qur'anic narrative about the crucifixion. This should be a point of reflection for Christians, for if the primary mission of Jesus was to die on the cross, then why did he pray to God to avoid the crucifixion?

As well as the Old and New Testaments, we find support for the Qur'anic crucifixion narrative in history. There were numerous first and second century Christian groups who denied the crucifixion of Jesus:

1. The Basilidians.

The first century scholar Basilides and his followers, the Basilidians, believed that Jesus was saved from the crucifixion and that another, Simon of Cyrene, was crucified in his place:

"The Unborn and Nameless Father seeing their miserable plight, sent his First-born, Nous (and this is the one who is called Christ) to deliver those who should believe in him from the power of the angelic agencies who had built the world. And to men Christ seemed to be a man and to have performed miracles. It was not, however, Christ who suffered, but rather Simon of Cyrene, who was constrained to carry the cross for him, and mistakenly crucified in Christ's stead..." [69]

The beliefs of Basilides matter because he was living very close to the time of the disciples, and there are even traditions that he got these teachings from disciples of Jesus, such as Peter [70]. From this account we can see that it's not the Qur'an that invented this claim of a substitutionary crucifixion, it goes back to the earliest time of Church history.

2. The Philadelphians.

The first century Church Father Ignatius wrote a letter to a Christian community, the Philadelphians, who seemed to deny that Jesus died and was resurrected on the basis that it was not found in the Old Testament Scriptures:

"And I exhort you to do nothing out of strife, but according to the doctrine of Christ. When I heard some saying, If I do not find it in the ancient Scriptures, I will not believe the Gospel; on my saying to them, It is written, they answered me, That remains to be proved. But to me Jesus Christ is in the place of all that is ancient: His cross, and death, and resurrection, and the faith which is by Him, are undefiled monuments of antiquity; by which I desire, through your prayers, to be justified." [71]

This community seemed to be one of Jewish Christians, as earlier in his letter Ignatius mentions that they should not fall into Judaism [72]. Moreover, we can see in the letter above that this community placed great significance on the Old Testament ("*If I do not find it in the ancient Scriptures, I will not believe the Gospel*"). In their view, the life of Jesus was to be interpreted through the Old Testament, and not vice versa as Ignatius maintained.

3. The Trallians.

Ignatius wrote a letter to a Christian group known as the Trallians, who seemed to believe that the death of Jesus was only in appearance, not reality. Here Ignatius tries to correct their understanding about the crucifixion:

> **"And when He had lived among men for thirty years, He was baptized by John, really and not in appearance; and when He had preached the Gospel three years, and done signs and wonders, He who was Himself the Judge was judged by the Jews, falsely so called, and by Pilate the governor; was scourged, was smitten on the cheek, was spit upon; He wore a crown of thorns and a purple robe; He was condemned: He was crucified in reality, and not in appearance, not in imagination, not in deceit. He really died, and was buried, and rose from the dead, even as He prayed in a certain place, saying, "But do Thou, O Lord, raise me up again, and I shall recompense them." [73]**

Now, critics tend to discredit groups such as the Basilidians, Philadelphians and Trallians by appealing to the writings of Church Fathers who condemned them as heretical. Sadly, nearly all the writings of such groups have perished, and we mostly know of them through the writings of their opponents. It is a well-known fact among historians that Church Fathers would exaggerate to the extreme when writing about other Christian sects with whom they did not agree. For example, the second century theologian Irenaeus claimed that the followers of Valentinus made indiscriminate copulation not only permissible but a desired act for those who are truly spiritual [74], and that the Carpocratians practised indiscriminate sex and that their theology compelled them to violate every conceivable moral law and ethical norm [75]. The third century historian Eusebius, who has been dubbed the "Father of Church History", claimed that Simon Magus and his followers engaged in activities "more disgusting than the foulest crime known" [76]. Perhaps the most outrageous example occurs near the end of the fourth century in the writings of the bishop Epiphanius who, in his discussion of a group of Gnostic Christians, outlines their beliefs and describes their orgiastic and cannibalistic practices. Epiphanius claimed that they indulged in sumptuous feasts, with married couples separating to engage in sexual intercourse with other members of the community [77]. The couples are alleged to have then collected the semen in their hands and ingested it together while proclaiming, "this is the body of Christ." The couples also collected and consumed the women's menstrual blood, saying "this is the blood of Christ" [78]. If for some reason the women became pregnant, the fetus was allowed to develop until it could be manually aborted. Then, claims Epiphanius, it was dismembered, covered with honey and spices, and devoured by the community as a special meal [79]. Can such extreme charges by Epiphanius against Gnostic Christians really be true? With the discovery of the Nag Hammadi library in the 20th century we have been able to study the actual writings of a bewildering variety of Gnostic Christians. A lot of the claims made by the Church Fathers against such groups were proven to be false, because, far from condoning, let alone promoting, such outlandish moral behaviour, their writings urge and assume just the opposite social and personal ethics. One of the few constants among all the Nag Hammadi writings is their ascetic orientation. Gnostic Christians appear to have believed, as a rule, in punishing the body, not indulging it. They endorsed ascetic lifestyles, far from the hedonistic debauchery that the Church Fathers alleged. Apparently then, Gnostics were consistently attacked by orthodox Christians as sexually perverse, not because they actually were perverse, but because they were the enemy. In summary, we should take any claims of heresy made against early Christian groups who believed that Jesus was not crucified with a pinch of salt. Recall from our earlier discussion on the Trinity the sheer variety of early sects and their differing beliefs about the nature of Jesus. History is written by the winners, and much of what we know about these early groups has been painted by their opponents.

A charge sometimes made against the Qur'an is that God 'deceived' people with the appearance of the crucifixion. The matter of the crucifixion was controversial in the formative years. The truth was "out there", as we've already seen that the Old Testament clearly states that the Messiah would not be harmed. So, the evidence that Jesus the Messiah could not be crucified is present within the Bible. Now, if some people of the past didn't have access to the Old Testament prophecies about the Messiah and they thought Jesus was crucified, then, according to the Qur'an, they would not be blameworthy in the sight of God: *"God does not burden any soul with more than it can bear..." [2:286].* Here the Qur'an states that God does not hold people to account for what is beyond their capacity. Now that the final revelation, the Qur'an, has been revealed and clears up the misconceptions about Jesus, people have no excuse for ignorance. The test of life is to see if truth is what matters to you, as opposed to what is convenient or fits your desires, and ultimately you are judged on your honest commitment to following the truth as it appears to you. It's important to realise that life is a test. God is testing us in this life to distinguish those who believe from those who disbelieve: **"Do the people think that they will be left to say, 'We believe' and they will not be tried? But We have certainly tried those before them, and God will surely make evident those who are truthful, and He will surely make evident the liars" [29:2-3]**. Such a claim about God deceiving us could be made about anything that seems confusing, contradictory or that needs a bit of investigation. Whilst we've focused a lot on the differences between Islamic theology and Christianity with regard to the crucifixion, it's important to note that Islam teaches, just like the New Testament, that Jesus will return in the End Times. The Prophet Muhammad ﷺ taught that on his return, Jesus will fight the anti-Christ, break the cross and rule the earth by God's law.

In conclusion, the Qur'an reveals the true reality of the crucifixion; although it appeared that Jesus was crucified, it wasn't actually him, and Jesus was in fact raised up to God, alive and well, a perfect fulfilment of a prophecy as foretold by the Old Testament. The Qur'anic narrative about the crucifixion does represent certainty because the Qur'an proclaims that it is divinely inspired, a claim supported by its coherent narrative and deep insight into the Bible. The Gospel authors, by virtue of not being divinely inspired or even eyewitnesses to the crucifixion, were limited to recounting the stories about Jesus that had been passed down to them. As such, they were merely reporting what was apparent: a crucifixion took place. But the Qur'an reveals the reality of what happened: it was not Jesus who was killed.

CHAPTER 6

THE PRESERVATION OF REVELATION

From our beliefs about God, to our worship rituals and even our morality, Scripture shapes virtually every facet of a believer's life. The preservation of Scripture is critical, because it is the foundation upon which everything else rests. Preservation is the difference between following God's true guidance, as revealed to His messengers such as Jesus, and man-made conjecture. This is why the pursuit of truth has to include a critical assessment of the religious texts we hold in our hands.

THE PROBLEM TRANSMITTING ANCIENT TEXTS

Have you ever thought about how the religious Scriptures that we have today have been passed down to us throughout history? Thanks to innovations like the printing press, we live in a world which allows for the mass distribution of information. So, we no longer have to worry about the loss of our religious Scriptures. In fact, we have probably taken their preservation for granted. But advances in technology, such as printing, only account for a small portion of the histories of most religious texts, which span thousands of years. The vast majority of religious texts today have been passed down to us by the scribal tradition, whereby manuscripts are manually copied, word for word, by hand, using materials like ink and leather. Is this method of preserving information reliable?

Have a think about communication in the modern world, such as email or text messages. Have you ever sent an email or text message that contains spelling and grammar mistakes, even with the benefit of spell check features that exist in modern computers and phones? Even professional media outlets often print newspapers and magazines with mistakes in spelling and grammar. Now imagine having to copy an entire book of hundreds of pages, by hand, using only paper and ink, without relying on modern technology. It would undoubtedly be filled with mistakes.

This is exactly what we find when we compare the manuscript copies of religious texts from the past. They are filled with spelling mistakes, missing words and sentences. There were even cases where scribes made intentional changes to suit an agenda. It was easy to do this without most people realising because literacy rates in the ancient past were very low and there were very few scribes. Now extend this copying process over hundreds or thousands of years. You can imagine how much a text can change over such a long span of time, as accidental and intentional changes gradually creep in.

Now imagine if you had the task of evaluating all these written copies with their differences. You would have to compare each of them to the original, word by word and line by line. This would be an extremely time-consuming task, but if you had enough time, or enough people helping you, eventually you could work out which copies are the most accurate when compared to the original.

Now imagine if you had to perform the same task of evaluating all these variations, but this time you do not possess the original to compare against. It would almost be impossible to determine their accuracy. This brings us to another major problem with relying on manuscripts for the preservation of information: over time they can be lost or become damaged. So, we don't always have access to the original or even early copies. Therefore, we lose the ability to determine which of the copies we possess is the most accurate.

THE TRANSMISSION OF THE NEW TESTAMENT

Now that we have a background to the transmission of ancient texts, we can better appreciate the transmission of the New Testament. The earliest physical manuscript evidence we have for the New Testament is a manuscript known as P52, dated to the early part of the second century [80], nearly 100 years after Jesus. It's from the Gospel of John and is about the size of a credit card:

The front contains parts of seven lines from the Gospel of **John 18:31-33** and the back contains parts of seven lines from verses 37-38, both in Greek. The earliest complete copy of the New Testament is the Codex Sinaiticus, dated to the 4th century [81], over 300 years after Jesus.

Just how many New Testament manuscripts are there, and how different are they to one another? The original language of the New Testament is Greek; this is the language of the most ancient manuscripts. There are almost 6,000 Greek manuscripts of the New Testament, with no two pages being identical. This is according to The Interpreter's Dictionary of the Bible: *"There is not one sentence in the New Testament in which the manuscript tradition is wholly uniform" [82].* The famous Alexandrian scholar Origen was aware of the scale of the variants of the New Testament even as early as the 3rd century:

> **The differences among the manuscripts [of the Gospels] have become great, either through the negligence of some copyists or through the perverse audacity of others; they either neglect to check over what they have transcribed, or, in the process of checking, they lengthen or shorten, as they please. [83]**

The Codex Vaticanus, one of the oldest surviving manuscripts of the New Testament, has a fascinating scribal comment in the margin which provides great insight into these variants from the point of view of a copyist:

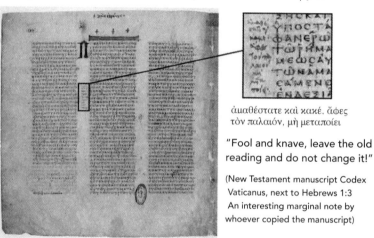

ἀμαθέστατε καὶ κακέ, ἄφες τὸν παλαιόν, μὴ μεταποίει

"Fool and knave, leave the old reading and do not change it!"

(New Testament manuscript Codex Vaticanus, next to Hebrews 1:3 An interesting marginal note by whoever copied the manuscript)

Some verses of the New Testament present a bewildering number of variant readings across the manuscripts; for example, **Colossians 2:2** has fifteen variations [84]. So, this raises an obvious question: which version of the New Testament is the inspired word of God when there are so many variants in existence? Faced with a massive number of variant readings, how do Christian scholars go about determining what may be the word of God? By way of example, let's take a look at the textual problem presented by **Luke 10:1:**

After this the Lord appointed <u>seventy-two others</u> and sent them

two by two ahead of him to every town and place where he was about to go. [New International Version]

After this the Lord appointed <u>seventy others</u>, and sent them on ahead of him, two by two, into every town and place where he himself was about to come. [Revised Standard Version]

As you can see, the editors for these two different versions of the Bible chose different readings (seventy v.s. seventy-two). But what did the original New Testament say, seventy or seventy-two? Bruce Metzger, a Christian expert on Greek biblical manuscripts and widely recognised as one of the most influential New Testament scholars of the 20th century, had this to say about his evaluation of the textual problem presented by **Luke 10:1**:

"The external evidence is almost evenly divided [meaning the manuscript evidence for both is strong]...

The factors bearing upon the evaluation of internal evidence, whether involving transcriptional or intrinsic probabilities, are singularly elusive...

It is likely that in most of the early manuscripts the numeral was written with letters of the alphabet...

It was easy, therefore, for either number to be accidentally altered to the other...

So evenly balanced are these two possibilities [i.e. both readings, seventy and seventy-two] that it is hazardous to dogmatize as to which is more probable...

A total appraisal of both the external and internal evidence bearing on these variant readings must remain indecisive. Though the reading "seventy-two" is supported by a combination of early witnesses and normally carries a high degree of conviction of originality, yet the witnesses that read "seventy" are so weighty and the internal considerations so evenly balanced that the textual critic must simply acknowledge an inability to decide with assurance between the two." [85]

As you can see, the criteria that have been developed by the textual scholars depend largely upon probabilities. Often the textual critics must weigh one set of probabilities against another. The range and complexity of textual data are so great that no mechanically-derived set of rules can be applied with mathematical precision. Each and every variant reading needs to be considered in itself and not judged according to a rule of thumb. Bruce Metzger concludes by saying the following about the evaluation of variant readings during the Bible editorial process:

> **"By way of conclusion, let it be emphasized again that there is no single manuscript and no one group of manuscripts that the textual critic may follow mechanically. All known witnesses of the New Testament are to a greater or lesser extent mixed texts, and even several of the earliest manuscripts are not free from egregious errors. Although in very many cases the textual critic is able to ascertain without residual doubt which reading must have stood in the original, there are not a few other cases where only a tentative decision can be reached, based on an equivocal balancing of probabilities. Occasionally, none of the variant readings will commend itself as original, and one will be compelled either to choose the reading that is judged to be the least unsatisfactory or to indulge in conjectural emendation. In textual criticism, as in other areas of historical research, one must seek not only to learn what can be known but also to become aware of what, because of conflicting witnesses, cannot be known." [86]**

So, before answering the question of whether the Bible is the word of God, we have the difficult task of identifying which version may be the word of God.

As we have seen, ultimately it is fallible editors that decide what goes into the New Testament – not Matthew, Mark, Luke and John. Now we can appreciate why there are so many different versions of the Bible in existence today. Scholars of the Bible, those who are experts in sifting through the huge number of variations that exist in the manuscript tradition, can't agree on which copies are the most accurate. This is because they have the tough task of estimating which copies are closest to the original without possessing the original to compare against. So, each version of the Bible that exists is a patchwork of different copies combined together, and represents what a particular scholar, or group of scholars, estimate to be the closest match to the original. Therefore, with texts like the New Testament that have relied on manual copying for preservation, at best, we can say that we have an estimate of the original words. We can't say with 100 per cent certainty that what we have today, however, is an accurate representation of the original.

THEOLOGICAL CONSEQUENCES OF THE NEW TESTAMENT VARIANTS

The response given by many Christian apologists on the issue of the New Testament variants is that they are not important as they are of no theological consequence. In other words, no matter which variants you take, the core message of the New Testament will still come through to the reader. The huge number of variants is negligible, they argue, because they amount to nothing more than minor spelling and grammatical mistakes. It's true that the majority of differences between manuscripts are down to spelling mistakes and similar scribal errors. These types of errors can be ignored because of the nature of copying manuscripts by hand. However, there are in fact changes that have important theological implications. Here are a few examples:

1. The mention of God being three

> **For there are three that bear record in heaven, the Father, the Word, and the Holy Ghost: and these three are one. [1 John 5:7]**

This verse is known as the Johannine Comma, and it is the only place in the Bible that clearly mentions the Trinity. It used to be present in all Bibles; it remains in some versions, such as the King James Version (KJV) today. However, the editors of modern versions of the Bible, such as the Revised Standard Version (RSV) and New International Version (NIV), have removed it. Compare **1 John 5:7** in these different versions of the Bible:

King James Version (KJV)	Revised Standard Version (RSV)	New International Version (NIV)
6 This is he that came by water and blood, even Jesus Christ; not by water only, but by water and blood. And it is the Spirit that beareth witness, because the Spirit is truth.	6 This is he who came by water and blood, Jesus Christ, not with the water only but with the water and the blood.	6 This is the one who came by water and blood—Jesus Christ. He did not come by water only, but by water and blood. And it is the Spirit who testifies, because the Spirit is the truth
7 For there are three that bear record in heaven, the Father, the Word, and the Holy Ghost: and these three are one.	7 And the Spirit is the witness, because the Spirit is the truth.	7 For there are three that testify:
8 And there are three that bear witness in earth, the Spirit, and the water, and the blood: and these three agree in one.	8 There are three witnesses, the Spirit, the water, and the blood; and these three agree.	8 The Spirit, the water and the blood; and the three are in agreement.

Notice how verse 7 in the RSV is different from verse 7 in the KJV. The RSV does not contain the mention of threeness. Also, notice that verse 7 in the NIV is different from not only the KJV but also the RSV. The NIV also does not contain the mention of threeness. Here is the NIV footnote regarding the Johannine Comma:

> **Late manuscripts of the Vulgate testify in heaven: the Father, the Word and the Holy Spirit, and these three are one. {8} And there are three that testify on earth: the (not found in any Greek manuscript before the sixteenth century)**

In other words, it is a later addition inserted into the New Testament over 1,500 years after Jesus. The Interpreter's Dictionary of the Bible echoes this conclusion: ***"The text about the three heavenly witnesses (1 John 5:7 KJV) is not an authentic part of the New Testament" [87].*** The Eerdmans Bible Dictionary states:

> *1 John 5:7 in the Textus Receptus (represented in the King James Version) makes it appear that John had arrived at the doctrine of the Trinity in explicit form ('the Father, the Son and the Holy Ghost'), but this text is clearly an interpolation since no genuine Greek manuscript contains it. [88]*

Without this verse, there is no clear mention of God's threeness in the Bible. One has to wonder, if the Trinity is a genuine doctrine of the Bible, why is the only explicit mention of God's threeness a later addition? It seems that it had to be inserted into the Bible in order to lend support to the doctrine.

2. The story of the adulteress

> *Then they all went home, but Jesus went to the Mount of Olives.*
>
> *At dawn he appeared again in the temple courts, where all the people gathered around him, and he sat down to teach them. The teachers of the law and the Pharisees brought in a woman caught in adultery. They made her stand before the group and said to Jesus, "Teacher, this woman was caught in the act of adultery. In the Law Moses commanded us to stone such women. Now what do you say?" They were using this question as a trap, in order to have a basis for accusing him.*
>
> *But Jesus bent down and started to write on the ground with his finger. When they kept on questioning him, he straightened up and said to them, "Let any one of you who is without sin be the first to throw a stone at her." Again he stooped down and wrote on the ground.*
>
> *At this, those who heard began to go away one at a time, the older ones first, until only Jesus was left, with the woman still standing*

there. Jesus straightened up and asked her, "Woman, where are they? Has no one condemned you?"

"No one, sir," she said.

"Then neither do I condemn you," Jesus declared. "Go now and leave your life of sin."

This section of the Gospel of John, verses **7:53-8:11**, is the famous story of the adulteress who is about to be stoned because of the charge of adultery. In these verses, Jesus, when questioned about her punishment, utters the famous words "Let he who is without sin cast the first stone." This whole story is another later addition as the earliest New Testament manuscripts do not contain it. In fact, the story does not even exist in any manuscripts before the 5th century, and the vast majority of those prior to the 8th century lack the story [89]. Here is a footnote regarding this verse from the New International Version of the Bible:

> **The earliest manuscripts and many other ancient witnesses do not have John 7:53—8:11. A few manuscripts include these verses, wholly or in part, after John 7:36, John 21:25, Luke 21:38 or Luke 24:53.**

Christian theology teaches that Jesus came to do away with the Old Testament laws of punishment for crimes of passion such as adultery, and these verses are commonly cited by Christians to support this claim. Without these verses, we can find no other examples of Jesus not following the Old Testament laws dealing with crime and punishment.

3. Believers being able to handle snakes and drink deadly poison

The New Testament manuscripts for the Gospel of Mark have multiple endings. The shortest ending is found in the oldest complete copies of the New Testament, known as the Vaticanus (350 CE) and Sinaiticus (360 CE), which stop at verse 16:8. Most of the later manuscripts contain some additional verses, **Mark 16:9-20**, which are not always the same and seem to have been added to the Gospel at later points in time. It is these additional verses that mention that believing Christians will be able to survive handling snakes and drinking deadly poison:

> *And these signs will accompany those who believe: In my name they will drive out demons; they will speak in new tongues; they will pick up snakes with their hands; and when they drink deadly poison, it will not hurt them at all; they will place their hands on sick people, and they will get well." [Mark 16:17-18]*

It's because of these verses that there are churches in America that handle venomous snakes as a test of faith. Sadly, many Christians have died doing such acts.

Here is the footnote regarding the ending of Mark's Gospel from the New International Version of the Bible:

> *The earliest manuscripts and some other ancient witnesses do not have verses 9–20.*

Nowhere else in the Bible does it say that believers will be able to survive handling snakes and drinking deadly poison.

4. The role of women in the Church

> *Women should remain silent in the churches. They are not allowed to speak, but must be in submission, as the law says. If they want to inquire about something, they should ask their own husbands at home; for it is disgraceful for a woman to speak in the church. [1 Corinthians 14:34-35]*

For many centuries women had not been allowed to lead or to teach in churches based on these verses. However, there is strong evidence to suggest that these verses were not originally Paul's writings, but were added by later scribes. For a start, these verses seem to contradict what Paul wrote earlier: *"But every woman who prays or prophesies with her head uncovered dishonors her head—it is the same as having her head shaved" [1 Corinthians 11:5].* Since it is quite clear that Paul had no issue with women openly prophesying and praying, it makes no sense that he would immediately follow this verse up by saying they had to be "silent" and not speak.

In addition, there is also manuscript evidence that these two verses were not part of Paul's original writing, but were added to the text by scribes or copyists. For example, verse **1 Corinthians 14:35** does not appear in the same place in every manuscript of **1 Corinthians**. The New International Version of the Bible has this to say about the verse:

> *1 Corinthians 14:35 In a few manuscripts these verses come after verse 40.*

This fact has led scholars to conclude these verses were added to the text at a later date. Professor Alan Johnson writes: "**A growing number of modern scholars believe that verses 34-35 are a later interpolation (gloss) added at an early stage in the manuscript transmission" [90].** New Testament scholar Richard Hays writes:

> **All things considered, this passage is best explained as a gloss [addition] introduced into the text by the second- or third-generation Pauline interpreters who compiled the pastoral epistles. [91]**

In summary, the weight of evidence leads to the conclusion that verses **1 Corinthians 14:34-35**, which say women should be silent and not speak in the church, were not part of the original New Testament, but rather were added at a later date, possibly by a copyist who had strong feelings against women's participation in Christian meetings. Without these verses, there is nothing in the New Testament to say that women must remain silent in church.

In this section, we've looked at a few examples of variants that do have theological impact. Critics may argue that, although there are fabrications that have made their way into the New Testament, thanks to modern scholarship we have managed to identify all the fabrications and therefore can be confident about the New Testament. This is actually not the case, as there is a big gap in the manuscript tradition. For example, let's examine the Gospels:

Gospel	Earliest Manuscript	Content	Date originally written (DOW)	Date of manuscript (DOM)	Gap between DOW and DOM
John	P52	John 18:31-33, 37–38	90 CE	125 CE	35 years
Matthew	P64 + P67	Matthew 3:9, 15; 5:20-22, 25-28; 26:7-33	80 CE	150 CE	70 years
Luke	P75	Luke 3:18-24, 53	80 CE	175 CE	95 years
Mark	P45	Mark 4-9, 11-12	70 CE	250 CE	180 years

We can see from the table above that the earliest surviving manuscript of all the Gospels is P52, a tiny scrap of the Gospel of John dating to 125 CE. That's a gap in transmission of around 35 years since it was originally written. The biggest gap is for the Gospel of Mark, around 180 years after it was original-ly written. Please note that these earliest surviving manuscripts are highly fragmentary; they only represent tiny portions of the Gospels. You have to go to as late as the third and fourth centuries before you find complete copies of the Gospels in the manuscript tradition. Given these big gaps in transmission, how can we be certain that what we possess today matches the earliest copies when there are no surviving early copies to compare against? Since the manuscripts that we do possess, most of which date to as late as the 10th century after Jesus, show evidence of tampering, then the chances are that there would also be tampering in the manuscripts that pre-date these. The problem is that these earlier manuscripts have not survived, and therefore there could well be fabrications which remain undetected in the New Testament today. We simply have no way of knowing for certain, and this is a big question mark of doubt that hangs over the New Testament.

THE TRANSMISSION
OF THE QUR'AN

What about the Qur'an? Has its preservation also been compromised? The author of the Qur'an makes a bold claim: **"We have sent down the Qur'an Ourself, and We Ourself will guard it" [15:9].** God blessed His final revela-tion, the Qur'an, with something that was not bestowed on any of the prior scriptures: He promised to protect and preserve it from any corruption. You might be wondering how such a bold claim can be true in the light of what we know about the consistent corruption of previous religious scriptures throughout history, including the New Testament.

Unlike other scriptures, the primary means of preserving the Qur'an has, and always will be, through memorisation: **"And We have certainly made the Qur'an easy for remembrance, so is there any who will remember?" [54:17].** Is memorisation really a practical way of preserving the Qur'an? One of the ways that God made the Qur'an easy to remember is the unique style of the Qur'an itself; it has a rhyming style much like poetry.

Have a think back to when you were at school. Most of us have probably forgotten many of the finer details of what we learnt at school, such as the dates of various events we studied in subjects like History, or the formulas and equations we learnt in subjects like Mathematics and Physics. This is because we haven't used the knowledge since leaving school and human beings naturally forget things over time. What's interesting is that many of us can easily recall the words of the nursery rhymes we used to sing in school, or even the lyrics of a song we haven't listened to in years. The difference is that the words of nursery rhymes and the lyrics of songs have a certain rhyme and rhythm that allows us to easily recall the information even without making a conscious effort to remember it. Much in the same way, the Qur'an rhymes like poetry and has a strong rhythm, making it easy to memorise.

The Prophet Muhammad ﷺ was tasked by God with memorising, transmitting and explaining the verses of the Qur'an to the Muslims, as they were revealed from God to him through the angel Gabriel: *"Truly, this Qur'an has been sent down by the Lord of the Worlds: the Trustworthy Spirit [angel Gabriel] brought it down to your heart [Prophet], so that you could bring warning" [26:192-194].* In turn, these Muslims who had learnt the Qur'an directly from the Prophet Muhammad ﷺ himself, known as the Companions, passed on what they had memorised to neighbouring tribes and nations. It must be re-highlighted here that the Qur'an was revealed gradually to the Prophet Muhammad ﷺ over a period of 23 years:

> *The disbelievers also say, 'Why was the Qur'an not sent down to him all at once?' We sent it in this way to strengthen your heart [Prophet]; We gave it to you in gradual revelation. [25:32]*

Gradual revelation facilitated the memorisation of the Qur'an by the early Muslims at large. It should be noted that the revelations of previous Prophets, such as Moses, were not gradual but rather given all at once. The Qur'an informs us about Moses:

> *We inscribed everything for him in the Tablets which taught and explained everything, saying, 'Hold on to them firmly and urge*

your people to hold fast to their excellent teachings. I will show you the end of those who rebel.' [7:145]

This legacy of mass memorisation has continued throughout Islamic history. Muslims today have no doubt about the perfect preservation of the Qur'an. This oral tradition spanning nearly 1,500 years has seen the Qur'an being passed down from teacher to student in an unbroken chain going all the way back to the Prophet Muhammad ﷺ himself. Today, it is estimated there are many millions of Muslims who have memorised the entire Qur'an, from cover to cover, in its original Arabic.

This is a testament to the promise made by God to protect the Qur'an. Orientalist scholar William Graham stated that the Qur'an is perhaps the only book, religious or secular, that has been memorised completely by millions of people [92]. Here are just a few examples of what some other non-Muslim textual scholars have to say about the preservation of the Qur'an:

Orientalist A.T. Welch writes:

For Muslims the Qur'an is much more than scripture or sacred litera-ture in the usual Western sense. Its primary significance for the vast majority through the centuries has been in its oral form, the form in which it first appeared, as the "recitation" chanted by Muhammad to his followers over a period of about twenty years... The revela-tions were memorized by some of Muhammad's followers during his lifetime, and the oral tradition that was thus established has had a continuous history ever since, in some ways independent of, and superior to, the written Qur'an... Through the centuries the oral tradition of the entire Qur'an has been maintained by the professional reciters. Until recently, the significance of the recited Qur'an has seldom been fully appreciated in the West. [93]

Bible scholar Kenneth Cragg reflects that:

This phenomenon of Qur'anic recital means that the text has traversed the centuries in an unbroken living sequence of devotion. It cannot, therefore, be handled as an antiquarian thing, nor as a historical document out of a distant past. The fact of hifdh (Qur'anic memorization) has made the Qur'an a present possession through all the lapse of Muslim time and given it a human currency in every generation, never allowing its relegation to a bare authority for reference alone. [94]

It must be pointed out that almost every Muslim of the estimated 1.5 billion Muslims in the world memorises at least some parts of the Qur'an in Arabic, in order to be able to pray like the Prophet Muhammad ﷺ. In fact, if every written copy of religious scriptures in existence today were to be somehow destroyed, then it is only the Qur'an that could be recreated perfectly, thanks to its mass memorisation. Those who memorise the Qur'an are people of all ages. The vast majority are not Arabs and don't even speak Arabic as a language.

The oral tradition of the Qur'an is a phenomenon unique to Islam. Is there any reason to doubt the reliability of the oral tradition? The estimated millions throughout the world who have memorised the Qur'an have learnt it via a direct transmission starting from the Prophet Muhammad ﷺ himself. The implications of this are astonishing. If millions of people who have memorised the Qur'an can trace their oral memorisation of the Qur'an, down the centuries of teachers and scholars, all the way back to the Prophet himself, who could doubt the authenticity of this oral tradition? Especially if these millions of memorisers live in different places in the world, and have learnt the Qur'an from different teachers and scholars. The amount of varying oral transmissions and the amount of people who have learnt the Qur'an, and the fact there are no discrepancies in what they have memorised, is not a historical accident. The conclusion can only be that the Qur'an memorised today is the one that was taught over 1,400 years ago. There is no other rational explanation for this unique oral phenomenon, unless someone argues that all of these memorisers throughout the ages - at different points in time and different places in the world - somehow came together to ensure that they all memorised and recited the exact same Qur'an. To pose such an argument, however, is conspiratorial and absurd.

Earlier we saw examples of numerous fabrications that made their way into the New Testament. Such changes to the Qur'an are impossible when we consider the nature of its revelation and transmission. Unlike the New Testament, the verses of the Qur'an were witnessed by multitudes of the Prophet Muhammad's ﷺ companions at their first point of revelation, so we have mass eyewitness testimony. Moreover, the entire Qur'an was memorised by a large number of companions during the Prophet Muhammad's ﷺ lifetime and then rapidly transmitted far and wide. This oral tradition of memorisation facilitated the rapid spread of the Qur'an because anyone can memorise and so, unlike the New Testament, the illiteracy of the masses did not hinder its preservation. It is literally impossible for anyone who transmitted the Qur'an to invent stories, like the stoning of the adulteress that we looked at earlier in the Gospel of John, and for those fabrications to then go on to become part of the accepted Qur'an because they would immediately be caught out by the other memorisers. Additionally, from the beginning, its transmission was on such a large scale by people whose opinions and concerns were so different that it would have been impossible for them to collude in corrupting the Qur'an.

TAJWEED

So far we have discussed the preservation of the Qur'an from the point of view of its linguistic content, the words and verses that make it up. Amazingly, we can take things a step further. In addition to the mass memorisation of the content of the Qur'an, another unique aspect of its preservation is that the rules and regulations for pronouncing each individual letter have also been safeguarded. This ensures that Muslims not only recite the same content as the Prophet Muhammad ﷺ, but also in exactly the same style.

You may be wondering to yourself, why is this important? Perhaps the easiest way to appreciate the significance of preserving the recitation style of the Qur'an is a comparison with the game of Telephone. Just in case you are not familiar with this game, the first person will whisper a message to the person next to them, who will then do the same with the person next to them and so on and so forth until the message reaches the last person in the chain. You then compare the message between the first and last person to see how much it has changed. Typically, what you find is that by the time the message reaches the final person, it has changed significantly.

Let's take a look at a simple example to make things clear. Imagine the first person says the following message to the person next to them:

"We are going to advance. Send reinforcements."

This person then passes on the message but shortens "We are" because the first person spoke very quickly:

"We're going to advance. Send reinforcements."

The next person then passes on the message as follows and changes "advance" because the second person didn't pronounce the letter 'v' correctly:

"We're going to a dance. Send reinforcements."

Finally, the last person changes the end of the message because English is not their first language and they are unfamiliar with the word "reinforcements":

"We're going to a dance. Send four cents."

As you can see there are various reasons why the message has changed by the time it reaches the ear of the last person. For example, the people in the group may speak at different speeds, they may intonate their words differently, and they may even have different regional accents, which could lead to letters of the alphabet being pronounced differently. Ultimately, what this demonstrates is that, without a systematic means of ensuring the preservation of the recitation style of the Qur'an - that is, the correct pronunciation of each letter of the Arabic alphabet, the speed of its recitation, the stopping points in the verses and so on - its mass memorisation would be like a giant unsupervised game of Telephone. Changes would inevitably creep in over time, as they did in the Bible.

What did inspire Muslims to pay such attention to detail? When God revealed the Qur'an to the Prophet Muhammad ﷺ, it was recited to him in a specific manner. The Qur'an itself commands Muslims to recite it in this same specific way: ***"...recite the Qur'an slowly and distinctly"*** **[73:4].** Therefore, Muslims throughout history have placed great importance on how they recite the Qur'an. This has led to the creation of an intricate science known as Tajweed.

Tajweed sets out rules and regulations to preserve the Prophet Muhammad's ﷺ recitation style. The fact that today we can find millions of Muslims of all different nationalities able to recite the Qur'an, as if they themselves were Arabs living during the time of the Prophet Muhammad ﷺ, is proof of the effectiveness of this science in preserving the aural integrity of the text. This is in spite of the fact that there is no internationally-centralised religious organisation to administer such preservation.

Further evidence for the reliability of this method of preserving the Qur'an lies in the recitation of the Qur'an itself. In millions of mosques throughout the world, every day, these memorisers who originate from different parts of the world, and learnt at the feet of different scholars, mix together and recite the Qur'an with one another. Any mistakes in recitation are immediately corrected by the congregation, and yet there is never any disagreement about the Qur'an itself. Now you can appreciate why Muslims have certainty in the perfect preservation of the Qur'an. Not only do we have to believe it from a theological perspective, but we also know it to be true from a historical and experiential one.

LANGUAGE

As has been discussed so far, the Qur'an has been preserved in both content and recitation style. To this we can add that the Qur'an has also been preserved in meaning. Why is this important? You can't separate language from scripture. As God states below, the Qur'an is tied to the Arabic language: *"We have made it a Qur'an in Arabic..." [43:3].* So if we were to lose the Arabic language, we would also lose the Qur'an. There is not much benefit in having the perfect preservation of the content of a scripture if we have lost the meanings of the words it is written in. You may be wondering, can languages really change in drastic ways over time? Let's take English as an example. If we were living in 14th century England, the word 'nice' would have a very different meaning from how we use it today. This word is derived from the Latin 'nescius', meaning "ignorant". The word began life in the 14th century as a term for "foolish" or "silly". Later, it took on the more neutral attributes of shyness and reserve. Later, in the 18th century, English society's admiration of such qualities brought on the more positive meanings of "nice" we know today. Even with this simple example, I'm sure you can appreciate the impact this can have on our understanding of a text. If we don't take great care in preserving the original meanings of words, then our understanding of ancient texts can become distorted. Even worse, languages can be lost completely. The ancient Egyptian Hieroglyphs are a good example. This language, which can be found in the Pyramids and is made up of pictures rather than words, was lost for thousands of years when the ancient Egyptian civilisation became extinct. These examples demonstrate the important role that language plays in the preservation of any text.

The oldest Arabic language dictionary in existence was published within two hundred years after the death of the Prophet Muhammad ﷺ. The early compilation of Arabic dictionaries has ensured that none of the meanings of the words of the Qur'an have ever been lost. To put this into perspective, with the Judaic tradition, the Torah was originally revealed to Moses over three thousand years ago, making it over 1,500 years older than the Qur'an. However, the first Hebrew dictionary wasn't created until the 10th century [95] – some two thousand years after the revelation of the Torah and three hundred years after the Qur'an. Hebrew was a dead language from the 2nd century CE until the foundation of Israel in 1948 [96]. As a consequence of this, Bible scholars had to turn to the vocabulary found in Arabic dictionaries to assist in understanding the many obscure and problematic Hebrew words in the Old Testament. Arabic and Hebrew are both part of the Semitic family of languages and so they have many similarities. This is why the Arabic language has been used since the Middle Ages to understand difficult words and expressions in biblical Hebrew. Even to the present day, commentaries and articles written by Bible scholars regularly cite evidence from Arabic in support of a particular meaning for a Hebrew word or passage [97]. It's a very interesting point that in order to fully understand Hebrew, the language of the Old Testament, Bible scholars have to rely on classical Arabic, the language of the Qur'an!

THE SCIENCE OF HADITH VERIFICATION

Is God's inspiration restricted to the scripture that He reveals, or were the Prophets also inspired to explain the scripture? It must be emphasised that the Prophets of God were not just mere delivery men for scripture; they were also teachers and as such performed the invaluable function of explaining God's revelation to mankind. Without this explanation given to them by God, we would have no certainty that we have the correct understanding and interpretation of scripture.

The Qur'an is unique because it is the only Scripture that comes with an explanation of how to interpret it correctly according to the understanding of its messenger. Earlier in the book, we discussed the Sunnah, which we defined as what the Prophet Muhammad ﷺ said, did, approved, and disapproved of. Recall that along with the Qur'an, the Sunnah is another source of guidance for Muslims. The Sunnah has been captured for us in the collections of hadith. The Arabic word "hadith" broadly means a narrative, or a story. In Islamic literature, it has the very specific meaning of the individual narrations about the Prophet Muhammad ﷺ, as conveyed to us by his companions.

Thanks to the hadith, we know more about the Prophet Muhammad ﷺ than any other historical figure, even down to the smallest of details such as how many white hairs he had in his beard. This treasure trove of information provides us with detailed explanations of the Qur'an. Hadiths are of critical importance in preserving the correct understanding and interpretation of the Qur'an. Each hadith consists of two parts: the report and chain of narration. The report represents what was said or done by the Prophet Muhammad ﷺ, as witnessed by his companions, and the chain is the sequence of people who have passed the report down to us. Knowing the chain that is associated with the report is crucial because without it anyone can make any claim they like about the Prophet Muhammad ﷺ and we would have no way of verifying whether it was an authentic report. Chains allow the scholars of Islam to distinguish authentic hadiths from weak and fabricated ones by scrutinising the individual narrators within the chains. This methodology was pioneered by the early Muslim scholars and is known as the science of hadith verification.

To help illustrate this science, imagine you have a friend called Jane and she informs you that 10 years ago, her friend John met a famous person that you really admire, and they spoke some words of wisdom that really inspired you. This is how you would represent the report and chain:

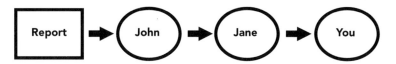

Before sharing this story all over social media, you decide to try and verify the report by analysing the people that have delivered the report to you. Now, ever since you've been friends with Jane you've observed that she has an excellent memory, and so you don't doubt that she has conveyed the report from John accurately. What about John? You don't know John personally, so you decide to ask Jane about him. Jane detects your scepticism and decides to reassure you by saying that John is a reliable person and wise beyond his years, in spite of his young age. This statement catches your attention and you ask how old John is. Jane informs you that he is 15 years old. With this information that has come to light, you decide against taking the report of the famous person as a fact. If John is now 15 years old, then this must mean he was 5 years old when he heard the wise words being uttered 10 years ago. How likely is it that a 5-year-old would be able to transmit such information accurately? In this case, the scholars of hadith would consider the weakness of John as a child narrator and might grade this particular report as a weak narration. Although this example is simple, it demonstrates that knowing the names of the people in the chain is insufficient; we also need to know information about them. The early scholars and historians of Islam compiled massive biographical works about each of those who transmitted the hadith. They listed the birth/death dates of narrators, descriptions of their lives, the strengths of their memories, their geographical locations, their students and their teachers, among other useful information. Such biographical information is exactly what the scholars of hadith utilise when verifying the reports attributed to the Prophet Muhammad ﷺ.

Going back to our example of Jane and John, you decide to investigate matters further. Although you don't trust that John as a 5-year-old could have accurately conveyed the report, you persevere in your investigation as the words were so inspiring that you're desperate to get to the bottom of whether or not they are authentic. You meet with John and ask him if anyone else heard the famous person utter the words. To your surprise, he says that he was in school at the time and his entire classroom witnessed the famous person utter the words. After finding out where he went to school, you speak to his teachers and they confirm that they were present when the famous person visited the school:

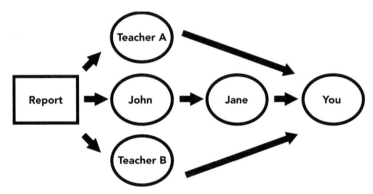

We now have a situation where multiple independent witnesses have corroborated the report, and you are certain beyond any doubt that the famous person really did say those inspiring words. All of these different factors – who conveyed the report, the biographical information about the witnesses, the number of independent witnesses and many other factors - are taken into account by the scholars of hadith. Having multiple, independent witnesses would mean that the scholars of hadith elevate the grading of Jane's report from weak to authentic. As with the mass memorisation of the Qur'an, the hadiths are part of a tradition going back all the way to the Prophet Muhammad ﷺ. The scholars of Islam have dedicated their lives to studying the intricate science of hadith verification in order to help us evaluate and grade each hadith. Without such a methodology, we would have no way of reliably distinguishing the authentic reports attributed to the

Prophet Muhammad ﷺ from the weak and even fabricated ones among the hundreds of thousands of reports that have been attributed to him.

Here is an example of an authentic hadith about fasting:

> **Abu Huraira reported the Prophet saying: [God the Exalted and Majestic said] Every act of the son of Adam is for him; every good deed will receive tenfold except fasting. It is [exclusively] meant for me, and I [alone] will reward it. He abandons his food for My sake and abandons drinking for My sake and abandons his pleasure for My sake. When any one of you is fasting he should neither indulge in sex nor use obscene language. If anyone reviles him he should say, "I am fasting." The one who fasts has two [occasions] of joy: one when he breaks the fast and one on the day when he will meet his Lord. And the breath [of a fasting person] is sweeter to God than the fragrance of musk. [98]**

Notice that the report starts with the statement "Abu Huraira reported". Abu Huraira is a famous companion of the Prophet Muhammad ﷺ and he is telling us he heard this statement directly from the mouth of the Prophet. This report reaches us through multiple chains, as Abu Huraira memorised the words of the Prophet and passed them onto the following people (the chart below should be read from right to left):

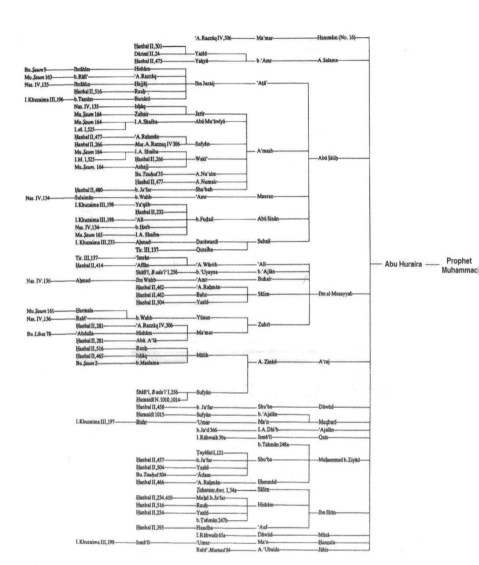

If we focus on the third generation of narrators from Abu Huraira, then there are over twenty narrators from different regions, such as Medina, Basra, Kufa, Mecca, Wasit, Hijaz and Khurasan. But Abu Huraira wasn't the only companion who heard the Prophet utter the words about fasting. Other companions, such as Ibn Masud, Uthman and Ali, also reported the same hadith:

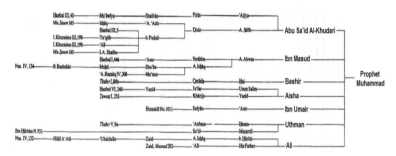

So, we can see that this hadith has a large amount of attestation. It would be virtually impossible to fabricate such a report given that there are multiple independent chains, consisting of people from different times and places, and yet they all report the same hadith [99].

Getting back to the interpretation of the Qur'an, Muslims have access to thousands of authentic statements of the Prophet Muhammad ﷺ where he explains the Qur'an in detail. These can be found in the famous collections of authentic hadiths in books such as Sahih Bukhari and Sahih Muslim. In fact, if you look at the references at the back of this book, you will notice that I have utilised many authentic hadiths from collections such as Sahih Bukhari and Sahih Muslim in my quotations of the Prophet Muhammad ﷺ throughout this book. There is always going to be the possibility of differences of interpretation; this is the case with any book. However, the Qur'an is unique because it is the only religious book that comes with an explanation of how to interpret it correctly according to the understanding of its messenger. Because of the clarity of the Qur'an and its detailed explanation in the form of the authentic hadiths, the scope for any such dispute and differing is minimised.

Let's look at the Bible for the sake of comparison. For example, here is the biblical commandment to keep the Sabbath holy: **"Remember the Sabbath day by keeping it holy" [Exodus 20:8].** When we search the Old Testament for specific laws regulating how to observe the Sabbath, we will find only basic information. So, the Old Testament alone is not sufficient for daily Jewish life. What is needed is a legal commentary to accompany the Old Testament. Jews claim that this can be found in the Talmud, an oral tradition they say originates from Moses and which they claim has been passed down over the centuries by their scholars. However, unlike the hadith, there is very little information about how the reports have reached us; there are no chains of narration which accompany the oral traditions. Therefore, there is no way of reliably distinguishing the genuine teachings of Moses from fabrications.

WHY THE QUR'AN'S PRESERVATION IS PROOF OF ITS DIVINE ORIGIN

Throughout history, the followers of God's messengers were entrusted to be the caretakers of revelation but they ultimately failed in this duty. This was not poor judgement on the part of God, as the revelation given to messengers, such as Jesus, were only ever meant to be time-bound messages. With the advent of the final messenger, Muhammad, and the revelation of the final message, God declared He would protect the Qur'an: **"We have sent down the Qur'an Ourself, and We Ourself will guard it" [15:9].** As we have seen, in every conceivable way, the Qur'an has been protected. Whether it's the preservation of its content, the meaning of its words, or its correct interpretation through the hadith, God has ensured that the Qur'an is the Scripture mankind can be certain of: **"This is the Scripture in which there is no doubt, containing guidance for those who are mindful of God..." [2:2]**

The preservation of the Qur'an is in fact proof of its divine origin. If the Prophet Muhammad ﷺ or any other human being for that matter were its author, then they could not have guaranteed that it would be perfectly preserved to this very day. This is because the track record of all other revealed books throughout history shows that their loss and tampering is the norm. The Qur'an, however, is the unique exception to this rule. Furthermore, it's proof that Muhammad is the final messenger of God. The fact that God didn't preserve other Scriptures reveals that they were never intended to be His final revelation. For the Qur'an to be uniquely preserved means that Muhammad must hold a special place in God's line of messengers.

The Qur'an even allows us to illuminate which parts of the New Testament have been corrupted, helping us to restore the true message of Jesus:

> *We sent to you [Muhammad] the Scripture with the truth, confirming the Scriptures that came before it, and with final authority over them: so judge between them according to what God has sent down... [5:48]*

This is why one of the names of the Qur'an is 'Al Furqan', meaning "the Criterion between truth and falsehood". So, the Qur'an not only confirms the Scriptures that came before it, but also acts as a guardian over them.

CHAPTER 7

PAUL – FAITHFUL FOLLOWER OF JESUS OR INVENTOR OF A NEW RELIGION?

Although the Old and New Testaments are bound together in today's Bible, their followers, the Jews and Christians, respectively, have a very different outlook on the fundamental question of how one is righteous in the sight of God. Is one made righteous by one's obedience to God's law, or are we made righteous by our faith alone? The Old Testament is filled with numerous commandments ('mitzvot' in Hebrew), 613 in total to be precise, and in Judaism one's standing as a believer is measured by one's keeping of the commandments. Total obedience to the Law of Moses is God's covenant with the children of Israel and the core message that all the Israelite Prophets brought. By contrast, Christianity teaches that whether you are Jew or Gentile, one's standing as a believer is not based on rigorously keeping God's laws, but rather on belief in Jesus. From this point of view, you can say that Judaism is characterised by the Law, and Christianity by its lack of it. We can see that a major distinguishing factor between these religions is that of their attitude towards the Law of Moses, and it's all because of one man – Paul. He is seen by Christians as an Apostle of God and he claims that his message was divinely sanctioned and represents a new covenant that replaced the old Mosaic one.

Just what did Jesus himself teach about the Mosaic Law? This is a question that many don't stop to consider. Is the message of Jesus and that of Paul one and the same? What was the outlook of the earliest followers of Jesus on the Law? These are just some of the questions that we are going to explore in this chapter, and the answers shake the very foundation of Christianity.

JESUS PRACTISED AND PREACHED THE LAW OF MOSES

Christians today view Christianity as representing a complete and total break from Judaism with the arrival of Jesus. However, if we analyse the teachings of Jesus, we will find overwhelming evidence that, throughout his ministry, he was Torah observant, obeying the Law and teaching others to do the same. His attitude towards the Law is exemplified in the Sermon on the Mount where he makes his position unequivocally clear:

> *"Do not think that I have come to abolish the Law or the Prophets; I have not come to abolish them but to fulfill them. For truly I tell you, <u>until heaven and earth disappear,</u> not the smallest letter, not the least stroke of a pen, will by any means disappear from the Law until everything is accomplished. Therefore anyone who sets aside one of the least of these commands and teaches others accordingly will be called least in the kingdom of heaven, but whoever practices and teaches these commands will be called great in the kingdom of heaven. For I tell you that unless your righteousness surpasses that of the Pharisees and the teachers of the law, you will certainly not enter the kingdom of heaven." [Matthew 5:17-20]*

We can see that Jesus links righteousness and success in the Hereafter with obedience to the Law. Now, Christians might argue that Jesus is simply saying that the entire Law will be in effect until he dies (*"until everything is accomplished"*). But Jesus is saying more than that; his followers must obey and teach the Law. None of it will pass away until the world is destroyed (*"until heaven and earth disappear"*). Jesus does not say, "Keep the Law until I die." He says he did not come to destroy the Law; it is still in effect and will be, for as long as heaven and earth last. This sermon was perfectly in line with the teachings of the Old Testament:

> *And the Lord commanded us to observe all these statutes, to fear the Lord our God, for our good always, that (for this purpose) He might preserve us alive, as it is this day. Then it will be righteousness*

for us, if we are careful to observe all these commandments before the Lord our God, as He has commanded us. [Deuteronomy 6:24-25]

Just how righteous does one have to be? Jesus set a standard in his sermon. One's obedience to the Law has to exceed that of the Pharisees and teachers of the Law (*"unless your righteousness surpasses that of the Pharisees and the teachers of the law, you will certainly not enter the kingdom of heaven"*). But why is this the case? There was a real problem with the righteousness of the religious leaders of his day. The heart of the matter was that their righteousness was defective, in that it was external only. They appeared to obey the Law to those who observed them, but broke God's Law inwardly, where it couldn't be seen by others. Notice Jesus's scathing denunciation of their hypocrisy in making a show of religion:

> *Woe to you, teachers of the law and Pharisees, you hypocrites! You are like whitewashed tombs, which look beautiful on the outside but on the inside are full of the bones of the dead and everything unclean. In the same way, on the outside you appear to people as righteous but on the inside you are full of hypocrisy and wickedness. [Matthew 23:27-28]*

Where many Christians jump to wrong conclusions about Jesus and the Law is in his confrontations with these religious leaders. Jesus was not pitting himself against the Mosaic Law. These confrontations were never over whether to keep the Law, only over how it should be kept. It must be noted that Jesus fully acknowledged the teaching authority of the Pharisees and advised others to follow what they teach, but not to act hypocritically as they did:

> *Then Jesus said to the crowds and to his disciples: "The teachers of the law and the Pharisees sit in Moses' seat. So you must be careful to do everything they tell you. But do not do what they do, for they do not practice what they preach" [Matthew 23:1-3]*

In actual fact, Jesus went a step further and extended the parameters of the Law. His move was to give a deeper and fuller understanding, to cover underlying attitudes and not just behaviours. For example, one of the most important commandments was not to murder. Jesus increased the scope of the Law to cover not only the act of murdering someone, but also anger towards others:

You have heard that it was said to the people long ago, 'You shall not murder, and anyone who murders will be subject to judgement.' But I tell you that anyone who is angry with a brother or sister will be subject to judgement. [Matthew 5:21-22]

So far from abolishing the Law, Jesus actually made its practice even more rigorous.

HOW JESUS' EARLIEST FOLLOWERS VIEWED THE LAW

In addition to the life and teachings of Jesus, there is further corroborating evidence for his pro-Law stance. It's to be found in the beliefs and practices of his immediate followers. The **Book of Acts** attests to the apostles' regular attendance at the Jewish Temple:

They devoted themselves to the apostles' teaching and to fellowship, to the breaking of bread and to prayer. Everyone was filled with awe at the many wonders and signs performed by the apostles. All the believers were together and had everything in common. They sold property and possessions to give to anyone who had need. Every day they continued to meet together in the temple courts. They broke bread in their homes and ate together with glad and sincere hearts, praising God and enjoying the favor of all the people. And the Lord added to their number daily those who were being saved. [Acts 2:42-47]

If these early Christians had been breaking the Jewish religious laws, then they would not have been welcome in the temple courts, and they would not have enjoyed the favour of the other Jews who had come to the temple to worship.

Here the description of the disciple Ananias as a **"devout observer of the law"** chosen by God to heal and baptise Saul (Paul) clearly confirms that the followers of Jesus had not yet abandoned the observance of the Law:

> *In Damascus there was a disciple named Ananias. The Lord called to him in a vision, "Ananias!" "Yes, Lord," he answered. The Lord told him, "Go to the house of Judas on Straight Street and ask for a man from Tarsus named Saul, for he is praying. [Acts 9:10-11]*

> *A man named Ananias came to see me. He was a devout observer of the law and highly respected by all the Jews living there. [Acts 22:12]*

We can see that Ananias was living in Damascus, far away from the Jerusalem Temple which was the centre of Jewish religious life, and yet he was still devout to the Law. Obviously, he considered obedience to the Law to be important enough, despite living outside of the Holy Land.

This attitude also extended to the close family members of Jesus. We are told that James is the flesh and blood brother of Jesus: *"**Isn't this the carpenter's son? Isn't his mother's name Mary, and aren't his brothers James, Joseph, Simon and Judas?" [Matthew 13:55].*** James preached a message of total obedience to the Law. He believed that one should not comply with the Law partially, keeping some commandments and breaking others. Rather, one should try and keep all of it as breaking part of it is equivalent to breaking all of it:

> *If you really keep the royal law found in Scripture, "Love your neighbour as yourself," you are doing right. But if you show favouritism, you sin and are convicted by the law as lawbreakers. For whoever keeps the whole law and yet stumbles at just one point is guilty of breaking all of it. For he who said, "You shall not commit adultery," also said, "You shall not murder." If you do not commit adultery but do commit murder, you have become a lawbreaker. [James 2:8-11]*

James's teachings mirror those of Jesus in his Sermon on the Mount. James was not just the brother of Jesus, but also a senior leader among Christians.

Paul acknowledges his seniority: *"James, Cephas and John, those esteemed as pillars, gave me and Barnabas the right hand of fellowship..." [Galatians 2:9]* Some years after his conversion, Paul pays a visit to the elders in Jerusalem. By this time many thousands of Jews had become believers in Jesus. The elders of Jerusalem describe (in a seemingly proud boast) the state of the believing Jews in their large congregation as being *"zealous for the Law"*:

> *When they heard this, they praised God. Then they said to Paul: "You see, brother, how many thousands of Jews have believed, and all of them are zealous for the law." [Acts 21:20]*

We've seen that the earliest believers in Jesus were, for all intents and purposes, Jewish. At this early stage, Christianity was just another movement within Judaism, not a separate religion. This is another piece of evidence for the Law-centric teachings of Jesus, for if the students of Jesus, his apostles and family members, had this positive attitude towards the Law, then it stands to reason that their teacher, Jesus, also had it.

TWO BRANCHES OF CHRISTIANITY BEGIN TO EMERGE

Soon after Jesus departed, an event took place that would change the face of Christianity, and the world, forever. According to the New Testament, Saul of Tarsus, or Paul as he is more commonly known, was a zealous Pharisee who intensely persecuted the followers of Jesus. Although he never met Jesus in person, he claims to have encountered him in a mystical vision on his travels and received instructions that he should stop persecuting Christians. Paul was to be God's chosen instrument to proclaim the message of Jesus to the Gentiles.

Immediately afterwards, Paul began to preach to the Gentiles about Jesus. With Gentiles becoming Christian in large numbers for the first time, an important question now arose: what is their status with regard to the Law of Moses, did it apply to Jew and Gentile converts alike? In other words, must non-Jews become Jewish in order to become Christian? In the eyes of Jesus's original Jewish followers, any Gentile who wanted to become a follower of Jesus was, in fact, becoming a follower of Judaism. But as Paul's evangelism brought in ever-larger numbers of Gentile converts, the issue of just how far these converts had to go in order to become followers became very contentious. New Gentile believers who were men would, quite understandably, want to put off circumcision, if at all possible. Jewish believers, on the other hand, were concerned that relaxing the circumcision requirement could potentially lead to an abandonment of all the requirements of the Mosaic Law. As Paul's ministry grew, the issue became increasingly urgent. Was any relaxation of the Law of Moses possible in these new circumstances? These are the questions that the Jerusalem Council was called to resolve. Chapter 15 of the **Book of Acts** goes into detail about this significant event:

> *Certain people came down from Judea to Antioch and were teaching the believers: "Unless you are circumcised, according to the custom taught by Moses, you cannot be saved." This brought Paul and Barnabas into sharp dispute and debate with them. So Paul and Barnabas were appointed, along with some other believers, to go up to Jerusalem to see the apostles and elders about this question. [Acts 15:1-2]*

We can see that this issue over the Gentiles and the Law was causing friction between Paul and other believers. The Council is convened and Paul attends it, along with the apostles and other elders of the Jerusalem congregation. Paul brings the Jerusalem congregation the news of his evangelising to the Gentiles and their entering into the faith:

> *The church sent them on their way, and as they travelled through Phoenicia and Samaria, they told how the Gentiles had been converted. This news made all the believers very glad. When they came to Jerusalem, they were welcomed by the church and the apostles and elders, to whom they reported everything God had done through them. [Acts 15:3-4]*

The Pharisaic Christians adopted a very strict view:

> **Then some of the believers who belonged to the party of the Pharisees stood up and said, "The Gentiles must be circumcised and required to keep the law of Moses." The apostles and elders met to consider this question. [Acts 15:5-6]**

Circumcision was closely linked to following the Jewish law. The strict view among the Pharisaic Christians was that it was necessary for Gentiles to be circumcised and keep the whole of the Law of Moses. Others, such as the disciple Peter, took a much more lenient view.

It is James who proposes the compromise:

> **The whole assembly became silent as they listened to Barnabas and Paul telling about the signs and wonders God had done among the Gentiles through them. When they finished, James spoke up... "It is my judgement, therefore, that we should not make it difficult for the Gentiles who are turning to God. Instead we should write to them, telling them to abstain from food polluted by idols, from sexual immorality, from the meat of strangled animals and from blood. For the law of Moses has been preached in every city from the earliest times and is read in the synagogues on every Sabbath." [Acts 15:12-21]**

We can see that James decreed that Gentiles don't have to be circumcised, though they should abstain from eating food offered to idols, strangled animals and blood, and from committing fornication. These are all ancient regulations found in the Law of Moses. In the section of the Law given in **Leviticus 17-18**, known as the Holiness Code, these same requirements are listed:

Jerusalem Council decree	Leviticus 17-18
"Abstain from food polluted by idols"	"They must no longer offer any of their sacrifices to the goat idols to whom they prostitute themselves. This is to be a lasting ordinance for them and for the generations to come. Say to them: 'Any Israelite or any foreigner residing among them who offers a burnt offering or sacrifice and does not bring it to the entrance to the tent of meeting to sacrifice it to the Lord must be cut off from the people of Israel.'" [Leviticus 17:7-9
"and from blood"	"'I will set my face against any Israelite or any foreigner residing among them who eats blood, and I will cut them off from the people.'" [Leviticus 17:10]
"from the meat of strangled animals"	"'Anyone, whether native-born or foreigner, who eats anything found dead or torn by wild animals must wash their clothes and bathe with water, and they will be ceremonially unclean till evening; then they will be clean.'" [Leviticus 17:15]*
"from sexual immorality"	Leviticus 18:6-26 lists a wide range of sexually immoral activities and ends with: "...The native-born and the aliens living among you must not do any of these detestable things"

This verse is interpreted by Rabbis to prohibit eating the meat of any animals which die by any means other than Kosher slaughter, which includes strangulation.

It is quite telling that James looked to the Old Testament for guidance on this issue. Notice that the Old Testament verses above apply to Israelites and "aliens" (foreigners or strangers) living among them. Rather than cancelling or withdrawing these Old Testament regulations, their scope is extended by applying them to the Gentile believers who do not live among the Israelites. Clearly, in the sight of James, the Law was considered to be important. A question then naturally arises: why didn't James apply the whole of the Law to the Gentile believers, and does this prove that the Law was ultimately meant to be abolished? The answer is absolutely not, because God's covenant as a whole in the Old Testament was specifically with the Israelites. What James did was take the four ancient commands from the Old Testament which applied to "aliens" living amongst the Israelites and logically equate them to the Gentile believers who were viewed as outsiders.

The apostles and elders agreed with the decision made by Jesus's brother James which indicates that James held a very senior position in the Jerusalem congregation. They put his decree in a letter that was to be distributed to the Gentile believers via Paul and his companion Barnabas:

> **Then the apostles and elders, with the whole church, decided to choose some of their own men and send them to Antioch with Paul and Barnabas. They chose Judas (called Barsabbas) and Silas, men who were leaders among the believers. With them they sent the following letter:**
>
> **The apostles and elders, your brothers,**
>
> **To the Gentile believers in Antioch, Syria and Cilicia:**
>
> **Greetings.**
>
> **We have heard that some went out from us without our authorization and disturbed you, troubling your minds by what they said. So we all agreed to choose some men and send them to you with our dear friends Barnabas and Paul— men who have risked their lives for the name of our Lord Jesus Christ. Therefore we are sending Judas and Silas to confirm by word of mouth what we are writing. It seemed good to the Holy Spirit and to us not to burden you with anything beyond the following requirements: You are to abstain from food sacrificed to idols, from blood, from the meat of strangled animals and from sexual immorality. You will do well to avoid these things.**
>
> **Farewell. [Acts 15:22-29]**

It's important to spend some time analysing this monumental event as it has many implications on the origins of modern Christianity. First, the outcome of this Council is that there was now a two-tiered church; one of Jewish believers in Jesus obedient to the whole of the Law, and another of Gentile believers who were only under obligation to keep those parts of the Law as decreed by the Council. We've seen that this decision was not arrived at easily, for there were many different opinions on the question of whether the Gentiles had to obey the Mosaic Law. Ultimately, a middle position was adopted, with James making the authoritative decision that Gentiles should follow some aspects of the Law, not all. It is quite telling that James and the other Law-observant believers looked to the Old Testament for guidance on this issue. We've seen that rather than cancelling or withdrawing the Old Testament legislation that governed Israelites and aliens (foreigners or strangers) among them, James and the apostles actually extended their scope by applying them to Gentile believers not living among the Israelites. So, the Law was obviously still considered to be important in the eyes of the apostles and elders even after the departure of Jesus. Had Jesus habitually violated the Law, or had Jesus instructed them that it was okay to do so, then no-one would have objected to a complete abandonment of the Law by the Gentiles. But Jesus was Law-observant, as were all of his earliest followers.

THE PARTING OF THE WAYS

We've seen that on the Jerusalem Council, Paul submitted to the decision taken by the apostles and elders that Gentile believers were to observe some aspects of the Law. Now, when we turn to Paul's own writings, a troubling picture emerges. What is clear from Paul's personal writings is that at some point after the Jerusalem Council, he started preaching a radically different message from that of the Jerusalem congregation. Whereas Jesus and his earliest followers taught righteousness through the Law, Paul started to promote a message of righteousness apart from the Law:

> **Know that a person is not justified by the works of the law, but by faith in Jesus Christ. So we, too, have put our faith in Christ Jesus that we may be justified by faith in Christ and not by the works of the law, because by the works of the law no one will be justified. [Galatians 2:16]**

So, according to Paul, no-one can be justified by obedience to the Law. A question then naturally arises: if no-one can become righteous through the Law, then why did God bother to give it to Moses in the first place? Paul offers the following reason:

> **Now we know that whatever the Law says, it says to those who are under the Law, that (for this purpose) every mouth may be stopped, and all the world may become guilty before God. Therefore by the deeds of the Law no flesh will be justified in His sight, for by the Law is the knowledge of sin. [Romans 3:19-20]**

Apparently, the purpose of the Law was to make man realise that he is guilty before God. In other words, it's to prove to us that it's impossible to keep the Law. This not only goes against Jesus, who believed that it was possible to keep, as he preached a message of total obedience to it, but also the Old Testament where God is clear: it is not too difficult to obey the commandments of the Law:

> *Now what I am commanding you today is not too difficult for you or beyond your reach. It is not up in heaven, so that you have to ask, "Who will ascend into heaven to get it and proclaim it to us so we may obey it?" Nor is it beyond the sea, so that you have to ask, "Who will cross the sea to get it and proclaim it to us so we may obey it?" No, the word is very near you; it is in your mouth and in your heart so you may obey it. [Deuteronomy 30:11-14]*

Paul even went so far as to say some very negative things about the Law. Here he calls it a curse:

> *For as many as are of the works of the law are under a curse. For it is written, "Cursed is everyone who doesn't continue in all things that are written in the book of the law, to do them. [Galatians 3:10]*

While Paul acknowledged his past zealousness in obeying the Law, he regarded all such efforts as garbage:

> *If someone else thinks they have reasons to put confidence in the flesh, I have more: circumcised on the eighth day, of the people of Israel, of the tribe of Benjamin, a Hebrew of Hebrews; in regard to the law, a Pharisee; as for zeal, persecuting the church; as for righteousness based on the law, faultless. But whatever were gains to me I now consider loss for the sake of Christ. <u>What is more, I consider everything a loss because of the surpassing worth of knowing Christ Jesus my Lord, for whose sake I have lost all things. I consider them garbage,</u> that I may gain Christ and be found in him, not having a righteousness of my own that comes from the law, but that which is through faith in Christ—the righteousness that comes from God on the basis of faith. [Philippians 3:4-9]*

Again, such negativity is at odds with what Jesus taught about how obedience to the Law makes one greatest in the kingdom of heaven, as well as what the Old Testament teaches about obedience to the Law bringing God's blessing and prosperity:

> *See, I set before you today life and prosperity, death and destruction. For I command you today to love the Lord your God, to walk*

in obedience to him, and to keep his commands, decrees and laws;
then you will live and increase, and the Lord your God will bless you
in the land you are entering to possess. [Deuteronomy 30:15-16]

Now, one may think that all such writings by Paul were directed to Gentiles only and do not apply to Jewish believers in Jesus. But this is not the case, as Paul clearly stated that in his eyes there is no longer any distinction between Jew and Gentile. In fact, he thought that the only Israel that God recognises anymore is a spiritual Israel made up of both Jew and Gentile who are no longer bound by the Law and live primarily by faith:

For as many of you as were baptised into Christ have put on Christ.
There is neither Jew nor Greek... [Galatians 3:27-28]

For when we were in the realm of the flesh, the sinful passions aroused by the law were at work in us, so that we bore fruit for death. But now, by dying to what once bound us, we have been released from the law so that we serve in the new way of the Spirit, and not in the old way of the written code. [Romans 7:5-6].

It must be reiterated that Paul's anti-Law sentiment isn't just restricted to Gentile Christians; he applied it to Jewish believers in Jesus as well. This is in direct conflict with the apostles and elders who practised the Law and expected other Jewish followers of Jesus to do the same. Now Christians may argue that the Jerusalem Council decree was merely provisional or temporary. They may think that, yes, initially Paul agreed with the apostles and elders that Gentiles had to obey some aspects of the Law, but then at a later stage they all changed their opinions. However, this is not the case, as we see that towards the end of his life, Paul visited Jerusalem again and met with the same apostles and leaders. During this visit, Paul re-confirmed his commitment to the Jerusalem Council decree:

When we arrived at Jerusalem, the brothers and sisters received us warmly. The next day Paul and the rest of us went to see James, and all the elders were present. Paul greeted them and reported in detail what God had done among the Gentiles through his ministry. When they heard this, they praised God. Then they said to Paul:

"You see, brother, how many thousands of Jews have believed, and all of them are zealous for the law. They have been informed that you teach all the Jews who live among the Gentiles to turn away from Moses, telling them not to circumcise their children or live according to our customs. What shall we do? They will certainly hear that you have come, so do what we tell you. There are four men with us who have made a vow. Take these men, join in their purification rites and pay their expenses, so that they can have their heads shaved. Then everyone will know there is no truth in these reports about you, but that you yourself are living in obedience to the law. As for the Gentile believers, we have written to them our decision that they should abstain from food sacrificed to idols, from blood, from the meat of strangled animals and from sexual immorality."

The next day Paul took the men and purified himself along with them. Then he went to the temple to give notice of the date when the days of purification would end and the offering would be made for each of them. [Acts 21:17-26]

Notice the charge that the elders brought to Paul's attention, ***"They have been informed that you teach all the Jews who live among the Gentiles to turn away from Moses"***. By submitting to the elders' command to undergo a purification ritual, Paul made a public declaration that he was loyal to the Law of Moses and innocent of all such allegations. Also, notice that the elders re-iterated their decree from the Jerusalem Council; the Old Testament laws pertaining to ***"food sacrificed to idols, from blood, from the meat of strangled animals and from sexual immorality"*** were still binding on Gentile believers. As readers, we are left with a perplexing situation – how is it that Paul denies the allegations of abandoning the Law and submits to the decree of the church elders in person, but preaches a message of Lawlessness for both Jews and Gentiles in his writings? It seems that either Paul is being deceitful to the elders, or that the history of the early Church, as it is recorded in the New Testament, is unreliable. Both scenarios are highly problematic for Christianity.

In any case, despite Paul's willingness to undergo the self-purification ritual, he continued to inspire hostility in those 'zealous for the Law' – who, a few days later, attacked him in the Temple. **"This"**, they proclaim, **"is the man who teaches everyone everywhere against our people and our Law"** **[Acts 21:28]**. The ensuing riot is no minor disturbance:

> **The whole city was aroused, and the people came running from all directions. Seizing Paul, they dragged him from the temple, and immediately the gates were shut. While they were trying to kill him, news reached the commander of the Roman troops that the whole city of Jerusalem was in an uproar. [Acts 21:30-31]**

Paul goes on to be rescued in the nick of time by some Roman troops who arrest him. Paul is subsequently put on trial in a Jewish court. Now the most fascinating thing about this whole episode is what is not said. At no point do we find the apostles of Jesus or elders, such as James, coming to Paul's rescue during the mob attack, despite the fact they and their supporters numbered in the thousands in Jerusalem, nor do they come to his defence at his trial in the Jewish court. The explanation that they were perhaps scared to show their public support doesn't work, as not only were they ardent supporters of the Law, a position that would have carried favour with the mob that attacked Paul, but these were men who were not afraid to stand up for the truth, even if it cost them their lives. This is according to Christian tradition which holds that many of these same apostles and elders would go on to be martyred for their beliefs at the hands of the pagan Roman Empire. Could it be that they believed that Paul was guilty of preaching against the Law, a fact we know to be true based on his personal writings? This would be the most rational explanation for their complete absence and seeming abandonment of Paul in the rest of the incidents that the **Book of Acts** narrates.

To demonstrate just how divergent the beliefs of Paul and the Jerusalem congregation had become, let's focus for a moment on the issue of eating meat that has been sacrificed to idols. We've seen that the Jerusalem Council explicitly and unconditionally prohibited such a practice; yet, Paul breaks away and makes it permissible:

> **So then, about eating food sacrificed to idols: We know that "An idol is nothing at all in the world" and that "There is no God but**

one." For even if there are so-called gods, whether in heaven or on earth (as indeed there are many "gods" and many "lords"), yet for us there is but one God, the Father, from whom all things came and for whom we live; and there is but one Lord, Jesus Christ, through whom all things came and through whom we live. But not everyone possesses this knowledge. Some people are still so accustomed to idols that when they eat sacrificial food they think of it as having been sacrificed to a god, and since their conscience is weak, it is defiled. But food does not bring us near to God; we are no worse if we do not eat, and no better if we do. [1 Corinthians 8:4-8]

Paul's reasoning is that since an idol is not a real thing, there is no harm in eating such meat. In doing so, Paul not only goes against the decision of the Jerusalem Council, but also other writers of the New Testament such as the author of the **Book of Revelation** where allusions to the Jerusalem Council decree can be found in multiple places:

Nevertheless, I have a few things against you: There are some among you who hold to the teaching of Balaam, who taught Balak to entice the Israelites to sin so that they ate food sacrificed to idols and committed sexual immorality. [Revelation 2:14]

Nevertheless, I have this against you: You tolerate that woman Jezebel, who calls herself a prophet. By her teaching she misleads my servants into sexual immorality and the eating of food sacrificed to idols. [Revelation 2:20]

It's important to point out that the **Book of Revelation** comes at the end of the Bible and was the last book to be written, indicating that the prohibition on idol meat was still in place long after Paul authored his works. An outright prohibition on idol meat was even understood by Christian communities that existed after Paul. For example, the work known as *The Didache* is an anonymous early Christian treatise, dated by most modern scholars to the first century [100]. It's seen as an early Christian church manual of sorts, and it has this to say on the permissibility of idol meat:

Now concerning food, bear what you are able, but in any case keep strictly away from meat sacrificed to idols, for it involves the

worship of dead gods. [The Didache 6:3]

The early Christian apologist Justin Martyr, considered a saint in the Catholic Church, stated that Christians must ***"abide every torture and vengeance even to the extremity of death, rather than worship idols, or eat meat offered to idols." [101]***

Just how did we go from this situation, where Paul's strand of Christianity was in a minority, to its position today, where it has absolute dominance and is considered the mainstream? While it's beyond the scope of this book to delve too much into why Paul's strand of Christianity ultimately 'won out', we will briefly mention some factors that may have served as catalysts. The destruction of the Jerusalem Temple in 70 CE by the Romans would have no doubt been devastating to the Jerusalem Christians. The Temple was at the heart of their daily lives with its courts being used for important rituals such as worship and animal sacrifices. For Gentile converts, the rigour and legalism of Judaic Christianity stood in stark contrast to the freedom that Pauline Christianity offered, an attractive prospect to those coming from a hedonistic pagan background. We can only speculate as to why Pauline Christianity ultimately triumphed, but what we can be certain of is that it by no means represented the views of Jesus or those who were closest to him.

One oddity worth highlighting is the amount of 'shelf space' that Paul takes up in the New Testament. We've seen that Paul was very much a secondary figure in **Acts**, with leaders such as James, the brother of Jesus, taking much more senior and even dominant roles over him. Recall that Paul submitted to James's decree at the Jerusalem Council, and even underwent the purification ritual at the command of the elders when he was confronted with the rumours of abandoning the Law. Yet, we have the strange situation of important figures like James having very little space in the New Testament, just one short letter that is the **Epistle of James**, whereas Paul by comparison dominates its pages; he is by far the most prolific New Testament writer, with almost half of the 27 New Testament books attributed to him. Such an imbalance reflects just how dominant Pauline Christianity had become by the time that the New Testament came to be canonised.

PUTTING PAUL'S CLAIMS OF DIVINE INSPIRATION TO THE TEST

The foundation of modern Christianity lies on one man; Paul. We've seen that much of what distinguishes Christianity as a stand-alone religion, separate from Judaism, are Paul's teachings of the abandonment of the Law. Remove Paul from the equation and Christianity is not much different to traditional Judaism, with the only significant difference being the acceptance of Jesus as the Messiah. Since Christianity hinges on Paul, then a question naturally arises: does Paul provide a solid foundation for Christianity? Paul's biggest claim to legitimacy is his proclamation of divine inspiration which can be found throughout his writings:

> **I want you to know, brothers and sisters, that the gospel I preached is not of human origin. I did not receive it from any man, nor was I taught it; rather, I received it by revelation from Jesus Christ. [Galatians 1:11-12]**

Was his message really divinely inspired? Since God is perfect, then it stands to reason that His true inspiration would also be perfect and free from error, so we will now turn our attention to Paul's writings:

A false Prophecy

There are numerous statements by Paul that suggest he believed the End Times and the return of Jesus was expected in his own lifetime:

> **According to the Lord's word, we tell you that we who are still alive, who are left until the coming of the Lord, will certainly not precede those who have fallen asleep. For the Lord himself will come down from heaven, with a loud command, with the voice of the archangel and with the trumpet call of God, and the dead in Christ will rise first. After that, we who are still alive and are left will be caught up together with them in the clouds to meet the Lord in the air. And so we will be with the Lord forever. [1 Thessalonians 4:15-17]**

Listen, I tell you a mystery: We will not all sleep, but we will all be changed— in a flash, in the twinkling of an eye, at the last trumpet. For the trumpet will sound, the dead will be raised imperishable, and we will be changed. [1 Corinthians 15:51-52]

Notice in the first passage that Paul begins by saying **"According to the Lord's word"**. This indicates that he received his information from God by divine inspiration. In the second passage, Paul states that **"we will not all sleep."** Sleep here is a metaphor for death, so Paul seems to be saying that not all of the believers in his day would die before the return of Jesus. Obviously, this is a false prophecy, as it has been nearly 2,000 years since Paul wrote those words, and return of Jesus still hasn't taken place. In fact, many New Testament scholars conclude that Paul and his followers expected the imminent end of the world during their lifetimes. For example, the distinguished New Testament scholar Professor C.K. Barrett wrote in his commentary on **1 Corinthians 15:52**:

Paul expects that at the parousia [Second Coming of Jesus] he himself will not be among the dead (of whom he speaks in the third person), but among the living (of whom he speaks in the first person). He expected the parousia within his own lifetime. [102]

Now some Christians try to defend Paul by claiming that he was speaking figuratively. For example, they argue that when Paul used the first person plural to refer to believers (**"we will not all sleep"**), this does not necessarily mean he included himself among them, but rather he was referring to a group of believers at some unspecified time in the future. So, what did Paul intend by his statement, should we interpret it literally or figuratively? In order to arrive at the correct understanding, we need to interpret Paul in the light of his other statements on the End Times:

...But those who marry will face many troubles in this life, and I want to spare you this. What I mean, brothers and sisters, is that the time is short. From now on those who have wives should live as if they do not; those who mourn, as if they did not; those who are happy, as if they were not; those who buy something, as if it were not theirs to keep; those who use the things of the world, as if not

engrossed in them. For this world in its present form is passing away. [1 Corinthians 7:28-31]

In this passage, Paul is commenting on the subject of marriage, and he advises that it is better not to get married because **"time is short."** This is a clear indication that Paul believed that the End was coming during his lifetime. Paul's statement regarding marriage only makes sense if he believed the End was coming very soon; it does not make sense if the End was supposed to come thousands of years later.

This mistaken prophecy, which Paul claimed was divinely inspired from God, is highly problematic when we consider the standard that the Old Testament lays out for true divine inspiration: **"If what a prophet proclaims in the name of the Lord does not take place or come true, that is a message the Lord has not spoken..." [Deuteronomy 18:22].** Therefore, we can see that, according to the Bible itself, anyone who makes a claim about the future which then fails to come true cannot be inspired by God.

Misquoting the Old Testament

Paul quotes the Old Testament to lend support to his theology that we are saved by faith, not the works of the Mosaic Law:

But what does it say? "The word is near you; it is in your mouth and in your heart," that is, the message concerning faith that we proclaim: If you declare with your mouth, "Jesus is Lord," and believe in your heart that God raised him from the dead, you will be saved. For it is with your heart that you believe and are justified, and it is with your mouth that you profess your faith and are saved. [Romans 10:8-10]

Paul's quotation **"The word is near you; it is in your mouth and in your heart"** is used to support his notion that it is faith alone in Jesus that saves you, and not obeying the Law. The problem is that Paul has taken the quote out of its original context in the Old Testament. Here is the full quote in **Deuteronomy**:

No, the word is very near you; it is in your mouth and in your heart so you may obey it. [Deuteronomy 30:14]

Notice that Paul has left out the part that states *"so you may obey it"*. In quoting the Old Testament, Paul seems to have omitted the instruction to obey the Law. The original passage of the Old Testament actually establishes the opposite of what Paul intended.

<u>Misinterpreting the Old Testament</u>

Here Paul makes the point that God's covenant promises to Abraham were fulfilled with the coming of Jesus:

Brothers and sisters, let me take an example from everyday life. Just as no one can set aside or add to a human covenant that has been duly established, so it is in this case. The promises were spoken to Abraham and to his seed. Scripture does not say "and to seeds," meaning many people, but "and to your seed," meaning one person, who is Christ. [Galatians 3:15-16]

Paul states that the Old Testament speaks of "seed", a singular, and not "seeds", a plural, and concludes that the single seed is a reference to Jesus. In making this point, Paul has referenced an Old Testament verse from **Genesis**:

and I will establish my covenant with him (Isaac) for an everlasting covenant, and with his seed after him. [Genesis 17:19]

The original Hebrew word used for "seed" is 'zera' which is a collective noun that can be used to refer to both a single descendant or many descendants; it depends on the context in which it appears. This is just like the English language; for example, the word "sheep" can mean one sheep or many depending on the context. So, how should we interpret the mention of "seed" in the Old Testament? We find an answer earlier in **Genesis**:

And I will make thy seed as the dust of the earth: so that if a man can number the dust of the earth, then shall thy seed also be numbered. [Genesis 13:16]

Here God promises Abraham that he will be blessed with a multitude of descendants, more than can be counted. Therefore, we can see that the correct context for seed is not a single seed, as Paul interprets, but rather many.

Distorting the Old Testament

Paul argues that no-one can be righteous in God's sight through the Mosaic Law:

> **As it is written:**
>
> **"There is no one righteous, not even one; there is no one who understands; there is no one who seeks God. All have turned away, they have together become worthless; there is no one who does good, not even one."**
>
> **"Their throats are open graves; their tongues practice deceit."**
>
> **"The poison of vipers is on their lips."**
>
> **"Their mouths are full of cursing and bitterness."**
>
> **"Their feet are swift to shed blood; ruin and misery mark their ways, and the way of peace they do not know."**
>
> **"There is no fear of God before their eyes."**
>
> **Now we know that whatever the law says, it says to those who are under the law, so that every mouth may be silenced and the whole world held accountable to God. Therefore no one will be declared righteous in God's sight by the works of the law; rather, through the law we become conscious of our sin. [Romans 3:10-20]**

What Paul quotes is a compilation of five separate passages from the Old Testament books of **Psalms** and **Isaiah**:

PAUL	OLD TESTAMENT
"There is no one righteous, not even one; there is no one who understands; there is no one who seeks God"	*The Lord looks down from heaven on all mankind to see if there are any who understand, any who seek God. All have turned away, all have become corrupt; there is no one who does good, not even one. [Psalm 14:2-3]*
"Their throats are open graves; their tongues practice deceit"	*Not a word from their mouth can be trusted; their heart is filled with malice. Their throat is an open grave; with their tongues they tell lies. [Psalm 5:9]*
"The poison of vipers is on their lips"	*They make their tongues as sharp as a serpent's; the poison of vipers is on their lips. [Psalm 140:3]*
"Their feet are swift to shed blood; ruin and misery mark their ways, and the way of peace they do not know"	*Their feet rush into sin; they are swift to shed innocent blood. They pursue evil schemes; acts of violence mark their ways. The way of peace they do not know... [Isaiah 59:7-8]*
"There is no fear of God before their eyes"	*I have a message from God in my heart concerning the sinfulness of the wicked: There is no fear of God before their eyes. [Psalm 36:1]*

We can see that Paul has linked together multiple passages of the Old Testament to come to the conclusion that no-one is able to keep the Law. The problem is that these Old Testament passages have been taken out of their original context. Let's examine one of the passages that Paul referenced from **Psalm 14**:

The fool says in his heart, "There is no God." They are corrupt, their deeds are vile; there is no one who does good. The Lord looks down from heaven on all mankind to see if there are any who understand, any who seek God. All have turned away, all have become corrupt; there is no one who does good, not even one. Do all these evildoers know nothing? They devour my people as though eating bread; they never call on the Lord. But there they are, overwhelmed with dread, for God is present in the company of the righteous. [Psalm 14:1-5]

We can see that, in this passage, a contrast is made between two distinct groups of people, with one group being described as **"corrupt"** and another described as **"righteous"**. The **"corrupt"**, those who say **"There is no God"**, are said to **"devour my people as though eating bread"**, with **"my people"** being a reference to those **"in the company of the righteous"**. Paul's quotation of this passage (**"There is no one righteous, not even one"**) implies that no-one is righteous, not even those who try to keep the Law. When we look at this passage in its original context, we can see that there are indeed those who are righteous, the opposite of what Paul would have us believe.

In this section, we've looked at a few examples which seriously challenge Paul's claims of divine inspiration. Even if we put aside the claim of divine inspiration, it's difficult to make excuses for such basic errors of interpreting the Old Testament because Paul himself claims to have been a student of the leading authority on Jewish Law in Jerusalem, the famous Rabbi Gamaliel:

I am a Jew, born in Tarsus of Cilicia, but brought up in this city. I studied under Gamaliel and was thoroughly trained in the law of our ancestors. I was just as zealous for God as any of you are today. [Acts 22:3]

So far from being ignorant, Paul was (in his own words) highly trained and sophisticated in his understanding of Jewish theology. Now an important point worth reflecting on is Paul's justification for his theology. We've seen that, throughout his writings, Paul makes a lot of effort to try and provide scriptural backing for his beliefs by quoting the Old Testament, but quite bizarrely, there is hardly ever an appeal by Paul to what Jesus said or did. In fact, the strongest argument that Paul could have put forward would have been an appeal to the practices and teachings of Jesus. That would have been a legitimate appeal to authority – see what Jesus said and did. But Paul did not make this argument, precisely because he couldn't – none of the teachings of Jesus advocate Paul's beliefs such as an abandonment of the Law. This is further proof that what Paul taught was at odds with Jesus himself. Far from being a faithful follower of Jesus, Paul in fact innovated a new religion. He morphed the very Jewish teachings of Jesus into an unrecognisable religion by basing it on misquotations of the Old Testament.

WAS JESUS REALLY SENT TO THE WHOLE WORLD?

Was Jesus the saviour of the whole world, or was he sent only to the Israelites? The answer really depends on whom you look to in the New Testament. We've seen that we had this confusing situation, early on, of multiple Christianities, each with opposing beliefs. When we looked at Paul's writings, we found that he proclaims Jesus abolished the Law and was sent to Jews and Gentiles alike. Looking at leaders such as James, we've found that the Mosaic Law was very much in effect in his eyes, and that Gentiles were seen as outsiders, hence his Jerusalem Council decree that the Old Testament Laws pertaining to foreigners living among Israelites were also binding on Gentiles.

When we look at the words of Jesus in the New Testament, we have a similarly confusing picture. On the one hand, we have unequivocal statements by Jesus where he states that he was only sent to save the Israelites: "*I was sent only to the lost sheep of Israel" [Matthew 15:24].* On the other hand, we have statements about him saying that he was sent to save the entire world: "*The next day John saw Jesus coming toward him and said, "Look, the Lamb of God, who takes away the sin of the world!" [John 1:29].* Christians try to make sense of this by saying that Jesus was initially sent to the Israelites and then subsequently to the Gentiles, and that ultimately there is no longer any distinction for either in belief or practice. This is very much

Paul's theology:

For I am not ashamed of the gospel, because it is the power of God that brings salvation to everyone who believes: first to the Jew, then to the Gentile. [Romans 1:16]

We have to bear in mind that many of the books of the New Testament were authored long after Paul, and so the authors of these books could very well have been influenced by Pauline Christianity when they were interpreting and subsequently recording the life and teachings of Jesus. Recall that we've already seen signs of bias towards Paul when it came to canonising the New Testament, as he dominates its pages with almost half of the 27 New Testament books attributed to him.

We can shed some light on the question of the true target audience of Jesus by looking at those who were closest to him. Who would have best understood the true message of Jesus, individuals such as Paul who never met him during his ministry on earth but claims to have experienced him in a vision, or the companions and family members of Jesus, such as his brother James, who were nearer to the source and knew Jesus personally in a way that Paul never did? Their understanding of his message is based on decades of living and speaking with Jesus, and not unverifiable mystical experiences on the road to Damascus. We can look at their handling of the Jerusalem Council incident to get an insight into the mission of Jesus. Recall that there was initially a lot of disagreement among the apostles and elders as to how to deal with the sudden influx of Gentiles, specifically on the question of whether they must follow the Law. We saw that in coming to a decision, there was no reference to any of the teachings of Jesus. Why didn't Jesus leave behind some instructions for how to deal with Gentiles? Apparently, the teachings of Jesus had nothing to say on this matter at all. In addition, if Gentiles originally were the target audience of Jesus and part of his mission all along, then, given the critical importance the Law had played in the lives of Jews since the time of Moses, surely the first question the apostles and elders would have asked Jesus is, "when we eventually come to evangelise to the Gentiles, what is their status with respect to the Law?" This is not what we find though; they had to convene a council in order to settle this question. This indicates that the sudden influx of Gentiles into the religion was an unplanned and unexpected turn of events and not something that Jesus had prepared them for, hence the friction that was happening and the disagreement over how to deal with them.

The answer to whom Jesus was sent to may just be the simplest one. Why did Jesus preach a message of total obedience to the Law? He preached a Law-centric message precisely because he was sent by God to the people of the Law, the Israelites. This is the view taken by many historians and theologians who believe that the historical Jesus saw himself as a Prophet of God sent exclusively to the Israelites. Professor Stanley E. Porter, a specialist in New Testament studies, states that Jesus **"looked to the house of Israel alone"**, and that **"the theocracy he proclaimed had nothing to do with non-Israelites at all." [103]**

The Qur'an also supports this understanding as it reveals to us that Jesus was primarily sent to the Israelites and not the whole world: "**He will teach him [Jesus] the Scripture and wisdom, the Torah and the Gospel, He will send him as a messenger to the Children of Israel..." [3:48-49].** Throughout this book, we've seen numerous examples of the tremendous insight that the Qur'an has into the true message of Jesus, and so the Qur'an's proclamation carries weight. Just as with the Trinity and the crucifixion, this is yet another stumbling block that the Qur'an removes, paving the way for the Jewish people to accept Jesus as the Messiah. The Qur'an presents a picture of Jesus that is in line with Jewish expectations of the Messiah, one whose target audience was the Israelites and one who would uphold the Law of Moses. Now, if Jesus was just another Israelite Prophet intended for the Israelites, then where does this leave Gentiles, the non-Jews? Are non-Jews really permanently outside of the fold of God's covenant? In the next chapter, we will see that the Jewish people don't have a monopoly on God's revelation, for Jesus brought glad tidings of one to come after him, a momentous individual who would be a light for the entire world, Jews and Gentiles alike.

CHAPTER 8

JESUS FORETOLD OF ANOTHER PROPHET AFTER HIM

Christianity teaches that Jesus is the final of God's representatives sent to mankind, there is no other after him. Such beliefs, however, are at odds with what Jesus taught in the New Testament. We find that Jesus spoke of one whom God would send after him:

> *And I will ask the Father, and he will give you another advocate to help you and be with you forever. [John 14:16]*

> *But the Advocate, the Holy Spirit, whom the Father will send in my name, will teach you all things and will remind you of everything I have said to you. [John 14:26]*

> *I have much more to say to you, more than you can now bear. But when he, the Spirit of truth, comes, he will guide you into all the truth. He will not speak on his own; he will speak only what he hears, and he will tell you what is yet to come. [John 16:12-13]*

We can see that Jesus foretold that God would send an advocate, the Holy Spirit, who would guide mankind into all truth. Just who is this 'Holy Spirit'? Christians typically interpret the mention of the Holy Spirit as a reference to the third person of the Trinity, God the Holy Spirit. Nonetheless, such an interpretation is unsatisfactory, especially in the light of our study into the Trinity and its absence in the Bible as a doctrine. Notice that Jesus says that this Holy Spirit would *"teach all things"* and *"remind you of everything I have said"*, an indication that the Holy Spirit would be a support for Jesus and that it plays a role in bringing knowledge to mankind. This perfectly describes the revelation of the Qur'an which, as we've seen throughout this book, restores the original message of Jesus, literally reminding mankind of his true teachings. The Qur'an also supports the notion that the Holy Spirit is not a divine person of God, but rather one that supported God's Prophets such as Jesus: **"And We gave Jesus, the son of Mary, clear proofs and supported him with the Holy Spirit" [2:87].** Muslims understand the Holy Spirit to be a reference to the angel Gabriel. The angel Gabriel is described in the Qur'an as the Spirit who brought the revelation of the Qur'an from God down to the Prophet Muhammad ﷺ: **"The Holy Spirit has brought it [the Qur'an] down from your Lord in truth to make firm those who believe and as guidance and good tidings to the Muslims." [16:102]**

The Qur'an sheds more light on the prophecy of Jesus:

> **Those who follow the Messenger, the unlettered prophet, whom they find written in what they have of the Torah and the Gospel... [7:157]**

We can see that the Qur'an makes the astonishing claim that the Prophet Muhammad ﷺ himself is mentioned in the Scriptures of the Jews and Christians. When we examine the Old Testament, we will find that there are indeed numerous prophecies that foretell the coming of an Arabian Prophet. We are going to look at two in particular: **Deuteronomy 33** and **Isaiah 42**.

THE PROPHECY IN DEUTERONOMY 33

We will start our discussion with the 95th chapter of the Qur'an, "The Fig":

> **By the fig and the olive and [by] Mount Sinai and [by] this secure city (Mecca). We have certainly created man in the best of stature. Then We return him to the lowest of the low. Except for those who believe and do righteous deeds, for they will have a reward uninterrupted. So what yet causes you to deny the recompense? Is not God the most just of judges?**

In the beginning of this chapter of the Qur'an, God refers to three locations. The land of Palestine is meant from the statement **"by the fig and the olive"**, as greater Palestine is known for its abundance in these fruits. The second location mentioned, **"Mount Sinai"**, is known to be in Egypt. The third statement, **"this secure city"**, refers to the city of Mecca in Saudi Arabia, as this is where the Prophet Muhammad ﷺ was living when this chapter of the Qur'an was revealed to him.

The Bible mentions exactly the same locations in a prophecy given by Moses, foretelling the emergence of a "fiery law" in Arabia:

> **And this is the blessing, wherewith Moses the man of God blessed the children of Israel before his death. The Lord came from Sinai, and rose up from Seir unto them; he shined forth from mount Paran, and he came with ten thousands of saints; from his right hand went a fiery law for them. [Deuteronomy 33:1-2]**

We are going to show that this prophecy is in fact a reference to the three Abrahamic faiths of Judaism, Christianity and Islam. This prophecy can be divided into two parts:

1. **The mention of Sinai, Seir and Paran**

2. **The emergence of ten thousand saints and a law**

We will now discuss each of these in detail:

The mention of Sinai, Seir and Paran

"The Lord came from Sinai, and rose up from Seir unto them; he shined forth from mount Paran..."

Here one can see clearly that three locations are mentioned. Sinai is in Egypt, where Moses came from with a message from God, as is evident from the statement **"the Lord came from Sinai"**. Seir is an allusion to Palestine, as mount Seir was situated within the ancient kingdom of Edom, which was in Palestine. This is according to commentators of the Old Testament: **"Seir is the mountain land of the Edomites to the east of Sinai"** [104]. Palestine is where Jesus appeared with a call to God: **"[the Lord] rose up from Seir"**.

The big question is: which location is being referred to in the final part of the verse whereby God proclaims *"he shined forth from mount Paran"*? The Bible tells us that Paran is the very place where Ishmael dwelt: *"While he (Ishmael) was living in the Desert of Paran, his mother got a wife for him from Egypt" [Genesis 21:21].* The dwelling place of Ishmael was none other than Arabia. It's important to note that biblical geographers differ as to the exact location of Paran. However, they are unanimous that Paran is somewhere within Arabia. From Clarke's Commentary on the Bible:

> *He dwelt in the wilderness of Paran – This is generally allowed to have been a part of the desert belonging to Arabia Petraea, in the vicinity of Mount Sinai; and this seems to be its uniform meaning in the sacred writings.*

Strong's Bible Dictionary also tells us that Paran is a desert of Arabia:

H6290 pâ'rân From H6286; ornamental; Paran, a desert of Arabia: – Paran.

Sebeos, a seventh century Armenian bishop and historian, when describing the Arab conquest of his time, wrote that the Arabs *"assembled and came out from Paran" [105].*

Encyclopaedia Biblica, edited by Reverend T. K. Cheyne, asserts: *"Paran refers to the Arab tribal names, farran or faran." [106]*

The Dead Sea Scrolls, which are dated to the second century BCE and represent the oldest surviving manuscript evidence for the Old Testament along with other apocryphal books, link Ishmael and his descendants to Arabia:

> *And Ishmael and his sons, and the sons of Keturah and their sons, went together and dwelt from Paran to the entering in of Babylon in all the land which is towards the East facing the desert. And these mingled with each other, and their name was called Arabs, and Ishmaelite. [107]*

The fifth century chronicler Sozomen, a Christian historian who wrote much about the history of the Church, wrote that Arabs descended from Ishmael the son of Abraham and were, as a result, originally called Ishmaelites. They practised circumcision like the Jews, refrained from the use of pork and observed many other Jewish rites and customs. *"Indeed there are some among them, even at the present day,"* he wrote, *"who regulate their lives according to the Jewish precepts." [108]*

Hence, the Paran (or Pharan) of Ishmael was certainly in the Arabian Peninsula. In fact, we can narrow this location down further. Modern academic research supports the claim that Ishmael's Paran was indeed in a specific part of Arabia known as Hijaz, modern-day Western Saudi Arabia. Irfan Shahid, one of the world's most renowned authorities on pre-Islamic, ancient Arabian geography/ history, stated that there was a place called Pharan in Hijaz, which belonged to the Sulaym tribe [109]. Professor Haseeb Shehada, an Israeli scholar and professor, in his translation of the Samaritan version of the Torah suggested an identification of the wilderness of Paran with the desert of Western Arabia which is known today as Hijaz. [110]

Some Christians claim that Paran is not in Arabia, but rather in the desert of Sinai in Egypt. But this can't be the case, as the Old Testament clearly distinguishes between Sinai and Paran as two separate places: *"Then the Israelites set out from the Desert of Sinai and traveled from place to place until the cloud came to rest in the Desert of Paran." [Numbers 10:12]*

The emergence of ten thousand saints and a law

This brings us onto the next part of the prophecy, *"he came with ten thousands of saints; from his right hand went a fiery law for them"*. The question we must now ask is: who came from/to Arabia with ten thousand saints and a law in his right hand? As we've seen, the third location, Paran, is a direct reference to Western Saudi Arabia. It just so happens that this is exactly where the Prophet Muhammad ﷺ was born, in the city of Mecca which is located in Western Saudi Arabia. At the time in the seventh century, the vast majority of Meccans were polytheistic in religion. Then, in 610 CE, God appointed Muhammad as His Prophet. He began to call his people to a new, monotheistic religion. Initially, Muhammad preached in private, and his early followers congregated in secret. When Muhammad eventually declared his message publicly, he and his early followers were met with increasing hostility. His mission to reform society, which included the call for his people to renounce idolatry and advocating for the rights of the poor and the weak, inevitably put him on a collision course with the rich and powerful tribes of Mecca.

The leaders of Mecca instigated a sustained campaign of violence against what they saw as a rival faith and a threat to their power structure. For over a decade, Muslims would go on to suffer severe persecution; they endured beatings, torture, imprisonment and some were even killed. The leaders of Mecca even signed a pact resulting in the complete social and economic boycott of Muslims along with the tribes associated with them. Muhammad and his followers were forced by these circumstances to leave their homes and wander in the outskirts of Mecca. Confined to the harsh and barren desert valley, they struggled to survive for three years, with even food and medicine being barred to them. During what is known as the Year of Grief, Muhammad's uncle Abu Talib passed away. Abu Lahab, early Islam's arch-enemy and Muhammad's bitterest foe, replaced Abu Talib as the chief of the tribe. The persecution of the early Muslim community in Mecca intensified and in 622 CE, after suffering for nearly a decade and a half, Prophet Muhammad ﷺ and his followers fled their home city of Mecca in order to escape persecution. They had to leave behind their possessions and properties which were confiscated by their enemies.

They arrived safely in the city of Medina. There, the early Muslim community regrouped and flourished. The persecution by their enemies had by no means come to an end, as over the next ten years the tribes of Mecca fought numerous wars against the Muslims. In 629 CE, the Meccans broke a mutual peace treaty with the Muslims. The Prophet Muhammad ﷺ then led a Muslim army of ten thousand in a triumphant return to their home city of Mecca, nearly a decade after they had been forced to flee it. This historic event is known as the Conquest of Mecca:

> *Narrated Ibn `Abbas: The Prophet left Medina (for Mecca) in the company of ten-thousand (Muslim warriors) in (the month of) Ramadan, and that was eight and a half years after his migration to Medina. He and the Muslims who were with him, proceeded*

on their way to Mecca. He was fasting and they were fasting, but when they reached a place called Al-Kadid which was a place of water between 'Usfan and Kudaid, he broke his fast and so did they. (Az-Zuhri said, "One should take the last action of God's Apostle and leave his early action (while taking a verdict.")). [111]

This is an exact fulfilment of the Bible's foretelling of the coming of ten thousand saints to Mecca. These saints are the ten thousand Muslims who accompanied Muhammad in the conquest and obeyed God and His Messenger in all matters.

The Prophet Muhammad ﷺ did not just arrive with an army, he also brought with him the Qur'an, the law that was divinely revealed to him from God through the angel Gabriel. The Qur'an was the book by which the Prophet Muhammad ﷺ judged all matters, and the fate of the Meccans was no exception. Before ordering the troops to enter Mecca, the Prophet instructed his men to lift their hands only against those who drew swords against them. He also directed them neither to lay their hands on any moveable or immovable property of the Meccans, nor to destroy anything [112]. The Muslim army entered the city peacefully. No house was robbed; no man or woman was harmed or even insulted. The Prophet Muhammad's ﷺ first act was to go to the Ka'aba, which Muslims believe was originally built by Abraham and Ishmael as a place of worship dedicated to the One God, but subsequently turned into a house of idolatry by the pagan Meccans. There he proceeded to destroy the idols and false gods within, whilst reciting the following verse of the Qur'an: ***"Say, the Truth has come and falsehood gone. Verily falsehood is bound to vanish" [17:81]***. Then the Prophet went before the defeated people whose hearts were trembling, waiting to see what the victorious conqueror would do with them. The Meccans were afraid because the Arabs had lived by the law of retaliation; their own practice was that of revenge and murder. Many of them were expecting some sort of punishment in accordance with the traditions of the Arabs, and Muhammad had the power to exact that punishment. But, instead, the Prophet granted a general amnesty to the entire population of Mecca, saying to them, ***"There is no censure on you on this day. May God forgive you, for He is the Most Merciful of the merciful" [113]***.

Muhammad could have taken vengeance against all those who had persecuted him and his people for so many years, but instead he forgave them. His merciful conduct was in accordance with the Qur'an's laws of justice: **"You who believe, uphold justice and bear witness to God, even if it is against yourselves, your parents, or your close relatives..." [4:135].** It's one thing to forgive others when you are in a position of weakness and have no choice, but it's very difficult to do so when you find yourself in a position of strength over your staunch enemies and brutal oppressors. This is one of the many beautiful qualities of the Prophet Muhammad ﷺ that changed the hatred in the hearts of his enemies to love for him, as the Qur'an testifies: **"And We have not sent you, [O Muhammad], except as a mercy to the worlds." [21:107]**

In summary, we can see that a Biblical prophecy was fulfilled to the letter with the advent of the Prophet of Islam. There is no other person in the entire history of mankind who emerged from Arabia in such circumstances, with ten thousand saints and a law, except the Prophet Muhammad ﷺ.

COMMON OBJECTIONS TO DEUTERONOMY ANSWERED

Probably the most common objection against **Deuteronomy 33** is that because it is written in the past tense, it therefore can't be a prophecy about Muhammad in the future:

> **"...he shined forth from mount Paran, and he came with ten thousands of saints; from his right hand went a fiery law for them"**

This is a literary technique that is actually very common in Biblical prophecy and is known as the prophetic perfect tense. It is used to describe future events that are so certain to happen that they are referred to in the past tense as if they have already happened [114]. The category of "prophetic perfect" was already suggested by medieval Hebrew grammarians, such as David Kimhi: **"The matter is as clear as though it had already passed"** **[115]**. Rabbi Isaac ben Yedaiah describes it as:

[The rabbis] of blessed memory followed, in these words of theirs, in the paths of the prophets who speak of something which will happen in the future in the language of the past. Since they saw in prophetic vision that which was to occur in the future, they spoke about it in the past tense and testified firmly that it had happened, to teach the certainty of his [God's] words - may he be blessed - and his positive promise that can never change and his beneficent message that will not be altered. [116]

There are numerous examples of this literary technique throughout the Old Testament. For example, in the story of Noah:

But I will establish my covenant with you, and you have come into the ark—you and your sons and your wife and your sons' wives with you. [Genesis 6:18]

Here God told Noah to build the ark. After telling him how to build it, the text reads that God said, *"and you have come into the ark"*. The ark was not even built at that time, and when it was eventually built God goes on to tell Noah, *"Go into the ark, you and your whole family..." [Genesis 7:1]*. The prophetic perfect in **Genesis 6:18** makes it clear that Noah would absolutely enter the ark. Most English versions, not wanting to confuse the reader, read something like, *"And you will enter the ark."*

Another example is the story of Joseph:

And seven years of famine have arisen after them, and all the plenty is forgotten in the land of Egypt, and the famine hath finished the land [Genesis 41:30]

We can see that when Joseph interpreted the King's dream, he foretold that there would be seven years of plenty and seven years of famine. When describing the seven years of famine, he speaks of them in the prophetic perfect tense, mentioning them in the past for emphasis. To avoid confusing the reader, almost every English version says that the famine *"will arise"*.

In the writings of Isaiah:

> *Therefore my people are gone into captivity, because they have no knowledge: and their honourable men are famished, and their multitude dried up with thirst. [Isaiah 5:13]*

The great captivity spoken of here is a reference to the Babylonian exile. Although this momentous event wouldn't take place until long after Isaiah's death, in his vision of the future he speaks of it as if it has already taken place to convey a sense of certainty.

The prophetic perfect tense can also be found in the New Testament. For example, when Paul speaks of being raised up to God:

> *And God raised us up with Christ and seated us with him in the heavenly realms in Christ Jesus [Ephesians 2:6]*

Notice that the verse speaks in the past tense when it says, *"And God raised us up with Christ and seated us with him."* The Biblical scholar F.F. Bruce writes specifically about **Ephesians 2:6**:

> *That God has already seated his people with Christ in the heavenly realm is an idea unparalleled elsewhere in the Pauline corpus. It can best be understood as a statement of God's purpose for his people—a purpose which is so sure of fulfillment that it can be spoken of as having already taken place. [117]*

So, in summary, just because a text in the Bible is written in the past tense does not rule it out as being a prophecy about the future.

Another common objection to **Deuteronomy 33** is that not all versions of the Bible translate it as *"ten thousands of saints"*. In this book, we have made use of the King James Version for this verse. However, some other versions of the Bible translate it slightly differently. For example:

> *He came with <u>myriads of holy ones</u> from the south, from his mountain slopes. [New International Version]*

and <u>with him thousands of saints</u>. In his right hand a fiery law. [Douay-Rheims Bible]

The original Hebrew word is 'rebabah' which carries the meaning of a "very large number" according to the Gesenius Hebrew lexicon:

Gesenius' Hebrew-Chaldee Lexicon [?]

רְבָבָה f. *a myriad, ten thousand*, Jud. 20:10; often used for a very large number, Gen. 24:60; Cant. 5:10. Pl. רְבָבוֹת *myriads*, 1 Sa. 18:8; commonly used of any very large number, Psalm 3:7; Deut. 33:17.

While most English versions of the Bible translate it as **"ten thousand"**, it must be noted that none of these alternative translations take away from this being a prophecy about Muhammad. Whether one translates it as **"ten thousand"**, **"myriads"** or **"thousands"**, they all point to the fact that some individual is going to arise from Arabia with a large number of followers and a fiery law. None other than the Prophet Muhammad ﷺ has fulfilled this prophecy in history. For those who still claim that it is not Muhammad ﷺ, then the question still stands: who came from Arabia with a fiery law and a multitude of followers?

THE PROPHECY IN ISAIAH 42

One of the most powerful and explicit prophecies about the Prophet Muhammad ﷺ in the Bible is Isaiah 42 which describes itself as a prophecy about the future: **"the former things have taken place, and new things I declare; before they spring into being I announce them to you" [Isaiah 42:9]**. *The entire chapter addresses the advent of one person: a messianic figure; a prophet king; someone with worldly as well as spiritual authority; someone connected to Arabia. We are now going to analyse some of the key verses of Isaiah 42:*

Characteristics of the coming servant

Here is my servant, whom I uphold, my chosen one in whom I delight; I will put my Spirit on him, and he will bring justice to the nations. [Isaiah 42:1]

Isaiah starts the 42nd chapter by drawing our attention to a very special person that God will send. He describes this person as:

"...my servant, whom I uphold, my chosen one in whom I delight..."

At least three of the names of the Prophet Muhammad ﷺ are mentioned - *"servant"*, *"chosen one"* and *"in whom I delight"*. The Prophet Muhammad ﷺ is known as God's servant, in Arabic 'abd – ullah'. This was mentioned by the Prophet Muhammad ﷺ *"Do not exaggerate in praising me as the Christians praised the son of Mary, for I am only a Servant (abd). So, call me the Servant of God (abd - ullah)."* [118]

"Chosen one" is 'Mustafa' in Arabic. This is another of the names of the Prophet Muhammad ﷺ: *"Indeed God chose the tribe of Kinanah over other tribes from the children of Ishmael; He chose Quraish over other tribes of Kinanah; He chose Banu Hashim over the other families of the Quraish; and He chose me from Banu Hashim"* [119]. The one in whom God "delights" shows that this person is beloved to God. 'Habibullah' in Arabic, which means "Beloved of God", also happens to be one of the Prophet Muhammad's ﷺ names.

Isaiah also indicates that God will support the coming servant:

"I will put my Spirit on him..."

The Qur'an confirms that the Spirit of God, who Muslims believe is the angel Gabriel, was sent down by God to Muhammad:

We have thus revealed a Spirit to you [Prophet] by Our command: you knew neither the Scripture nor the faith, but We made it a light, guiding with it whoever We will of Our servants. You are indeed guiding to the straight path. [42:52]

Isaiah further states that the coming servant will not just be concerned with his own people, but rather the nations of the entire world:

"and he will bring justice to the nations"

The word translated as "justice" in Isaiah is the Hebrew 'mishpat', which also means judgement according to Biblical Hebrew dictionaries. The very fact that this prophet will bring judgement to the nations is a point to be noted. Israelite prophets did not preach to non-Israelites. The Prophet of Islam brought judgement for the entire world, as is clear from history. Moreover, some of the foremost authorities commenting on the book of Isaiah interpret this judgement to be comprehensive in the sense of a complete way of life, which is what Islam represents. Professor of Hebrew Christopher North stated in his commentary on **Isaiah 42:1** that:

> **Most commentators remark that mishpat is here used absolutely, without the definite article, and that it has the comprehensive sense of the Islamic din ("judgement'), which embraces both faith and practice. [120]**

Isaiah goes on to give us some insight into the special person's personality:

"He will not shout or cry out, or raise his voice in the streets." [Isaiah 42:2]

Here the phrase "not cry" is meant as "not complain about the duty that God gave him". Throughout his life, the Prophet Muhammad ﷺ never once cried out in complaint at the mission that was given to him by God, in spite of its immense difficulty and hardship. Also, it's interesting to note that the personality and character of the Prophet Muhammad ﷺ was exactly as this verse describes; his companions bore witness to the fact that he was soft in speech and did not raise his voice in the marketplace [121].

The rest of **Isaiah 42** goes on to provide further details about God's coming servant.

The Location of God's servant

"Let the wilderness and its towns raise their voices; let the settlements where Kedar lives rejoice. Let the people of Sela sing for joy; let them shout from the mountaintops." [Isaiah 42:11]

Here Isaiah reveals the location of God's servant. The two key words used are *"Kedar"* and *"Sela"* which together pinpoint an exact location for this special person. Out of all the places on earth that Isaiah could have mentioned, he chose to highlight Kedar and Sela's location so we should pay special attention.

Who is Kedar, and where did he settle? The Old Testament tells us that Kedar was one of the sons of Ishmael: *"These are the names of the sons of Ishmael, listed in the order of their birth: Nebaioth the firstborn of Ishmael, Kedar, Adbeel, Mibsam." [Genesis 25:13]*

As we saw with his father Ishmael, Kedar and his own sons are also specifically linked to Arabia: *"Arabia and all the princes of Kedar were your favored dealers in lambs, rams, and goats; in these they did business with you." [Ezekiel 27:21]*

Smith's Bible Dictionary defines Kedar as:

> *"...the name of a great tribe of Arabs settled on the northwest of the peninsula... That they also settled in villages or towns we find from Isaiah (Isaiah 42:11). The tribe seems to have been one of the most conspicuous of all the Ishmaelite tribes..." [122]*

The Keil-Delitzsch Commentary on the Old Testament discusses Isaiah's use of Kedar: *"The name Kedar is here the collective name of the Arabic tribes generally." [123]*

These two ancient Assyrian inscriptions, dating to the seventh century BCE, associate the king of the Arabs with the land of "Qedar":

Hazael, king of Arabs, with a sumptuous gift,
came over to Nineveh, city of my sovereignty,

he kissed my feet
and begged me for his gods. And I had pity.
[King Esarhaddon, Prism A IV, lines 6 - 9]

Iauta son of Hazael
king of the land of Qedar paid homage to me.
He approached me concerning his gods (and) begged my kingship
[King Assurbanipal, Prism B VII, lines 93 - 96]

Compare the description of King Hazael, described as **"king of the Arabs"**, with that of his son King Iauta, who is described as **"king of the land of Qedar"**. This shows us that the land of the Arabs was associated with Kedar even in ancient times.

We've established that Kedar dwelt in Arabia. In fact, Kedar dwelt within a specific part of Arabia known as Hijaz, modern-day Western Saudi Arabia. This can be established from Biblical geography which places the Ishmaelites in a land called Midian:

Typical Bible map   Modern day map

We know that Biblical Midian is linked to Kedar, the son of Ishmael, because the terms "Midianite" and "Ishmaelite" are used interchangeably in the Old Testament. This is according to Harper's Bible Dictionary [124]. We can see this from the story of Joseph in Genesis:

> *So when the <u>Midianite</u> merchants came by, his brothers pulled Joseph up out of the cistern and sold him for twenty shekels of silver to the <u>Ishmaelites</u>, who took him to Egypt... Meanwhile,*

the <u>Midianites</u> sold Joseph in Egypt to Potiphar, one of Pharaoh's officials, the captain of the guard. [Genesis 37:28-36]

The Old Testament scholar Charles Foster also confirms that Kedar dwelt in Western Saudi Arabia (Hijaz/Hedjaz):

"Namely, of the land of Kedar; which every reader conversant with Arabian geography will recognise as a most accurate delineation of the district of Hedjaz [Western Saudi Arabia], including its famous cities of Mecca and Madina." [125]

A very ancient, pre-Islamic Arab tradition states that Kedar settled in Western Saudi Arabia, and that his descendants have ruled there ever since [126].

In summary, we have established that Kedar and his descendants settled in modern-day Saudi Arabia. In fact, we can narrow the location down further; recall that Isaiah mentions Kedar in association with "Sela":

"... let the settlements where Kedar lives rejoice. Let the people of Sela sing for joy..."

Just what is "Sela"? There are two ways that this Hebrew word can be interpreted. It can be interpreted in terms of its meaning, which represents a description of a general location. But it can also be interpreted as a proper noun, in other words, as the name of a specific place. To appreciate this, let's take the example of the city of Bethlehem. In Hebrew, the word "Bethlehem" is 'Bet Lehem', meaning "house of bread". So, if we interpret this word in terms of its meaning, it could refer to any place associated with bread, such as a marketplace or bakery. However, if we interpret the word as a proper noun, then it can only refer to one place on earth, the city of Bethlehem in the Holy Land. If we apply this principle to Sela, then it pinpoints two possible locations within Saudi Arabia, the cities of Mecca and Medina. The word 'Sela' means "craggy rock" in Hebrew. Isaiah mentions the villages of Kedar, so if we use the villages of Kedar as the reference point, then the "craggy rock" mentioned by Isaiah is a reference to Muhammad's city of birth, Mecca. Not only was Mecca inhabited by the children of Kedar (the tribe of Quresh) during the time of the Prophet Muhammad ﷺ, but Mecca also best fits the description of "craggy rock" as Mecca is surrounded by rocky mountains.

If we interpret 'Sela' as a proper noun, as the name of a specific place, then the location being spoken of must be the city of Medina because Sela is the name of a famous mountain in Medina:

Figure 1 - Masjid Nabawi, Prophet Muhammad's ﷺ mosque in modern-day Medina. The foot of Sela mountain can be seen to the right of the mosque.

Recall that Medina was the Prophet Muhammad's ﷺ adopted city whilst in exile after the Muslims fled Meccan persecution. You can find mention of Sela mountain throughout the statements of the companions of the Prophet Muhammad ﷺ. For example:

> *...while I was sitting in the condition which God described, my very soul seemed straitened to me and even the earth seemed narrow to me for all its spaciousness, there I heard the voice of one who had ascended the mountain of Sala calling with his loudest voice, 'O Ka'b bin Malik! Be happy (by receiving good tidings).' I fell down in prostration before God, realising that relief has come...* [127]

> *...by God, we did not see any cloud or any patch of it, and there*

was neither any house or building standing between us and Sala...
[128]

As we've seen, all possible interpretations of "Sela" in the light of Kedar, whether understood as Mecca or Medina, are direct references to the Prophet Muhammad ﷺ. As well as being linked to Kedar and Sela geographically, the Prophet Muhammad's ﷺ genealogy is also linked. His lineage can be traced back to Ishmael and Abraham directly through Kedar:

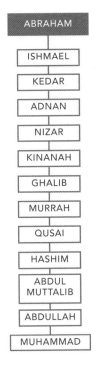

One of the earliest biographies of the Prophet Muhammad ﷺ, Tabaqat Ibn Sa'd (d. 845 CE), documents one of the chains of genealogy, which confirms that the Prophet was a direct descendant of Ishmael through his second son Kedar. Hayden's Bible dictionary states: ***"Mohammad is said to have been of the Bene-Kedar [sons of Kedar]." [129]***

Isaiah not only reveals to us the location of God's servant, but also describes how the people will react when the awaited one arrives:

"...Let the people of Sela sing for joy; let them shout from the mountain-tops..."

We are told that the people of Sela will be so overjoyed that they will sing with joy. Amazingly, this again applies to both Mecca and Medina. With regard to Mecca, the Prophet Muhammad ﷺ brought the obligation of Hajj (once in a lifetime mandatory pilgrimage to Mecca) with him as the fifth pillar of Islam and it is during the event of Hajj when millions of Muslims sing the song: **labaik Allahumma labaik, labaika la sharika laka labaik... ("O my Lord, here I am at Your service, here I am. There is no partner with You, here I am")**. The pilgrims sing the above song from the top of the mountains and all of this takes place in Mecca. With regard to Medina, Isaiah describes exactly what happened when the Prophet Muhammad ﷺ arrived in Medina, its inhabitants were overjoyed and cried out in happiness:

> *I never saw the people of Medina so happy with anything as they were with his arrival. I even saw the little boys and girls saying, "Here is the Messenger of God; he has come!"* [130]

> *The people hurried quickly to meet the Messenger of God when he arrived in Medina. They cried, 'The Messenger of God has arrived! The Messenger of God has arrived!'* [131]

> *Then men and women climbed upon house-tops; the boys and servants scattered in the way, and they were all calling out: 'Muhammad! Messenger of God! Muhammad! Messenger of God!'* [132]

It's important to note that, historically, we know there was a presence of various Jewish tribes in Medina before the advent of the Prophet Muhammad ﷺ. Both Jewish historians and Islamic history record this fact. The American historian Salo Baron, the most noted historian of the Jews of his generation, recorded the following in his book "Social and Religious History of the Jews":

Judaic presence and influence throughout the region burgeoned steadily throughout the first few centuries of the Common Era. The process is substantiated by solidly sympathetic references to Jews and Judaism in pre-Islamic Arabic literature. By the sixth century, it is clear that Jewish tribes dominated Yathrib (Medina)... [133]

Alexander Marx, an American historian, and Max Margolis, an American philologist, wrote the following in their book "A History of the Jewish People":

In the northwest of the peninsula the Jews occupied the oases on the line of the caravan route running from north to south. Taima, Fadak, Khaibar, Wadi-I-Kura (Vale of Villages) were in their hands and Yathrib (later Medina) was in all probability founded by them... [In] Yemen, their industry and enterprising spirit helped to revive the prosperity of the country. [134]

According to Watt, a Scottish historian and professor in Arabic and Islamic Studies, the Jewish tribes had previously dominated the political, economic and intellectual life of Medina [135].

A question then arises: why were there numerous Jewish tribes within Medina? The answer is that the scholars among them were aware of this prophecy in Isaiah and were anxiously awaiting the coming of a new prophet. Islamic history records the fact that before the advent of Muhammad's Prophethood, whenever a dispute arose between the Jewish tribes and Arabs in Medina, they would taunt their pagan Arab neighbours, by saying: *"when our prophet arrives we shall obliterate you..." [136]*. The Qur'an also affirms this. God says: *"Is it not a sign to them that the learned men of the Children of Israel knew it (as true)?" [26:197]*

One possible objection is that the "Sela" referenced is actually Sela in the city of Petra, modern-day Jordan, and not the Sela in Saudi Arabia. For example, the following verse may be cited to support this argument: *"He was the one who defeated ten thousand Edomites in the Valley of Salt and captured Sela in battle..." [2 Kings 14:7]* The Edomites were a people who inhabited the land of Edom, the Biblical name for modern-day Jordan. Let's consider the entire verse of Isaiah in question:

Let the wilderness and its towns raise their voices; let the settlements where Kedar lives rejoice. Let the people of Sela sing for joy; let them shout from the mountaintops. [Isaiah 42:11]

Now, if Isaiah had intended to identify the Sela of Edom, then he would have mentioned the rejoicing of the Edomites, not Kedar. The Edomites and Kedarites were two different groups that inhabited entirely different lands, the land of Edom (modern-day Jordan) and the land of Midian (modern-day Western Saudi Arabia):

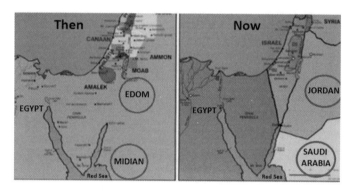

The fact is that Isaiah mentions Sela in conjunction with Kedar's location, so this should lead us to conclude that Sela is in relation to Western Saudi Arabia. Moreover, the Sela of Edom does not fit the context of the chapter of Isaiah, which talks of the coming of God's special person. Which Prophet or Messenger of God ever travelled to Edom and was received by overjoyed people? The Bible mentions no such incident.

Another way that we can come to a resolution on the identity of Sela is to consider the nature and purpose of prophecy. Prophecies allow those who receive them to be aware of things that are going to happen in the future. If a prophecy causes confusion, or raises more questions in the minds of its recipients, then that defeats its purpose. Now, if Kedar has no significance in the verse, then there is no certainty as to which site is being mentioned. Given that there were multiple Selas at the time Isaiah was writing, how would his audience be able to determine which Sela is being spoken of? Shouldn't we expect Isaiah to specify which one he's talking about? That must be why Isaiah spoke about Kedar, as it allows us to pinpoint a specific Sela, that of the Prophet Muhammad ﷺ.

Global justice and new revelation

"He will not falter or be discouraged till he establishes justice on earth. In his teaching the islands will put their hope." [Isaiah 42:4]

The first part of this verse mentions:

"He will not falter or be discouraged till he establishes justice on earth..."

Early into his mission when the Muslims were in a position of weakness, the Prophet Muhammad ﷺ was offered every worldly gain imaginable to try and persuade him to stop preaching the message of Islam:

> *If you desire money and wealth by preaching what you are preaching, we will collect enough for you from our own. We will make you the wealthiest of all of us. If it is chieftainship that you desire, we are ready to make you our paramount chief, so that we will never decide on a matter without you. If you desire rulership, we will make you our ruler...* [137]

The Prophet Muhammad ﷺ responded by saying:

> *Even if they place the sun in my right-hand, and the moon in my left-hand in return for giving up this matter, I will never stop, until either God makes it triumph or I die defending it.* [138]

What this incident demonstrates is that Muhammad was not motivated by money or power, but rather he was sincere about the message he was preaching. When his enemies realised that nothing would discourage him from preaching his message, they turned to more aggressive tactics. The Prophet Muhammad ﷺ went on to face extreme persecution and hostility in Mecca but he still did not give up the message of Islam. He did not rest until the just rule of Islam was firmly established within his lifetime. Even though he often faced extraordinary odds in battles, the Prophet was not discouraged. Instead, the Qur'an talks about the faith of Muhammad and his companions rising when they were outnumbered by their enemies. The Prophet Muhammad ﷺ survived several attempts on his life, until he completed his mission and established justice by judging people according to the laws of God. Indeed, the message of Islam was completed: *"Today I have perfected your religion for you, completed My blessing upon you, and chosen as your religion Islam..."* **[5:3]**

The second part of the verse in Isaiah mentions:

"...In his teaching the islands will put their hope"

Here Isaiah informs us that God's servant will bring forth a new law. The word translated as "teaching" is the Hebrew "Torah" which means instruction or law. According to commentators on the Bible, this word *"has in the total context of this passage almost the sense of 'revelation'"* **[139].** Notice that Isaiah states that the islands will put their hope in *his* law, implying he will bring forth something new, something different, as the Law of Moses already existed at the time Isaiah made this prophecy. Another point is that the islands are said to put their hope in his new Torah in the future tense, again implying it is a new law and therefore cannot be a reference to the Torah of Moses which already existed at the time that Isaiah made this prophecy. The Qur'an given to the Prophet Muhammad ﷺ fits this description perfectly as it was a new book revealed after the time of Isaiah:

> *We sent to you [Muhammad] the Scripture with the truth, confirming the Scriptures that came before it, and with final authority over them: so judge between them according to what God has sent down...* **[5:48]**

The law of Islam spread as far east as northern China and as far west as southern France. In fact, many isles did wait for his law and when the Islamic law came to them with the Muslim armies, they welcomed their liberators. This happened in Syria, Egypt and Spain. With the advent of Islam, all the oppressive powers surrounding Arabia fell one after another and the masses could live in peace from then on. In the Qur'an, God commanded the Muslims to go on a rescue mission:

Why should you not fight in God's cause and for those oppressed men, women, and children who cry out, 'Lord, rescue us from this town whose people are oppressors! By Your grace, give us a protector and give us a helper!'? [4:75]

This mission was so successful that even the Christians attributed the Muslim success to God. John Bar Penkaye, a Christian monk and contemporary of the early Islamic conquests, expressed his feelings as follows:

We should not think of the advent (of the children of Hagar) as something ordinary, but as due to divine working. Before calling them, (God) had prepared them beforehand to hold Christians in honour; thus they also had a special commandment from God concerning our monastic station, that they should hold it in honour. Now when these people came, at God's command, and took over as it were both kingdoms, not with any war or battle, but in a menial fashion, such as when a brand is rescued out of the fire, not using weapons of war or human means, God put victory into their hands in such a way that the words written them might be fulfilled, namely, "One man chased a thousand and two routed ten thousand." How otherwise, could naked men, riding without armour or shield, have been able to win, apart from divine aid, God having called them from the ends of the earth so as to destroy, by them "a sinful kingdom" and to bring low, through them, the proud spirit of the Persians [140].

Some Christians claim that **Isaiah 42** is a prophecy about Jesus. When we analyse the life of Jesus as portrayed in the New Testament, we will see that this cannot be the case. The new law cannot refer to Jesus, because he obeyed and followed the Law of Moses throughout his life. In the Gospel of Matthew, Jesus taught adherence to the Law of Moses, not a new law:

For truly I tell you, until heaven and earth disappear, not the smallest letter, not the least stroke of a pen, will by any means disappear from the Law until everything is accomplished. Therefore anyone who sets aside one of the least of these commands and teaches others accordingly will be called least in the kingdom of heaven, but whoever practices and teaches these commands will

be called great in the kingdom of heaven. [Matthew 5:18-19]

Also, when Jesus was asked whether he was the King of the Jews, he stated that his kingdom was not of this world (**John 18:36**). This again rules Jesus out, as the passage of Isaiah announces the advent of a messianic figure with worldly powers who will establish global justice. For one to establish justice on the earth, one has to have spiritual as well as worldly capacity. The Qur'an talks in a similar fashion: **"It is a promise of God to those who believe among you and do righteous deeds that He will grant you succession over the present rulers in the earth, like He granted it to those before you." [24:55]**

Who he will be sent to

"I, the Lord, have called you in righteousness; I will take hold of your hand. I will keep you and will make you to be a covenant for the people and a light for the Gentiles." [Isaiah 42:6]

Here Isaiah emphasises the universal mission of the coming person. Gentiles means non-Jews, and the Qur'an confirms that the Prophet Muhammad ﷺ was sent to the whole of mankind, Jews and Gentiles alike: **"We have sent you [O Prophet] as a bearer of glad tidings and a warner for the whole of mankind, but most people have no knowledge." [34:28]**

The verse in Isaiah cannot apply to Jesus because in the Gospel of Matthew Jesus said: **"I was sent only to the lost sheep of Israel." [Matthew 15:24]**

Isaiah further states that God will:

"...lead the blind by ways they have not known, along unfamiliar paths I will guide them..." [Isaiah 42:16]

The pagan Arabs at the time of the Prophet Muhammad ﷺ fit this description perfectly because they had not been sent a messenger prior to Muhammad ﷺ. The Qur'an bears witness to this, God states that Muhammad ﷺ was sent to: **"...warn a people to whom no warner has come before..." [32:3]**

Isaiah also highlights the worship of idols:

"I am the Lord; that is my name! I will not yield my glory to another or my praise to idols. [Isaiah 42:8]

This again is a very specific point in this prophecy. The whole of Arabia at the start of Muhammad's Prophethood consisted of idol worshippers. In fact, Muhammad's people, the Meccans, had 360 different idols for worship and each of these idols was thought to be taking care of a specific duty. The Qur'an talks about them in the following manner:

> **Say [O Muhammad] "who is the Lord of the heavens and the earth?" Say "God." Say "have you then taken [for worship] protectors other than Him, such as have no power either for benefit or for harm to themselves?" Say "is the blind equal to the one who sees? Or darkness equal to light? Or do they assign partners to God who created the like of His creation, so that the creation seem alike to them?" Say "God is the creator of all things; and He is the One, the Irresistible. [13:16]**

It is very clear in the verse above that God is condemning the idol worshippers and their attribution of divine qualities to carved wood and stone. The verse from **Isaiah 42** states that God will never give His glory to another and his praise will not be attributed to carved images. The Prophet of Islam was clearly facing people who had attributed the qualities of God to graven images and the Prophet's main task was to reclaim the glory of God to God alone.

This is less likely to be a reference to Jesus because, unlike Muhammad ﷺ whose lifetime opponents were primarily idol worshippers, Jesus's opponents during his ministry were the Jewish religious leaders, the Sadducees and Pharisees. His people, the Israelites, were monotheists and not idol worshippers. On one occasion, Jesus even told his disciples to stay away from the idol-worshipping Gentiles, the exact opposite of what Isaiah prophesied. The Gospel of Matthew tells us that: **"These twelve Jesus sent out with the following instructions: 'Do not go among the Gentiles...'" [Matthew 10:5]**

A Warrior Who Will Fight God's Enemies

Isaiah gives us a list of momentous achievements for God's servant. Chief of these is that:

"The Lord will march out like a champion, like a warrior he will stir up his zeal; with a shout he will raise the battle cry and will triumph over his enemies." [Isaiah 42:13]

Here Isaiah, in Biblical language, is asserting that the foretold servant will triumph against the enemies of God. Throughout history, God has dealt sternly with those who are sent guidance and persist in disbelief. If one was to pay little attention to the life of the Prophet of Islam, one will see, without a shadow of a doubt, that this prophecy was fulfilled with his arrival. The Prophet Muhammad ﷺ was sent as a "man of war" for those who opposed justice and mercy. He fought 27 battles in person and was victorious against all the enemies of God who fought him. They employed all possible means to destroy the Prophet but they failed, as God had promised to protect His messenger. In the battle of the ditch (also known as the battle of armies [Ahzab] owing to the participation of many tribes), over ten thousand men besieged Medina but they failed to defeat the Prophet and his companions. Islam was victorious and Islam endured. Historian Howard Johnston describes the triumph of Islam: *"Seldom, if ever, has a set of ideas had so great an effect on human societies as Islam has done, above all in the first half of the seventh century. In little more than twenty years, the religious and political configuration of Arabia was changed out of all recognition. Within another twenty all of the rich, highly developed, militarily powerful world enveloping Arabia was conquered, save for Asia Minor and North Africa." [141]*

By comparison, Jesus did not triumph over his enemies; according to Christians, he was crucified by them. Moreover, Jesus wasn't interested in fighting, he was not a man of war; he was a pacifist, according to the New Testament. He said such things as: *"for all who draw the sword will die by the sword." [Matthew 26:52]* and *"My kingdom is not of this world: if my kingdom were of this world, then would my servants fight..." [John 18:36]*.

Isaiah further states that the enemies of God mentioned earlier are in fact idol worshippers and that they will be defeated:

"But those who trust in idols, who say to images, 'You are our gods,' will be turned back in utter shame." [Isaiah 42:17]

There is a very clear reference to idol worshippers here. God is informing us that the idol worshipers will be shamed owing to their disbelief in the One true God, the God of Abraham, Moses, Jesus and Muhammad. The Prophet Muhammad ﷺ fought most of his battles against idolaters and they were eventually put to shame on the day of the conquest of Mecca when all 360 idols worshipped by the Meccans were destroyed. The idolaters lost their power forever and were utterly ashamed, with two thousand Meccans renouncing idol worship and embracing Islam. As we've already seen, it is this incident which was foretold in **Deuteronomy 33:2**, as the Prophet was accompanied by ten thousand men in this expedition and the law of Islam was presented to the people of Mecca. It was this city which contained the biggest idol worshipping establishment in Arabia. However, in just 23 years of Prophethood, it ceased to function as a centre of idolatry. Not only did the Prophet Muhammad ﷺ conquer Mecca, the pagan capital of Arabia, but by the end of his life much of Arabia had shunned idol worship and now worshipped the One true God of Abraham.

HOW EARLY MUSLIMS
VIEWED ISAIAH 42

If we examine the Islamic sources, the Qur'an and hadith, it seems that the early Muslims were made aware of the prophecy found in **Isaiah 42**, at least in its overall meaning, if not verbatim. For example, we find the following statement by a companion of the Prophet Muhammad ﷺ:

> *Ata bin Yasar reported: "I met Abdullah bin 'Amr bin al-'As and asked him, 'Tell me about the description of the Messenger of God which is mentioned in the Torah.'" He replied, "Yes. By God, he is mentioned in the Torah with his qualities found in the Qur'an as follows, O Prophet! We have sent you as a witness, and a giver of glad tidings, And a warner, and guardian of the illiterates. You are My servant and My Messenger. I have named you al-Mutawakkil (meaning 'one who depends upon God'). You are neither discourteous, harsh, nor a noise-maker in the markets; You do not do evil to those Who do evil to you, but you deal with them with forgiveness and kindness. God will not let him die till he makes upright the crooked people by making them say: None has the right to be worshipped but God, with which will be opened blind eyes, deaf ears and enveloped hearts." [142]*

If we compare this hadith to **Isaiah 42:1-3; 6-7,** you cannot help but notice the remarkable resemblance between them. I have highlighted in bold the portions that are similar:

HADITH	ISAIAH 42:1-3; 6-7
"You are My servant and My Messenger. I have named you al-Mutawakkil (meaning 'one who depends upon God')."	*Here is my servant, whom I uphold,* *my chosen one in whom I delight;* *I will put my Spirit on him,* *and he will bring justice to the nations.*
"...You are neither discourteous, harsh, nor a noise-maker in the markets"	**He will not shout or cry out,** **or raise his voice in the streets.**
"...You do not do evil to those Who do evil to you, but you deal With them with forgiveness and kindness."	*A bruised reed he will not break,* *and a smoldering wick he will not snuff out.* *In faithfulness he will bring forth justice;*
"...**God will not let him die** till he makes upright the crooked people"	*I, the Lord, have called you in righteousness;* ***I will take hold of your hand.*** ***I will keep you** and will make you to be a covenant for the people and a light for the Gentiles,*
"...**with which will be opened blind eyes,** deaf ears and enveloped hearts."	**to open eyes that are blind,** *to free captives from prison and to release from the dungeon those who sit in darkness.*

How the companions of the Prophet Muhammad ﷺ could have come to know of this prophecy in the Jewish Scriptures is an interesting question. The most probable answer is that they came to know of such prophecies from the Jewish converts to Islam, especially Rabbis such as Abdullah ibn Salaam and Ka'ab Al Ahbar [143] who were leading scholars of the Torah at the time of the Prophet Muhammad ﷺ.

If we examine the Qur'an, we also find an acknowledgement that the Prophet Muhammad ﷺ is found in the Jewish and Christian Scriptures:

Those who follow the Messenger, the unlettered prophet, whom they find written in what they have of the Torah and the Gospel, who enjoins upon them what is right and forbids them what is wrong and makes lawful for them the good things and prohibits for them the evil and relieves them of their burden and the shackles which were upon them. So they who have believed in him, honoured him, supported him and followed the light which was sent down with him – it is those who will be the successful. Say, [O Muhammad], "O mankind, indeed I am the Messenger of God to you all, [from Him] to whom belongs the dominion of the heavens and the earth. There is no deity except Him; He gives life and causes death." So believe in God and His Messenger, the unlettered prophet, who believes in God and His words, and follow him that you may be guided. [7:157-158]

When you compare these verses of the Qur'an to **Isaiah 42:4-7**, again you cannot help but notice the remarkable resemblance between them. I have highlighted in bold the portions that are similar:

QUR'AN 7:157-158	ISAIAH 42:4-7
"...who enjoins upon them what is right and forbids them what is wrong and makes lawful for them the good things and prohibits for them the evil"	he will not falter or be discouraged till he establishes justice on earth. In his teaching the islands will put their hope.
"...[from Him] to whom belongs the dominion of the heavens and the earth. There is no deity except Him; He gives life and causes death."	This is what God the Lord says— the Creator of the heavens, who stretches them out, who spreads out the earth with all that springs from it, who gives breath to its people, and life to those who walk on it:
"...Say, [O Muhammad], "O mankind, indeed I am the Messenger of God to you all"	"I, the Lord, have called you in righteousness; I will take hold of your hand. I will keep you and will make you to be a covenant for the people
"...and followed the light which was sent down with him – it is those who will be the successful."	and a light for the Gentiles
"...and relieves them of their burden and the shackles which were upon them."	to open eyes that are blind, to free captives from prison and to release from the dungeon those who sit in darkness."

COMMON OBJECTIONS TO ISAIAH ANSWERED

Some might raise the objection that the references in the Qur'an that associate Muhammad ﷺ with the Jewish Scriptures are in relation to the Torah, and **Isaiah 42** is not part of the Torah. It's true that, in its most limited sense, the Torah refers to the five Books of Moses (Genesis, Exodus, Leviticus, Numbers and Deuteronomy). However, in a broader sense, the Torah actually includes all Jewish law and tradition. The Hebrew word "torah" just means instruction or law, and so in Judaism it is also used in a general sense to refer to the entire Old Testament which includes Isaiah. Rabbi Alfred J. Kolatch informs us:

> **"In Jewish tradition the word 'Torah', which literally means 'teaching', is often used to describe the entire gamut of Jewish religious learning. When so used, 'Torah' refers not only to the five books of Moses, but also to the Prophets, Holy Writings, Talmud, and Midrash -- In fact all religious writings from earliest times to the present." [144]**

It's interesting to note that Jesus does exactly this in the New Testament: **"Jesus answered them, Is it not written in your law, I said, Ye are gods?" [John 10.34].** Here Jesus has quoted **Psalm 82:6** from the Old Testament: **"I said, 'You are "gods"; you are all sons of the Most High."** Clearly, Jesus refers to the Psalms of David as the Torah ('law'), even though technically it is not part of the five books of the Torah. In the same way, when the Qur'an and companions of the Prophet Muhammad ﷺ refer to the Torah, it is a reference to the complete collection of Scriptures that the Jews had in their possession at the time of Muhammad, which included the Book of Isaiah. So, for the sake of convenience, it is referred to as the Torah collectively.

Another objection might be that Muslims shouldn't be using prophecies like those found in Isaiah as we also make the claim that the Bible is corrupted. In other words, we can't have it both ways. Earlier in this book, we looked at the preservation of the New Testament and saw that there is strong evidence that the text we hold in our hands today has been changed over the centuries. However, this does not mean that we have to reject the entire Bible outright. We can use the Qur'an as a guide to help us identify the truth that remains within it. Recall that one of the names of the Qur'an is 'Al Furqan', meaning "the criterion between truth and falsehood". As such, the Qur'an represents the ultimate authority for truth. Earlier, we saw how it is the most reliable religious Scripture in existence today owing to its flawless preservation. This preservation, along with the numerous examples we've seen of its phenomenal insight into ancient history and the Scriptures of the past, are compelling arguments for the Qur'an's divine origins. Since the Qur'an is the pure, undistorted word of God, we can be certain that what it is says is correct. Hence, Muslims have no doubt that the Prophet Muhammad ﷺ is mentioned in the Bible because the Qur'an proclaims it.

THE PROBLEMATIC PORTRAYAL OF ISHMAEL IN THE BIBLE

Prophet Abraham is a pivotal figure in Judaism, Christianity and Islam, so much so that the three faiths are referred to as "Abrahamic faiths". Jews, Christians and Muslims believe that Abraham is the forefather of many great prophets. It is through his offspring that individuals such as Jacob, Moses, David and Solomon, arose. Abraham is not just significant from a spiritual perspective, but also a genealogical one. Arabs trace their lineage back to his first son Ishmael, who is considered the father of the Arabs, and Jews trace their lineage back to his second son Isaac, who is considered the father of the Jews.

Ishmael's story starts out very promisingly in the Old Testament. God promises to establish His covenant with all of Abraham's "seed" ('zera' in Hebrew) without exception:

> *I will establish my covenant as an everlasting covenant between me and you and your descendants after you for the generations to come, to be your God and the God of your descendants after you. [Genesis 17:7]*

God informs Abraham that the sign of the covenant shall be circumcision: *"This is my covenant with you and your descendants after you, the covenant you are to keep: Every male among you shall be circumcised."* *[Genesis 17:10]* We are told that Abraham immediately circumcised himself and Ishmael, thus establishing God's covenant with Ishmael:

> *On that very day Abraham took his son Ishmael and all those born in his household or bought with his money, every male in his household, and circumcised them, as God told him. [Genesis 17:23]*

We can see that the Bible sets up a promising picture for all of the offspring of Abraham. Strangely, Ishmael's story culminates in him and his mother being cast into a barren desert to the advantage of his brother Isaac:

> *and she said to Abraham, "Get rid of that slave woman and her son, for that woman's son will never share in the inheritance with my son Isaac." [Genesis 21:10]*

Strange still, we are told that Ishmael's crowning achievement will be that he will have many descendants:

> *And as for Ishmael, I have heard you: I will surely bless him; I will make him fruitful and will greatly increase his numbers. He will be the father of twelve rulers, and I will make him into a great nation. [Genesis 17:20]*

The picture presented by the Bible is that God's blessings amounted to nothing more than being successful at procreation. Did not disbelieving people, those outside of the lineage of Abraham and outside of the fold of the covenant, also make up large numbers and have great nations? Perhaps strangest of all, we are told that Ishmael would grow up to be "a wild donkey of a man":

> *He will be a wild donkey of a man; his hand will be against everyone and everyone's hand against him, and he will live in hostility toward all his brothers. [Genesis 16:12]*

Therefore, we can see that the Bible presents a greatly juxtaposed picture of Ishmael: on the one hand, he is included in the covenant of Abraham and told that he will be blessed by God, and on the other, an anti-climactic, and somewhat negative picture, is painted of him. Something does not quite add up here. You may be wondering to yourself, why does any of this matter? Well, the Bible's negative portrayal of Ishmael is a barrier for Christians and Jews to recognising that prophecies such as **Deuteronomy 33** and **Isaiah 42** are about the Prophet Muhammad ﷺ. This is due to misconceptions that Ishmael and his descendants have been excluded from God's covenant with Abraham, and therefore Isaac's descendants have a monopoly on Prophethood.

We will spend the remainder of this chapter clarifying such misconceptions about the family of Abraham. In doing so, we are going to uncover what is perhaps the biggest cover-up in the Bible, the role of Ishmael in God's plan of salvation for mankind.

THE GREAT COVER-UP: EVIDENCE OF TAMPERING IN THE BIBLICAL ACCOUNTS OF ISHMAEL AND ISAAC

Muslims believe in the original Scripture given to Moses:

Indeed, We sent down the Torah, in which was guidance and light... *[5:44]*

And when the anger subsided in Moses, he took up the tablets; and in their inscription was guidance and mercy for those who are fearful of their Lord. [7:154]

The verses of the Qur'an above show that it speaks of the original revelation given to Moses in an extremely positive light. The original Torah is described as being "guidance", "light" and a "mercy", just as all divinely inspired Scriptures are. The Qur'an also claims that the Israelites, who were entrusted with safeguarding the Torah, were responsible for corrupting it:

> **So woe to those who write the "scripture" with their own hands, then say, "This is from God," in order to exchange it for a small price. Woe to them for what their hands have written and woe to them for what they earn. [2:79]**

Muslims believe that the reason for the Bible's juxtaposed portrayal of Ishmael and Isaac can be explained by human tampering of the Bible. Is this just a conspiracy theory? Is it wishful thinking on the part of Muslims? The Qur'an presents an important principle in evaluating whether a scripture really is from God. The Qur'an tells us that if a scripture is not from God, then you will find therein much discrepancy: **"Then do they not reflect upon the Qur'an? If it had been from [any] other than God, they would have found within it much contradiction" [4:82].** We find that when we scrutinise the stories of Ishmael and Isaac in the Bible we have today, many inconsistencies emerge, a tell-tale sign of human tampering, just as the Qur'an proclaims.

1. Who was the son of sacrifice?

Like the Qur'an, the Bible tells us that God tested Abraham with the sacrifice of his son. Unlike the Qur'an, the Bible makes the claim that it was Isaac to be sacrificed and not Ishmael:

> **Then God said, "Take your son, your only son, whom you love—Isaac—and go to the region of Moriah. Sacrifice him there as a burnt offering on a mountain I will show you." [Genesis 22:2]**

Not only does the Bible contradict the Qur'an, but it also contradicts itself. Notice the words **"your only son"**. Why does Genesis specifically refer to Ishmael as Abraham's progeny in one place and then refer to Isaac as his "only son" in another place? The sacrificial son cannot have been Isaac, for the simple fact that Isaac was Ishmael's younger brother and was therefore never Abraham's only son. Such a description can only apply to Ishmael who was around 13 years older than Isaac.

The claim that it must have originally referred to Ishmael is reinforced when we examine the Hebrew of the text. The Hebrew word 'yachid', translated as "only son" in the verse above, actually means "only begotten", according to the Gesenius Hebrew lexicon:

Gesenius' Hebrew-Chaldee Lexicon

יָחִיד m. יְחִידָה f. (from יָחַד).—(1) *only*, especially *only begotten, only child,* Gen. 22:2, 12, 16; Jer. 6: 26; Zec. 12:10; Pro. 4:3; and fem. יְחִידָה Jud. 11:34.

(2) *solitary;* hence forsaken, wretched, Ps. 25: 16; 68:7.

(3) f. יְחִידָה *only one,* hence that which is most dear, that which cannot be replaced, poet. for *life,* Ps. 22:21; 35:17; [does not this pervert both the passages?] comp. בָּבוֹר.

Clearly, Isaac was at no point Abraham's "only begotten" son; Ishmael is the only one who fits such a description. This understanding of the text is supported by the New Testament, where Paul quotes the verse from Genesis:

By faith Abraham, when he was tried, offered up Isaac: and he that had received the promises offered up his only begotten son. [Hebrews 11:17]

The Greek word that Paul uses, 'monogenes', carries the meaning of "only begotten", according to Strong's dictionary:

Strong's Definitions [?] (Strong's Definitions Legend)

μονογενής monogenés, mon-og-en-ace'; from G3441 and G1096; only-born, i.e. sole:—only (begotten, child).

There are some who make the claim that Ishmael was not a legitimate son of Abraham, an accusation that is demonstrably false from a number of different angles:

– The Bible itself bears witness to the fact that Ishmael was Abraham's son:

On that very day <u>Abraham took his son Ishmael</u> and all those born in his household or bought with his money, every male in his

household, and circumcised them, as God told him. [Genesis 17:23]

– Some claim that Ishmael is a "lesser" son than Isaac because his mother, Hagar, was a slave woman. This is not the case according to the Bible:

> *So after Abram [Abraham] had been living in Canaan ten years, Sarai his wife took her Egyptian slave Hagar and gave her to her husband to be his wife. [Genesis 16:3]*

So, the Bible confirms that Hagar was Abraham's legitimate wife. Were Ishmael an illegitimate child, as some Christians and Jews allege, then that would imply that Abraham had an illegitimate relationship with Hagar, a serious accusation indeed! From all the evidence, we can see that Abraham undoubtedly had a legitimate relationship with Hagar, and so Ishmael was a legitimate son.

– Moreover, the Bible tells us that Ishmael remained the legitimate son of Abraham until even after Abraham's death:

> *Then Abraham breathed his last and died at a good old age, an old man and full of years; and he was gathered to his people. His sons Isaac and Ishmael buried him in the cave of Machpelah near Mamre, in the field of Ephron son of Zohar the Hittite. [Genesis 25:8-9]*

Clearly, Ishmael is every bit the legitimate son of Abraham, just as Isaac is. Now, there is a variant in the manuscript tradition of the Old Testament that makes it even more explicit that Ishmael was to be sacrificed, not Isaac. One of the great Muslim exegetes of the Qur'an, Ibn Kathir (born c. 1300 CE), argued that the Old Testament was corrupted by changing the sacrificial son from Ishmael to Isaac. In his book Tafsir Ibn Kathir, he states the following when explaining the meaning of chapter 37 of the Qur'an:

> *"My Lord, grant me [a child] from among the righteous." So We gave him good tidings of a forbearing boy. [37:100-101]*

> *(So We gave him the glad tidings of a forbearing boy.) This child was Ishmael, peace be upon him, for he was the first child of whom glad tidings were given to Ibrahim [Abraham], peace be upon him,*

and he was older than Ishaq [Isaac]. The Muslims and the People of the Book agree, and indeed it is stated in their Book, that Ishmael, peace be upon him, was born when Ibrahim, peace be upon him, was eighty-six years old, and Isaac was born when Ibrahim was ninety-nine years old. According to their Book, Allah commanded Ibrahim to sacrifice his only son, and in another text it says his firstborn son. But here they falsely inserted the name of Isaac. This is not right because it goes against what their own Scripture says. They inserted the name of Isaac because he is their ancestor, while Ishmael is the ancestor of the Arabs. They were jealous of them, so they added this idea and changed the meaning of the phrase "only son" to mean `the only son who is with you,' because Ishmael had been taken with his mother to Mecca. But this is a case of falsification and distortion, because the words "only son" cannot be said except in the case of one who has no other son. Furthermore, the firstborn son has a special status that is not shared by subsequent children, so the command to sacrifice him is a more exquisite test.

This suggests that perhaps Ibn Kathir was aware of a variant "firstborn son" in the Old Testament tradition that was possibly in circulation during his time in the fourteenth century. Such a reading makes it even more explicit that it was Ishmael that was to be sacrificed, as he was 13 years older than Isaac and thus Abraham's firstborn. The Dead Sea Scrolls, a collection of texts discovered between 1946 and 1956 inside caves near the Dead Sea, support Ibn Kathir's claims about the Old Testament. These texts are of great religious significance because they include the earliest known surviving manuscripts of the Old Testament. The scrolls date from approximately 150 BCE – 70 CE. One of the books found in the Dead Sea Scrolls was the Book of Jubilees which is another version of Genesis. This book mentions the words "firstborn son" in relation to the one to be sacrificed by Abraham [145]:

And I said unto him: 'Lay not thy hand upon the lad, neither do thou anything to him; for now I have shown that thou fearest the Lord, and hast not withheld thy son, thy first-born son, from me.' [18:11]

Therefore, the claim by Ibn Kathir is remarkable, when we consider that he was writing in the fourteenth century, nearly 7 centuries before the discovery of the Dead Sea Scrolls. For him to be aware of such a variant must mean that the Book of Jubilees was being widely circulated and considered a valid book of the Old Testament. In fact, even today there are Christians who consider the Book of Jubilees to be canonical; the Ethiopian Orthodox Church, for example, includes it in their Bible, as do Ethiopian Jews who refer to the book as "The Book of Division".

In summary, evidence suggests that the Old Testament scribes altered the story in Genesis by swapping the name "Ishmael" for "Isaac" in order to make Isaac the son of sacrifice. Why would they do such a thing? We find an answer in the recorded sayings of the Prophet Muhammad's ﷺ companions. In the following narration, we are given an answer to this question by a Jewish scholar who converted to Islam and was alive at the time of the Prophet Muhammad ﷺ:

> **Then he [Umar, the commander of the Muslims] sent for a man who was with him in Syria, a Jew who had become a Muslim and was committed to Islam, and he thought that he had been one of their scholars.**
>
> **Umar said to him, "Which of the two sons of Abraham was he commanded to sacrifice?"**
>
> **He [the convert Jewish scholar] said, "Ishmael. By God, O Commander of the faithful, the Jews know this, but they were jealous of you Arabs because it was your father about whom God issued this command and the virtue that God mentioned was because of his patience in obeying the command. So they denied that and claimed that it was Isaac, because he is their father." [146]**

2. The age of Ishmael when he was cast into the desert.

There is a story in Genesis where Ishmael is portrayed as a bully to his younger brother Isaac and, as a consequence, Ishmael and his mother Hagar are cast out of Abraham's household into the desert. Now, this entire episode is odd for a number of reasons. The reaction by Isaac's mother Sarah is extreme, for casting Hagar and Ishmael into the barren desert is effectively a death sentence. Even stranger yet is that the details of the story seem to contradict the age of Ishmael. It is clear from the account of Genesis that Ishmael was a young child, perhaps a baby, when he was condemned to the desert:

Early the next morning Abraham took some food and a skin of water and gave them to Hagar. He set them on her shoulders and then sent her off with the boy. She went on her way and wandered in the Desert of Beersheba.

When the water in the skin was gone, she put the boy under one of the bushes.

Then she went off and sat down about a bowshot away, for she thought, "I cannot watch the boy die." And as she sat there, she began to sob.

God heard the boy crying, and the angel of God called to Hagar from heaven and said to her, "What is the matter, Hagar? Do not be afraid; God has heard the boy crying as he lies there. Lift the boy up and take him by the hand, for I will make him into a great nation."

Then God opened her eyes and she saw a well of water. So she went and filled the skin with water and gave the boy a drink. [Genesis 21:14-19]

It is possible to calculate the approximate age of Ishmael when he was sent into the desert with his mother. According to **Genesis 16:16,** Abraham was 86 years old when Ishmael was born:

Abram was eighty-six years old when Hagar bore him Ishmael.

And, according to **Genesis 21:5,** Abraham was one hundred years old when Isaac was born:

Abraham was a hundred years old when his son Isaac was born to him.

It follows that Ishmael was already thirteen years old when his younger brother Isaac was born. According to **Genesis 21:8-10,** the desert incident took place after Isaac was weaned:

> *The child grew and was weaned, and on the day Isaac was weaned Abraham held a great feast. But Sarah saw that the son whom Hagar the Egyptian had borne to Abraham was mocking, and she said to Abraham, "Get rid of that slave woman and her son..."*

According to tradition, Isaac was two years old when he was weaned. Three years is the Biblical age of weaning mentioned in **2 Chronicles 31:16** and **2 Maccabees 7:27**. Thus, it follows that when Hagar and Ishmael were taken away, Ishmael was a fully-grown teenager, around fifteen or sixteen years old. The problem is that the profile of Ishmael in **Genesis 21:14-19** is a small child and not a fully-grown teenager:

- Remember that it is Hagar that carried all the supplies into the desert **(Genesis 21:14)**. If Ishmael were a teenager, then surely Abraham would have made him carry at least some of the supplies to lessen the burden on his mother.

- She put the boy under the bush **(Genesis 21:15)**. Now the original Hebrew used is the word 'shalak' which has the meaning "to throw, cast, hurl, fling", according to Strong's Hebrew Lexicon. One does not "throw", "cast", "hurl" or "fling" a teenager, especially when one is an old woman and suffering from the fatigue of a harsh desert environment.

- Even though it was Ishmael who was crying, God consoles the mother **(Genesis 21:17)**. This could be taken to imply that Ishmael was too young to converse with.

- Hagar is asked to lift up the boy **(Genesis 21:18)**. Again, one would not expect a woman suffering from the fatigue of a harsh desert environment to be able to lift up a fully-grown teenager.

Finally, it's worth mentioning that the Septuagint version of the Old Testament has the following for **Genesis 21:14**:

> *And Abraham rose up in the morning and took loaves and a skin of*

water, and gave them to Agar, and he put the child on her shoulder, and sent her away, and she having departed wandered in the wilderness near the well of the oath.

There is simply no way that a woman would be able to carry both the supplies and a fully-grown teenager on her shoulders, so the Septuagint is even more explicit in conveying that Ishmael was a young child when he was sent into the desert.

Furthermore, the proof of Ishmael's actual age can be established from the use of Hebrew in the text. The Hebrew word used to describe Ishmael in the desert incident is 'yeled', translated by the New International Version of the Bible as "boy" in **Genesis 21:15**. Yet, within the same chapter, in **Genesis 21:8,** when the same Hebrew word is used to refer to the 2-year old Isaac, it is translated as "child":

Genesis 21:15	Genesis 21:8
When the water in the skin was gone, she put the boy [yeled] under one of the bushes.	The child [yeled] grew and was weaned, and on the day Isaac was weaned Abraham held a great feast.

Why is the same Hebrew word translated differently within the same chapter? If there is any lingering doubt as to the real meaning of the word, we should consider that it is almost exclusively used in the Bible to literally describe young children or infants. Examples of its usage in the Bible are in the following passages:

But when she could hide him no longer, she got a papyrus basket for him and coated it with tar and pitch. Then she placed the child in it and put it among the reeds along the bank of the Nile. [Exodus 2:3]

Then Naomi took the child in her arms and cared for him. The women living there said, "Naomi has a son!" And they named him Obed. He was the father of Jesse, the father of David. [Ruth 4:16-17]

When we look at the Jewish Rabbinical tradition, it is clear that the word refers to a child, specifically one who is less than 13 years of age. In the commentary on **Ecclesiastes 4:13,** the famous Rabbi Rashi, who authored a comprehensive commentary on the Old Testament, explains that any boy less than 13 years of age was considered a child, whereas anyone 13 years or older was considered a man: *"...why is it called a child? Because it does not enter man until thirteen years."* [147]

From all of the evidence, it is clear that the outcast Ishmael was a helpless infant, rather than an able-bodied teenager; thus, the account in **Genesis 21** is chronologically wrong. The claim that Ishmael mocked Isaac and that this had anything to do with Hagar's exile is an obvious fabrication, since Isaac was not even born yet when this story occurred as Ishmael was still a baby. The Interpreter's Bible compares the texts of **Genesis 21:14-19** with **Genesis 16:1-16** and concludes that they are sufficiently different to be inconsistent:

> *The inclusion in Genesis of both stories so nearly alike and yet sufficiently different to be inconsistent, is one of the many instances of the reluctance of the compilers to sacrifice any of the traditions which has become established in Israel.*

Contrast this account of the desert incident from the Bible with the version of the story narrated by the Prophet Muhammad ﷺ :

> *"Abraham brought her (Hagar) and her son Ishmael while she was suckling him, to a place near the Ka'ba under a tree on the spot of Zam-zam, at the highest place in the mosque. During those days there was nobody in Mecca, nor was there any water. So he made them sit over there and placed near them a leather bag containing some dates, and a small water-skin containing some water, and set out homeward. Ishmael's mother followed him saying, "O Abraham! Where are you going, leaving us in this valley where there is no person whose company we may enjoy, nor is there anything (to enjoy)?" She repeated that to him many times, but he did not look back at her. Then she asked him, "Has God ordered you to do so?" He said, "Yes." She said, "Then He will not neglect us, ..."* [148]

So not only do Islamic sources have the correct age of Ishmael, he is a baby, but the reason for them being cast out into the desert is a test by God, similar to Abraham being commanded to sacrifice his son, rather than the jealous whims of Sarah as put forth by the Bible. Evidently, the Biblical account is chronologically flawed and self-contradictory, whereas the Islamic tradition is consistent.

3. Tarnishing the reputation of Ishmael.

In the Bible, Ishmael is described in rather unflattering terms:

> *He will be a wild donkey of a man; his hand will be against everyone and everyone's hand against him, and he will live in hostility toward all his brothers." [Genesis 16:12]*

This verse does not fit the context of the chapter of Genesis, as, in the verses that precede this, we are told that an angel of the Lord met Hagar and gave her the good news that God was going to bless her and her offspring. Her descendants would be so many that they would be innumerable. Her child would be a boy, and she was to name him Ishmael (meaning "God hears"), because God had indeed listened to Hagar's sorrowful cries in her affliction:

> *The angel added, "I will increase your descendants so much that they will be too numerous to count." The angel of the Lord also said to her: "You are now pregnant and you will give birth to a son. You shall name him Ishmael, for the Lord has heard of your misery." [Genesis 16:10-11]*

So, doesn't it seem rather odd that in the very next verse, the angel abruptly starts talking in a derogatory way about the child he has just named "God hears" and promised to be blessed greatly, by calling him *"a wild donkey of a man"*, that *"his hand will be against everyone and everyone's hand against him"*, and that *"he will live in hostility toward all his brothers"*? Saying that Ishmael would be a "wild donkey" who would be constantly at odds with everyone else sounds like a strange fulfilment of God's promise to bless Ishmael. Such a fate for anyone is surely a curse, rather than a blessing.

But this dilemma of the abrupt switch from 'blessing' to 'cursing' is easily solved when it is understood that the Hebrew word used for "wild donkey", transliterated to pereh or pere' in English letters, is very similar to another Hebrew word, para', which means "fruitful". Is there any evidence for this or is it pure speculation? It turns out that the same promise by the angel is repeated later in **Genesis 17** and, in this chapter, it is the Hebrew word para' ("fruitful") that is used:

> **And as for Ishmael, I have heard thee: behold, I have blessed him, and will make him fruitful, and will multiply him exceedingly; twelve princes shall he beget, and I will make him a great nation. [Genesis 17:20]**

So, even though it's a different word in Hebrew, it shows that the intended meaning of **Genesis 16:12** in the original text was in fact "fruitful", not "wild donkey", which fits the context of the chapter perfectly. It seems that whoever changed the word from "fruitful" to "wild donkey" in **Genesis 16:12** forgot to do so here in **Genesis 17:20**! The word 'fruitful' obviously fits very nicely in the context of the chapter – it doesn't stand at odds with the surrounding verses. The angel had just promised Hagar an innumerable number of descendants, so it would be very appropriate to describe him as a 'fruitful' man.

Let's move onto the next part of **Genesis 16:12** which makes the claim that **"his hand will be against everyone and everyone's hand against him, and he will live in hostility toward all his brothers"**. Again, in the context in which Ishmael is to be blessed by God, it's very strange that the angel would abruptly say that this man who is blessed by God will be antagonistic to everyone, and vice versa. The word which is translated "against" **("his hand will be against everyone and everyone's hand against him")** is a single consonant in Hebrew. Langenscheidt's dictionary says the following concerning the meaning of this word:

> **"in, at, to, on, among, with, towards; according to, by, because of."**

It is the context of the verse which determines how we should translate the word and whether it carries a positive or negative meaning. As we will now discuss, in the context of **Genesis 16:12**, the positive meaning of "with" or "towards" would appear to be a more appropriate translation than the negative meaning "against". There is absolutely nothing in the context of **Genesis 16:12** that would indicate it should have the negative meaning of "against". The only reason it would be read that way is because of prejudice against Ishmael. In summary, when we consider the context of the verse, an alternative, and perhaps even more accurate, translation of **Genesis 16:12** would be:

> *"He will be a fruitful man: his hand shall be with everyone, and every man's hand shall be with him..."*

What was at the outset a very negative picture about Ishmael has now become a very positive one. Compare the difference between the two readings of **Genesis 16:12**:

"He will be a wild donkey of a man; his hand will be against everyone and everyone's hand against him..."	*"He will be a fruitful man: his hand shall be with everyone, and every man's hand shall be with him..."*

Is there any scriptural backing for such a reading of the verse? It just so happens that this exact reading can be found in another version of Genesis found in the Samaritan Torah [149]:

> *"He will be fertile of man. His hand will be with everyone. And everyone's hand will be with him. And he will live among all his brothers."*

The Samaritan version of the Torah is written in the Samaritan alphabet which is derived from the paleo-Hebrew alphabet used by the Israelite community prior to the Babylonian captivity. The Samaritans represent a sect of Judaism that split off from the mainstream. There are still a few hundred Samaritans living in modern-day Israel.

THE QUR'AN GIVES THE CORRECT UNDERSTANDING OF ISHMAEL

Ishmael's story in the Qur'an begins with a supplication by Abraham. His call on God for a righteous child is greeted with the glad tidings of a special son: ***"My Lord, grant me [a child] from among the righteous." So We gave him good tidings of a forbearing boy [37:100-101].*** Similarly for Isaac, God makes a promise to Abraham: ***"And We gave him good tidings of Isaac..." [37:112].*** We see a fulfilment of these promises in the Prophethood of Ishmael and Isaac:

> ***Say, [O believers], "We have believed in God and what has been revealed to us and what has been revealed to Abraham and Ishmael and Isaac and Jacob and the Descendants and what was given to Moses and Jesus and what was given to the prophets from their Lord..." [2:136]***

From this verse we can see that both Ishmael and Isaac were blessed with the greatest station that a human being can attain: Prophethood. We can see that the stories presented by the Qur'an about both sons are coherent; all of God's promises to Abraham are fulfilled by their Prophethood.

Now, notice what the Qur'an doesn't say. The glad tidings that God gave to Abraham wouldn't make sense, had the Qur'an gone on to say that Isaac was raised to be an evil man, or that his greatest achievement was a worldly, materialistic affair such as being wealthy. This is not to say that wealth isn't a blessing. However, from the point of view of Isaac's father and one of the great Prophets of God, Abraham, this promise of God could only mean one thing: a great spiritual blessing, rather than material blessing, a son who would follow in his noble footsteps.

We can see that the picture painted by the Qur'an with regard to Ishmael and Isaac is coherent: God's glad tidings of Ishmael and Isaac are fulfilled by both of them becoming great Prophets of God. Readers might be interested to know that the Qur'an mentions Isaac a total of 17 times, and Ishmael a total of 12 times. This is a remarkable point if we reflect on it. For the sake of argument, if the Qur'an were nothing more than an invention of the mind of the Prophet Muhammad ﷺ, or had it been tampered with by those who were first tasked with preserving it, i.e. the Arabs, then one has to wonder why Isaac is mentioned more times than Ishmael. Given the tribalistic nature of Arabian society and the importance they placed on lineage, wouldn't you expect the focus to be on Ishmael, the forefather of the Arabs, over that of Isaac, the forefather of the Jewish people? Would it be unreasonable to expect their nationalism to leak into the pages of the Qur'an by playing down Isaac's importance, or even for his character to be attacked? Yet, what we find is the complete opposite: both Isaac and Ishmael are glorified as great Prophets. Thus, the Qur'an is perfectly harmonious in its telling of the stories of Ishmael and Isaac.

By contrast, a careful analysis of the Bible's stories about Ishmael reveals irreconcilable contradictions and prejudiced readings in the text. No doubt, Jewish and Christian apologists have gone to great lengths to explain these problems, but an objective analysis can only lead to one conclusion: these inconsistencies are real and cannot be resolved by mental gymnastics. Since God is perfect, then it stands to reason that His true revelation is perfect, too. We must conclude that the issues present in the Biblical account are not the words of a perfect God. Rather, the best explanation appears to be that the original stories about Ishmael have been corrupted by human hands and passed off as "scripture", exactly as the Qur'an reveals.

It's important to mention that these issues with the Biblical narrative have been raised not to upset or offend the reader, but rather to arrive at the truth. Without the correct bearings, it's impossible for one to navigate and arrive at the correct destination. Likewise, with Biblical prophecy, without the correct foundation, one will not be able to correctly interpret Scripture. Many Jews and Christians write off Muhammad ﷺ because they cannot accept the possibility of an Arabian Prophet owing to their misunderstanding about the role of Ishmael as portrayed in the Bible. We've seen that, far from the door of Prophethood being shut on Ishmael, it is in fact wide open for him and his descendants in God's plan of salvation for mankind. Furthermore, the examples we've looked at in **Deuteronomy 33** and **Isaiah 42** which proclaim the coming of an Arabian Prophet, only serve to confirm this understanding

---

BEING FAIR AND BALANCED IN ASSESSING PROPHECIES

The idea that the Bible contains prophecies about the coming of Muhammad ﷺ surprises many people. It isn't difficult to understand why, since the general perception people have of Muhammad ﷺ is that of a man with no connection to biblical Prophets or prophecies. However, taking a closer look at Muhammad's life, it becomes clear that he upheld the basic tenets that the biblical Prophets came with. Indeed, it is because of the teachings of Muhammad ﷺ that billions of Muslims, since his time and until today, have revered the persons of Jesus, Moses and Abraham. Isn't this exactly the kind of legacy we would expect of Muhammad ﷺ were he a genuine Prophet of God?

Sadly, in my experience there are people who won't even contemplate the possibility of Muhammad ﷺ being foretold in the Bible, no matter how much evidence is provided, and no matter how many misconceptions are corrected. Those who reject the notion often do so for no other reason than that it's not what they expect. We should be fair and balanced when evaluating Jesus and Muhammad ﷺ; doing so is a sign of one's sincerity in seeking the truth. There are many vague prophecies that Christians take and apply to Jesus. If Christians have no issue accepting such standards for Jesus, then in the name of fairness and consistency they should adopt at least a similar standard for Muhammad ﷺ. As we have seen, however, the evidence for Muhammad ﷺ in **Deuteronomy 33** and **Isaiah 42** is clear and unambiguous by comparison. We should adopt a methodology that is fair and consistent when it comes to finding prophecies of Jesus and Muhammad ﷺ in the Old Testament. We can't have one set of standards for Muhammad ﷺ, and another for Jesus.

The main proof of Muhammad's Prophethood is the miraculous Qur'an which was revealed by God to him through the angel Gabriel. God Almighty also provided additional proof to mankind for his Prophethood which can be found in other Scriptures, such as the Bible. As we've seen, the Old Testament clearly foretells the coming of a special person with the following qualities:

- *He will be God's servant and associated with the Arabian cities of Mecca and Medina,*

- *He will be accompanied by ten thousand saints and a fiery law,*

- *He will be a warrior who will battle with an idolatrous people,*

- *He will bring light to the Gentiles,*

- *He will spread peace and justice in the world.*

In the thousands of years since these prophecies were foretold in **Deuteronomy 33** and **Isaiah 42,** which personality in history can such things be attributed to? It can be none other than Muhammad ﷺ; the successor to Jesus and the Seal of the Prophets.

SOME FINAL THOUGHTS

Today, churches teach that the Creator became His creation in order to condemn Himself to a humiliating death on the cross. Throughout this book, we've seen that the concept of a divine, crucified Messiah who abolished the Law of Moses is at odds with everything that is taught in the Old Testament. As a consequence, Jesus has long been a stumbling block to the Jewish people recognising him as the Messiah. It shouldn't have been this way, as we've also seen that the original message of Jesus was perfectly in line with the Prophets of old like Abraham and Moses.

God, out of His mercy, did not leave mankind in a state of confusion. The Qur'an was revealed and unravels centuries of myth-making around Jesus and, in the process, bridges this millennia-old Judeo-Christian divide. Therefore, the Qur'an unites the three Great Abrahamic faiths, not by revolutionising the person of Jesus, but rather by restoring his original message. The Qur'an is not a radical departure from these other messages, but rather a continuation of the message and teachings that God has revealed throughout time. The core message of the Qur'an does not differ except in one important regard: the message given to the Prophet Muhammad ﷺ was intended by God to be universal, whereas the messages given to other Prophets were localised.

This fact is reflected in the nature of the miracles that God gave to His Prophets. The miracles of Moses, such as the parting of the sea, and the miracles of Jesus, such as the healing of the sick, are not signs that we can witness for ourselves today. This shows that these Prophets were localised, in the sense that they were only meant for a specific time and place in history. With the advent of the final Prophet, Muhammad ﷺ, a miracle that could only be witnessed and experienced by a single generation would not be sufficient. Rather, God gave him a miracle that was universal, one that could be experienced by people of all times and places so that it can be continually examined and experienced by later generations until the Day of Judgement. Prophet Muhammad's ﷺ miracle is the Qur'an, and it is a sign that is timeless because its miracle is intrinsic to the message itself.

During the course of this book, we've covered many incredible aspects of the Qur'an, such as its pure and clear concept of God's nature, its insight into the crucifixion and unique standing as the only flawlessly preserved book of revelation that survives to the present day. When all of these factors are combined together, they represent compelling evidence for the divine origins of the Qur'an. Yet, what we've seen only represents the tip of the iceberg. There is so much to the Qur'an that no other book can do it justice. Whatever is said or written about the Qur'an will always fall short in describing and exploring its words and their meanings: ***"Say [Prophet], 'If the whole ocean were ink for writing the words of my Lord, it would run dry before those words were exhausted'– even if We were to add another ocean to it"*** ***[18:109].*** The Qur'an is a miracle which, without doubt, has to have come from God. Since the Qur'an is God's message to mankind, then it stands to reason that Muhammad ﷺ is God's Messenger, since he was the one given the message.

At the heart of the Qur'an is a very simple, but profound, message: that there is nothing worthy of worship except God Almighty, and that Muhammad ﷺ is His Messenger. Abraham, Moses and Jesus, peace be upon them all, are also God's Messengers. Islam teaches us to have a direct relationship with God. It reminds us that since God created us, no-one should be worshipped except God alone. It also teaches that God is nothing like a human being or like anything that we can imagine. This is the core belief of every Muslim. The word "Muslim" simply means somebody who is doing Islam. "Islam", in the Arabic language, means somebody who submits to God. Although Islam is the youngest of the Abrahamic faiths, it is not something new. In fact, Muslims believe that Jesus himself was a Muslim as he submitted to God and came with a message of submission. The only way to truly follow Jesus, and all of God's Messengers for that matter, is to be a Muslim. Muslims are the true followers of Jesus and all the Messengers, as (thanks to the Qur'an) we have access to and follow their true, undistorted messages.

This is why those who choose to become Muslim do not abandon Jesus, but rather return to his original teachings. Guidance is from God alone, but the sincerity to acknowledge and worship Him comes from our own free will. I invite you to submit to your Creator by embracing the original message of

Jesus. In order to become a Muslim and enter the fold of Islam, one has to simply confess in their heart and utter with their tongue the following declaration of faith:

I am a witness that there is nothing worthy of worship except God Almighty, and that Muhammad is His Messenger (or in Arabic: "Ash shadu an laa il laaha il Allah wa ash hadu anna Muhammadan rasul lu lah").

You can get support as a new Muslim by contacting "Muslim Now":

www.muslimnow.com

May God's peace, blessings and guidance be upon you.

REFERENCES

1 – James White, "Loving the Trinity," Christian Research Journal, vol. 21, no. 22.

2 – Catechism of the Catholic Church, no. 234.

3 – The Catholic Encyclopedia, Constitution, "De fide. cath.", iv.

4 – Harold Lindsell and Charles Woodbridge, A Handbook of Christian Truth, pp. 51-52.

5 – Ehrman, Bart D., The Orthodox Corruption of Scripture: the effect of early Christological controversies on the text of the NT; New York, Oxford: Oxford University Press, 1993, p. 48.

6 – Tertullian, Against Praxeas, chapter 9 – The Catholic Rule of Faith Expounded in Some of Its Points. Especially in the Unconfused Distinction of the Several Persons of the Blessed Trinity.

7 – Ibid., chapter 3 – Sundry Popular Fears and Prejudices. The Doctrine of the Trinity in Unity Rescued from These Misapprehensions.

8 – W. H. C. Frend, The Rise of Christianity, p. 636.

9 – Mansi, III, col. 560.

10 – Alister E. McGrath, A Life of John Calvin: A Study in the Shaping of Western Culture, 1990, pp. 118-120.

11 – Keith Hopkins, A World Full of Gods: The Strange Triumph of Christianity, p. 191

12 – W. H. C. Frend, The Rise of Christianity, p. 319.

13 – R. Gerberding and J. H. Moran Cruz, Medieval Worlds (New York: Houghton Mifflin Company, 2004) pp. 55–56.

14 – Diarmaid MacCulloch, A History of Christianity, p. 214.

15 – Emperor Constantine as quoted in History of the Christian Church, vol. 3, p. 626.

16 – Philip Schaff, History of the Christian Church, Volume 3, pp. 627-628.

17 – Diarmaid MacCulloch, A History of Christianity, p. 214.

18 – Catechism of the Catholic Church, Joseph Cardinal Ratzinger, p. 74.

19 – Encyclopedia Britannica 14th ed., vol. 16, pp. 410-411.

20 – Richard E. Rubenstein, When Jesus Became God, p. 83.

21 – Brown HOJ. Heresies: Heresy and Orthodoxy in the History of the Church. Hendrickson Publishers, Peabody (MA), 1988, pp. 332 – 333.

22 – Ammianus Marcellinus, as cited by Schaff, History of the Christian Church (Grand Rapids: Eerdmans, 1985), III:632.

23 – Charles D. Levy, The Arian Christian Doctrines: The Origins of Christianity, p. 78.

24 – The New Catholic Encyclopedia, 1967, Vol. 1. Arianism, by V.C. Declercq, p. 793.

25 – Catechism of the Catholic Church. Imprimatur Potest, Joseph Cardinal Ratzinger. Doubleday, p. 72.

26 – Harold Brown, Heresies: Heresy and Orthodoxy in the History of the Church, p. 140.

27 – Theodosian Code XVI.1.2. Cited in Bettenson H, ed., Documents of the Christian Church, London: Oxford University Press, 1943, p. 31.

28 – Roberts JM. Antiquity Unveiled: Ancient Voices from the Spirit Realms Disclose the Most Startling Revelations, Proving Christianity to be of Heathen Origin, University of Michigan, May 21, 2007, p. 468.

29 – Grudem, Systematic Theology: Chapter 26 – The Person of Christ, 1994, p. 554.

30 – The Catholic Encyclopedia, "De pud.", xxi.

31 – Bruce Metzger and Michael D. Coogan (eds.), The Oxford Companion to the Bible (Oxford University Press, 1993) pp. 782 – 783.

32 – Origen, Commentary on John, Book II, chapter 2.

33 – Homilies on John, tractate CV, chapter 17.

34 – Eusebius, Book III of his History, Chapter 5, Section 2.

35 – Bruce Metzger and Michael D. Coogan (eds.), The Oxford Companion to the Bible (Oxford University Press, 1993) pp. 782-783.

36 – The New Catholic Encyclopedia – vol. 14, p. 295.

37 - New Bible Dictionary, Grand Rapids, MI, 1975, p. 559.

38 – See article by Don Stewart, BlueLetterBible.Org (accessed 22/11/2015): https://www.blueletterbible.org/faq/don_stewart/don_stewart_1203.cfm

39 – John William Charles Wand. 1955. The Four Great Heresies, p. 39.

40 – Justin Martyr, The First Apology, Chapter 21.

41 - Dr. H Wolfson, The Philosophy of the Church Fathers, pp. 361-363.

42 – Angelos Chaniotis, The Ithyphallic Hymn for Demetrios Poliorcetes and Hellenistic Religious Mentality, p. 160.

43 – Iris Sulimani, Diodorus' Mythistory and the Pagan Mission: Historiography and Culture, p. 288.

44 – Hans-Josef Klauck, Religious Context of Early Christianity: A Guide To Graeco-Roman Religions, p. 296

45 – Walter Kasper, The Petrine ministry: Catholics and Orthodox in dialogue: academic symposium held at the Pontifical Council for Promoting Christian Unity, p. 188.

46 – Tirmidhi, vol. 4, book 13, Hadith #2597.

47 – The Life of Muhammad, A Translation of Ishaq's Sirat Rasul Allah, translation by A. Guillaume, 2004, pp. 151 – 152.

48 – Sahih Bukhari, Hadith #1229.

49 – Tirmidhi, Hadith #2641.

50 – Riyad as- Salihin, Book #1, Hadith #23.

51 – Sunan of Abu Dawood, Hadith #1359.

52 – Reuters article (valid as of 26/05/2016): http://www.reuters.com/article/2007/08/24/us-teresa-letters-idUSN2435506020070824

53 – Mark Goodacre, The Synoptic Problem: A Way Through the Maze, p. 16.

54 – The Harper Collins Study Bible, p. 1089.

55 – The New English Bible, Oxford Study Edition, p. 788.

56 – Craig Blomberg, The Case for Christ, p. 22.

57 – E P Sanders, The Historical Figure of Jesus, pp. 63-64.

58 - Harris, Understanding the Bible, p. 355.

59 – Meir Bar-Ilan, "Illiteracy in the Land of Israel in the First Centuries C.E." in Essays in the Social Scientific Study of Judaism and Jewish Society, Vol 2, pp. 46-61.

60 – Christopher Tuckett, Christology and the New Testament: Jesus and His Earliest Followers, p. 106.

61 – Christopher Tuckett, Christology and the New Testament: Jesus and His Earliest Followers, pp. 151-152.

62 – Richard Bauckham, Jesus and the Eyewitnesses: The Gospels as Eyewitness Testimony, p. 410.

63 – Mike Licona, The Resurrection of Jesus, p. 527.

64 – Ibid., p. 530.

65 – Ibid., p. 306, 548, 552 and 553.

66 – Ibid., p. 34.

67 – William Lane Craig, Will the Real Jesus Stand Up?, p. 165.

68 – Al-Nasa'i, Al-Kubra, 6:489.

69 – Irenaeus, Against Heresies, Book I, Chapter 24, section 4.

70 – Nicholas P. Lunn, The Original Ending of Mark: A New Case for the Authenticity of Mark 16:9-20, p. 349.

71 – Ignatius, The Epistle Of Ignatius to the Philadelphians, 8:2.

72 – Ignatius, The Epistle Of Ignatius to the Philadelphians, 6:1.

73 – Ignatius, The Epistle of Ignatius to the Trallians, Chapter 10.

74 – Irenaeus , Against Heresies 1,6,3–4.

75 – Irenaeus , Against Heresies, 1,25,4.

76 – Eusebius, Ecclesiastes History II, 13, 8.

77 – Epiphanius , Panarion 26.4.4.

78 – Epiphanius , Panarion 26.4.5–8.

79 – Epiphanius , Panarion 26.5.4–6.

80 – Roger S. Bagnall, The Oxford Handbook of Papyrology, p. 596.

81 – Helmut Koester, Introduction to the New Testament, vol. 2, p. 25.

82 – G. A. Buttrick, The Interpreter's Dictionary of the Bible, vol. 4, p. 595.

83 – Bruce Metzger, The Text of the New Testament: Its Transmission, Corruption, and Restoration, 4th ed. (2005), p. 200.

84 – Ibid., p. 334.

85 – Ibid., p. 341.

86 – Ibid., p. 343.

87 – The Interpreter's Dictionary of the Bible – vol. 4, p. 711.

88 – The Eerdmans Bible Dictionary, p. 1020.

89 – Bruce Metzger, The Text of the New Testament: Its Transmission, Corruption, and Restoration, 4th ed. (2005), p. 320.

90 – Alan F. Johnson, The IVP New Testament Commentary Series; 1 Corinthians, p. 271.

91 – Richard Hays, Interpretation: A Bible Commentary for Teaching and Preaching: 1 Corinthians, p. 247.

92 – William Graham, Beyond the Written Word, p. 80.

93 – The Encyclopedia of Islam, 'The Quran in Muslim Life and Thought.'

94 – Kenneth Cragg, The Mind of the Quran, p. 26.

95 – Sa'adyah Gaon (892 – 942) a religious leader in present-day Iraq, author of the first grammar and dictionary of the Hebrew language.

96 – Chaim Rabin, A Short History of the Hebrew Language, Jewish Agency and Alpha Press, Jerusalem, 1973.

97 – John Kaltner, The Use of Arabic in Biblical Hebrew Lexicography, 1996, pp. 78-79.

98 - Sahih Bukhari, Hadith #1761.

99 – Mustafa al-Azami, On Schacht's Origins Of Muhammadan Jurisprudence, p. 157.

100 – The Oxford dictionary of the Christian Church, p. 482.

101 – Dialogue of Justin With Trypho, Chapter 34.

102 – First Epistle to the Corinthians by C.K. Barrett, commentary on verse 52, p. 381.

103 – Stanley E. Porter, Handbook for the Study of the Historical Jesus, p.766.

104 – Keil-Delitzsch, Commentary on the Old Testament", 1991, p. 497.

105 – Sebeos, The Armenian History of Sebeosi, pp. 95-97.

106 – Reverend T. K. Cheyne, Encyclopaedia Biblica, p. 3583.

107 – Dead Sea Scrolls, Book of Jubilees, p.118, verses 12-13.

108 – Sozomen, The Ecclesiastical History of the Church, p. 309.

109 – Irfan Shahid, Byzantium and the Arabs in the Fourth Century, p. 325.

110 – Professor Haseeb Shehada, Translation of the Samaritan Torah, p. 90.

111 – Sahih Bukhari, 59:574.

112 – Seerah ibn Hisham, vol. 2, p. 409.

113 – Al-Tabaqat Al-Kubra, vol. 2, p. 142.

114 – Roy B. Zuck, Basic Bible Interpretation, p. 117.

115 – Bruce Waltke and M. O'Connor, An Introduction to Biblical Hebrew Syntax, p. 464.

116 – Robert Chazan, Daggers of Faith, p.87.

117 – F. F. Bruce, The New International Commentary on the New Testament, The Epistle to the Colossians, to Philemon, and to the Ephesians, p. 287.

118 – Sahih Bukhari, Kitab Ahadees al-Ambiyaa (Prophets) 60, Chapter 48, Hadith #654.

119 - Sahih Muslim, Hadith #2276.

120 - Christopher North, The Second Isaiah: Introduction, Translation and Commentary To Chapters XL–LV, p. 108.

121 - Sahaih Bukhari, Kitaab al-Buyu' (Book of Sales and Trade), Chapter 50 (The dislike of raising voices in the market).

122 - Smith's Bible Dictionary, 1884, p 370.

123 - Keil-Delitzsch, Commentary on the Old Testament, 1991, p. 253.

124 – Paul Achtemeier, Harper's Bible Dictionary, San Francisco: Harper and Row, 1985.

125 – Charles Foster, The historical geography of Arabia, p. 130.

126 – Abulfeda, Historia Anteislamica, Fleischer edition, p. 192.

127 – Sahih Bukhari, Kitab al-Maghazi (Book of Expeditions led by the Prophet) Chapter 80, Hadith #702.

128 – Sahih Muslim, Book 4, Chapter 169 (Supplication in prayer for rain), Hadith #1955.

129 – A Bible Dictionary, Hayden Series, edited by Rev. Charles Boutell, p. 386.

130 – Sahih Bukhari, Book of Prophetic Commentary, Hadith #4560.

131 – Tirmidhi, Book of the Description of the Day of Resurrection, Softening of Hearts, and Piety, Hadith #2409.

132 – Sahih Muslim, The Account of the Prophet's Emigration, Hadith #7150.

133 – Salo Baron, Social and Religious History of the Jews, Chapter XVI The Pre-Islamic World.

134 – Max L. Margolis and Alexander Marx, A History of the Jewish People, NY. 1927, p. 248.

135 – Watt, Montgomery, Muhammad in Medina, (OUP, 1988 impression), p. 192.

136 – Rodinson, Maxime, Mohammed, (Pelican, London, 1973), p.143, quoting the Sira of Ibn Hisham.

137 – Seerah ibn Hisham, vol. 1, pp. 293-294.

138 – Ibid., pp. 265-266.

139 – Christopher North, The Second Isaiah: Introduction, Translation and Commentary To Chapters XL-LV, p. 109.

140 – John Bar Penkaye, quoted by Walter E. Kaegi, Byzantium and the Early Islamic Conquest, Cambirdge, 2000, p. 216.

141 – James Howard-Johnston, Witnesses to a World Crises, 2010, pp. 357-358.

142 – Bukhari Kitaab al-Buyu' (Book of Sales and Trade) Chapter 50 (The dislike of raising voices in the market).

143 – Bukhari Kitab Manaqib al-Ansaar (Merits of the Helpers in Madinah), Chapter 45 (The emigration of the Prophet and his Companions to Al-Madina).

144 – Alfred J. Kolatch, This is the Torah, 1988, p. 1.

145 – You can view the Book of Jubilees online here. Accessed 23rd August 2016:
http://www.pseudepigrapha.com/jubilees/18.htm

146 – Tafsir Ibn Al Kathir, verse 37:105.

147 – Rashi's commentary can be found here. Accessed 23rd August 2016:
http://www.chabad.org/library/bible_cdo/aid/16465#showrashi=true

148 – Sahih Bukhari 4.583.

149 – The Israelite Samaritan Version of the Torah: First English Translation Compared with the Masoretic Version Hardcover, by Benyamim Tsedaka.